CABIN FEVER

This riveting comedy of menace features three ma[...] country porch in an imaginary New England, reciti[...] about the customs of their nearest neighbors.

"The real world of the play is the familiar haunted by the unknown, parody colliding into cartoon, as if an antic Samuel Beckett has allowed himself to be kidnapped by a gloomily playful Charles Addams." **—Village Voice**

"A compellingly ambiguous static drama, at times suggesting an allegory of a society gone sour on itself or a spiteful game played by malevolent gods atop some Appalachian Olympus." **—Los Angeles Times**

Cabin Fever has been produced around the globe.

SIGNS OF LIFE

Signs of Life is a bizarre and elegantly witty drawing room comedy presenting eminent Victorians—actual and fictitious—as they perform their lives and experiment on their loved ones. The novelist Henry James rifles the imagination of his powerful sister Alice, who stages public fits, keeps a private journal, and has a female lover who prefers Henry dead; the drunken impresario P. T. Barnum exhibits his miraculous "Elephant Woman," Jane Merrit, who is too like Alice James for anyone's comfort; and the suave and sinister Dr. Sloper is far too interested in the scientific possibilities of the bodies of both ladies.

At the center of the play is a mad tea party at which Dr. Sloper and Henry James continually toast the health of "the ladies"—who meet only in the men's stories of them.

"An original drama on a provocative theme, advanced in an elegant and literate voice...What more can anybody ask from a new play?" **—New York Post**

"A true gem...full of surgical imagery and brilliant giggly horridness." **—Village Voice**

Signs of Life is one of the most widely produced experimental comedies of its kind.

FULFILLING KOCH'S POSTULATE

In this internationally acclaimed dark comedy, cooking and death, art and science are served up in wonderfully delectable forms in both the kitchen and the laboratory. *Koch's Postulate* features Typhoid Mary as the live-in chef of Dr. Koch, the scientist who identifies the bacillus she spreads so liberally through her cooking. In its up-to-the-minute, comic book, Katzenjammer style, *Koch's Postulate* balances the beauties of art and the dangers of science in a murderously funny comedy of cooking and eating for four unforgettable characters.

"...darkly hilarious and brilliantly creepy." **—Village Voice**

"Schenkar is an original: her narrative drive springs from menace."
—Time Out (London)

THE LAST OF HITLER

In this brilliant and timely comedy of menace, a post-war Adolf Hitler and Eva Braun are trapped in a Jewish retirement community in Florida, surrounded by the people they so recently tried to exterminate. This dazzling language-opera is staged as a 1940s radio broadcast complete with announcers, commercials for Rinso-Blue, and a "How to Cook a Kosher Chicken" show—in which much more than the kosher chicken is cooked. It features singing and dancing Russian nurses, Edgar Bergen–Charlie MacCarthy routines with a talking skeleton, the psychoanalysis of Adolf Hitler by Dr. Wilhelm Reich, and a radio appearance by the Dionne Quintuplets.

THE UNIVERSAL WOLF

The Universal Wolf, one of the most-produced comedies in colleges and little theaters for the last two years, is the quintessential send-up of both the Little Red Riding Hood tale and modern French criticism. Featuring the Wolf as a French Structuralist, Grandmother as a retired butcher with a very good cutting arm, Little Red Riding Hood as the insufferable brat everyone wants to eat, and a role for the Audience, *The Universal Wolf* delivers a side-splitting comedy for four characters that has delighted theatergoers across the country and around the world.

BURNING DESIRES

An entirely new and fiercely comedic reinvention of the story of Joan of Arc: this time Joan is a teenager in 1950s Seattle, where it's far too wet to burn her. She drives a Triumph convertible, goes on the warpath with a fabulous Native American Princess, and is advised by those mid-twentieth-century icons, Saint Marlene Dietrich, Saint Gertrude Stein, Saint Emily Brontë, and Saint Emily Dickinson. Featuring mad doctors, bad girl and boy scouts, and a teen-aged Gilles de Raix, *Burning Desires* is a wonderfully rollicking and literate comedy for all ages.

SIGNS OF LIFE

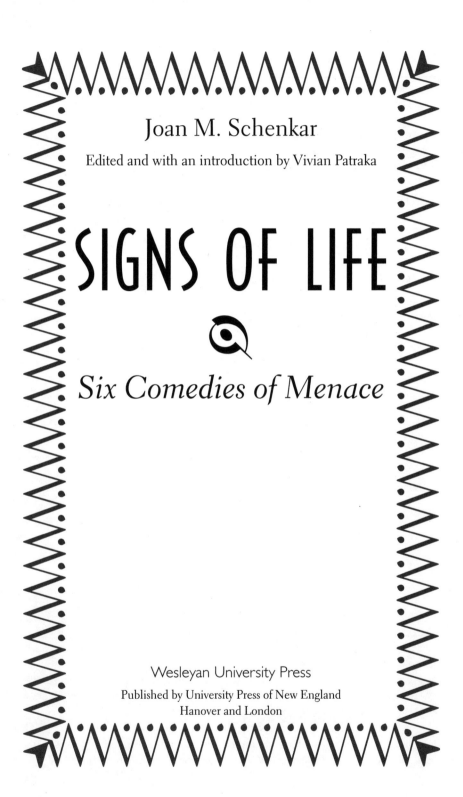

Joan M. Schenkar

Edited and with an introduction by Vivian Patraka

SIGNS OF LIFE

Six Comedies of Menace

Wesleyan University Press
Published by University Press of New England
Hanover and London

Wesleyan University Press
Published by University Press of New England, Hanover, NH 03755

Printed in the United States of America

5 4 3 2 1

CIP data appear at the end of the book

SIGNS OF LIFE

is for Maureen, Marlene, Maurice, and Sara

—responsible, as usual, for everything.

FAMILY PRIDE IN THE 50's (*Photo by Sylvia Plachy*)

Left to right: RICKY, DAVID, LOUIS, DOROTHY, JOAN, MARLENE, MAURIE, MAUREEN. Theatre for the New City production, 1987, directed by Liz Diamond.

JOAN: That's right. That's right we are related. And it's totally the worst kind of relation. It's <u>blood</u> relation. (*spooky tone*) You know what I mean. There's one big vein that runs down this dinner table and one big heart in the kitchen pumping the blood through all that same vein. And the knife that cuts one, cuts all.

Contents

Preface

At This Performance . . .

Joan M. Schenkar

Writing is a life sentence to solitude. Writing for theatre is a life sentence to standing on a stage with your skirt up over your head. Between utter seclusion and total exposure, I have tried to locate an even more extreme position: the theatricalization of feelings so complex that the only way to access them is laughter. I cannot forget that The Last Laugh is always (literally) on us. After the flesh is gone, every skeleton sports a persistent smile.

Each of these plays was composed as much as possible as a piece of music. Each one has movements, developed themes, arias, duets, etc. I have always meant to mark the plays for performance much as music is marked—for prose language does not offer us the nice distinctions of pitch, stress, tempo, and juncture that music does. In this edition, I settled for underlinings (rather like *crescendi*) to indicate stressed words or syllables, and for different styles of spelling and presentation to express what is unique and inalienable to each work. I have always paid more attention to the sound of language than to the sense of it, figuring that if I get the sound right, the sense will take care of itself. It usually does.

Each of these plays has been influenced by my own private Himalayas of Art and Thought: Elizabethan and Jacobean drama, 19th and early 20th-Century highbrow Novels, Expressionist painting, Feminist theory and practice, Modernist literature (including Miss Barnes and Mr. Beckett), Post-Structuralist theory and code, the entire Classic Comics series, and rock n' roll. Although *Family Pride In the 50's* is not included in this volume, a photograph from the New York production is on the dedication page. It represents the last, brilliant stage set Reagan Cook—who designed the premieres of half the plays in the book and whose ability to extend a metaphor into constructed meaning for no money at all was without peer—made for me before his death.

Plays happen, for an audience, in the dark. Reading them requires a very good light. I love this apparent contradiction and am encouraged by it, for it turns the act of reading plays—which for me is often more interesting than seeing them—into a waking dream. In order to stage plays in your head, you must first allow the comforting illusions that light your inner life to be switched off—and find the darkness inside yourself. Only then can you perform that singular act of Higher

Personal Mathematics that reading these plays makes available to you: the division, the multiplication, the fractioning of your very Self.

(At this performance, the role of the Author was played by Joan M. Schenkar.)

Introduction

Vivian Patraka

"All my plays have their own lives. They're like living things in that they have an aesthetic, they have a physical body, they have an amatory life, they have a spiritual life, and they have a linguistic life, a metaphorical one."

—Joan Schenkar[1]

"In the best of all productions I've made you laugh at something dreadful, just dreadful."

—Joan Schenkar[2]

Joan Schenkar, whose plays have been staged throughout the English-speaking world, is best known for her "comedies of menace for the mental stage." Critics have praised her "powerful, disturbing theatre" for its "unorthodox and bold experimental staging," "its echoing, austere, and dazzling language," and its "darkly hilarious and brilliantly creepy" comedy that gives no quarter to easy answers or mass popularity. Using an embroidered tapestry of the real and the invented and a lyrical, witty language, Schenkar's plays create disturbing, surreal landscapes of collective mind.

Signs of Life: Six Comedies of Menace is the first collection of Schenkar's work and allows us to sense the weight of her continuing influence on both theatrical writing and staging. These plays demonstrate the rich and varied history of theatre and performance on which Schenkar draws, and clarify the ways in which Schenkar renders and alters that tradition for her own unique theatrical ends.

Schenkar is fascinated by epistemology, by how people know what they know, why they know it, and what they do with it. Tracking this knowledge by means of condensed, unusual theater metaphors drawn from cannibalism and cooking, from pathology and freakishness, from gardening and comic strips, from fairy tales and Amazon myth, and from performance and ritual, Schenkar's theatre creates a continuing exploration of gender politics and sexuality, fascism and violence, language and invention, and memory and history in relation to our psychic lives. The world of these plays is, as one critic described it, "the familiar haunted by the unknown," a world that elicits "a shudder of recognition" from audiences in the midst of their own laughter.

Schenkar's plays were initially written to be read, and one of the great pleasures in store for the reader lies in Schenkar's brilliant use of metaphor. Schenkar calls her plays "language operas, theatrically-enhanced linguistic experiences, composed as carefully as music and designed to be staged in the imagination." Her stage directions are unusually vivid, precise, and visually persuasive; her metaphors are equally evocative and often humorous. Schenkar uses metaphors—especially those clichéd encodings based on convention, authority, or custom that gain their power by seeming natural and inevitable—to break down our psychological defenses. Her metaphors are physicalized—on every level—on stage and in the reader's imagination, infecting the audience through humor, eliciting laughter and a shudder of recognition as they work to displace and distort everyday experiences. Schenkar uses metaphor as a catalyst to explode the usual tropes by which we structure experience. In so doing, she forces us to examine at a gut level how we assimilate, recreate, and extend dominant discourse.

Repetition, stagnation, desire, illusion, and obsession play critical roles in Schenkar's theatrical world. Nothing is as it seems, and everything has larger consequences and more complex associations than what can first be imagined. As Schenkar told me in our 1996 interview: "I have an extremely tragic vision of life and a highly comic vision of living and those two things coexist in a kind of uneasy *extente cordiale*. They inform and reflect and infect each other always. If you have to think dimensionally, the comedy is on top, the tragedy underneath" (Schenkar interview, 375). This constant negotiation through metaphor of the comic and the tragic, the real and the illusory, the progressive and the stagnant, recurs throughout the work of Joan Schenkar and stamps each play with her highly unusual and immediately recognizable imagination.

Take, for example, her earliest work, *Cabin Fever*. In this comedy of menace, three characters sit rocking on a dilapidated porch through an interminable winter and a lifeless spring. These three, little more than "indiscriminate shapes," have nothing to define them except their own language. Speaking in "hard New England accents," the characters invent vague statements of menace such as "things could happen" and "that's how it starts" to structure the blankness of their existence through story, in this case the story of macabre deaths. The characters are laconic and sly in the way they embed their discussions of cannibalistic acts around town within gossipy narratives. Here, as in all her plays, Schenkar makes us aware of the larger implications of some mode of ordinary conversation. Passing the time through gossip invokes a fascination with insanity, violence, and death: "all this sitting around turns the mind to blood 'n gore." In *Cabin Fever*, the way cannibalism is encased in the structure of gossip suggests that gossip itself is cannibalistic—as casual but devouring discourse.

In all the plays in this collection, the two-halved brain serves as a kind of template for the stage set, as if all of what we see is being staged inside a giant mind. Within this mind, every character is a different aspect of the consciousness of the play and of the cultural moment this consciousness represents. The characters obsessively embody a set of interrelated metaphors to reveal how the structures that define a particular historical moment—those structures under which power and knowledge are organized, justified, and used—are themselves obsessional.

For example, *Signs of Life*, set in nineteenth-century America, exposes the creepy theatrics of Victorian gender politics. The play is embedded with enough "factual" material and historically known "characters" (the winter Henry James, his sister Alice, her companion Kathryn Loring, and sideshow impresario P. T. Barnum) that Schenkar's obsessional version of history supplants the "real" one. Some of her characters might never have met (Henry James and P. T. Barnum); some don't even meet in the play, although they are connected by repeating motifs (Alice James and Jane Merritt, the Elephant Woman); and some are particularly apt conglomerates of real and fictive figures (Dr. Sloper is a character from James's novel *Washington Square*, as well as a version of Dr. J. Marion Sims, the "father" of American gynecology and actual inventor of the "uterine Guillotine"). As the play progresses, the distance between our present world, the world of the past, and the invented past on stage begins to collapse, provoking us to recognize how our present cultural moment is produced by our historical past.

Frequently, Schenkar emphasizes the "frame of mind" of a particular historical moment by setting the play within the discourse of a form of mass culture or popular entertainment. For *Cabin Fever*, it is the newspaper; for *Signs of Life*, it is the carnival sideshow; for *The Last of Hitler*, it is the radio; and for *Fulfilling Koch's Postulate*, it is the comic strip. Mass culture operates as a kind of conceptual proscenium, and as such is visually represented on stage. As a result, we as audience for the play are also resituated as the audience of the mass culture form, a position that forces us to reexamine our own pleasure in the conventions of each form. For example, *Signs of Life* is framed by P. T. Barnum's urging to the audience at the outset to view a freak show from his American Museum. Performance in this freak show, then, serves as a metaphor for what the play in a larger sense depicts: the self-conscious performing of women and men within the narrative of nineteenth-century gender ideology.

In *Fulfilling Koch's Postulate*, the mouth emerges as the border zone between inside and out, as the point of circulation for food, disease, sex, and ideas. In this play, the confusion of what we take into our stomachs and what we take into our heads is revealed in the imaging of the mouth as consumer of, as singer and kisser, as maker of speech, and as maker of infectious letters rendered like the balloons emerging from the mouths of comic strip characters. The play is framed by a giant mouth, with the uvula dividing the stage into two equivalent compartments across which the action flows. *Fulfilling Koch's Postulate* undermines the border between revulsion for the Cook (a.k.a. Typhoid Mary) as contaminating pariah and idealization of the Koch (a.k.a. Dr. Robert Koch, the famous bacteriologist) as hero of medicine by showing that the structures of medical and social pathologies are deeply intertwined. Devaluating the status of the scientist (as a "cooker"), the play erodes the disciplinary separation between the scientist experimenting and the cook (Koch being German for cook) testing and manipulating food. In an outsized, "very Katzenjammer" comic-strip way, the laboratory, scalpel, and huge phallic test tubes match the kitchen, butcher knife, and big cooking pots. In both kitchen and lab they "cut and cut and peel and peel" to produce dead animals. Thus, Schenkar arranges the language of cooking to expose the violent underside of this activity along with the violence of scientific experimentation.

Schenkar again implicates her audience in the horrific infectious humor of death in *The Last of Hitler*, her sendup of 1940's American radio shows. The play is staged in a huge radio console with two miked broadcasters ensconced among cathode tubes at the top of the set. In *The Last of Hitler*, Schenkar uncovers 1940's fascism in 1940's America without ever abandoning the particularity of American references and patterns of speech, especially those expressed in radio culture. In the play, the Holocaust is viewed from an American distance that obscures both its material reality and the reality of the people subjected to it. Turning references to the ovens, soaps, and showers of the Nazi concentration camps into obscene innuendo, the playwright marks a kind of pornographic fascination with the paraphernalia of death. The radio show is organized around a group of escalating metaphors that are shifted from character to character, revealing the process by which we project onto the Other that which is most feared, identify it as contagious, and imagine ourselves as its victims.

The discourse of fascism and anti-Semitism litters the stage with distorted and grotesque versions of "Jewishness." Countering the pathology Nazism attached to Jews, the play configures anti-Semitism itself as a plague. Taking Hitler's construction of the threat of the Jewish Other literally, Schenkar's characters are subject to contamination. They not only project "Jewishness" onto each other, they "catch it" like a disease that transforms them into burlesqued stereotypes that underscore the vulgarity of their conceptions. Schenkar's revenge is to literalize how hate speech works: those characters who espouse vulgar, burlesque stereotypes of Jews turn into those very stereotypes, including a continually more "Jewish" Hitler and Eva Braun. The discourse of anti-Semitism materializes on the bodies of those who speak it so that they become their own hated, fear-filled projections. Thus there are no actual Jewish characters in *The Last of Hitler*, only the "suppositious" imaginings of Jews as Other that the other characters "catch," invent, and so become. What's left is an engineered absence at the heart of the play that evokes the historical reality of the Holocaust.

Spectators are frequently enjoined to be the consumers, en masse in the dark, of the theatrical event. But acquiescent bystanders have no place in the theatre of Joan Schenkar. Schenkar, as she told Elin Diamond in an interview, gives spectators "the opportunity to withdraw from the hideous oneness [of a passive, monolithic audience]".[3] Schenkar's irreverent fairy tale, *The Universal Wolf*, contains multiple revisions of the story of Little Red Riding Hood and asks the audience to choose between them. Comically inserted into the fairy tale frame are the wolf as a French Structuralist, Little Red as an "insufferable brat," and Grandmother as "a retired butcher with homicidal instincts living in the Bois de Boulogne." The play also features a Reader who creates the voices of a panoply of French Structuralists and Post-structuralists from Jacques Lacan to Julia Kristeva. This Reader embodies stage directions that the actor's "can't, won't, or don't do," thereby creating a simultaneous text that is not embodied by the characters. These characters compete not only for the power to tell the story, but for the power to decide which version of the story is to be told. By implicating us in this struggle, Schenkar directs our attention to the allure of the single, uncontested narrative, itself a fantasy world predicated on a "once upon a time" nostalgia with its promise of a "happily ever after" unblemished by multiple points of view. *The Universal Wolf* makes us aware of the danger of uncritically consuming narrative without considering the consequences, which includes being eaten in the process.

In her most recent work, *Burning Desires*, Schenkar revisions the story of Saint Joan, thus posing the question "Whatever happened to Joan of Arc?" She answers this question by playfully moving between Seattle in the 1950's and her own ideally constructed space outside of the constraints of that historical moment. In Schenkar's version, Joan is allowed to narrate her own story. Near the opening of the play, young Joan reports to the audience: "This is the story of Joan of Arc, and how she came to be born into a new fate. It's been my story for a long time and now it's going to be yours. Listen to me carefully. I have never told it like this before." This new telling of Saint Joan permits her to start fires, wage war, cross-dress, and hear her voices with impunity.

The play's multiple, overlapping images of smoke and fire incorporate a wide range of meanings, from the exuberance of young Joan's newly-discovered sexuality to the barely repressed incestuous lusts of her brothers. The smoking of cigarettes, a signature gesture of 1950's America, emerges as a central motif in the play; the lethal flames of the original legend are replaced in *Burning Desires* by the women who energetically "smolder like cigarette paper." Young Joan's triumph is powerfully literalized. She drives a 1957 Triumph convertible bracketed by her "beatified" guardians Marlene Dietrich, Emily Brontë, Emily Dickinson (who refuses to come out of Joan's closet), and Gertrude Stein. They assist her in uniting the pyromaniacal Bonfire girls (Schenkar's twisted version of the Girl Scouts) with Angelina, Warrior Princess of the Salish Indians, to vanquish both the Salish men of her tribe and all the Boy Scouts in Seattle.

The six plays collected here are exuberant, disturbing, and deeply funny. They are written in a highly witty, allusive, elegant language that is informed in its conception by traditions of Western literature. Too often, at least in the U.S., readers of plays and readers of literature do their work in separate worlds. Because these plays are so deeply literate and intensely visual, they offer themselves persuasively to both groups of readers. As Schenkar says: "all theatre begins with an act of writing and continues with an act of reading. The life it will have in the future will be in a book." (Schenkar interview, 377–78)

I have been thinking about and publishing articles on the plays of Joan Schenkar for over ten years.[4] In that time, I have read or seen staged nearly everything she has written. And I hold to my original opinion: We have precious few avant-garde playwrights of her stature who continue to write experimental work. I believe we ignore them at our peril.

Notes

I acknowledge the invaluable assistance of Heath A. Diehl, my 1997 research assistant, in the preparation of the Introduction. His work was funded by a Graduate Research Assistant Award from Bowling Green State University.

1. From page 68 of my interview with playwright Joan Schenkar, in *Speaking on Stage: Interviews with Contemporary American Playwrights*, eds. Philip Kolin and Colby Kullman (Tuscaloosa: University of Alabama Press, 1996), 365–378. Subsequent references to this interview will appear in the text as Schenkar interview, accompanied by its page number.

2. Schenkar interview, page 370.

3. "Crossing the Corpus Callosum: An Interview with Joan Schenkar" by Elin Diamond. *The Drama Review* 35.2 (Summer 1991), p. 111.

4. These articles include: Introduction to Joan Schenkar's *The Lodger*, with Annette Wannamaker, in *Amazon All Stars*, ed. Rosemary Keef Curb (New York: Applause Books, 1996), 397–400; "Feminism and the Jewish Subject in the Plays of Sachs, Atlan, and Schenkar," in *Performing Feminisms: The Critical Act*, ed. Sue Ellen Case (Baltimore: Johns Hopkins University Press, 1990), 160–74; "Mass Culture and Metaphors of Menace in Joan Schenkar's Plays," in *Making a Spectacle: Feminist Essays on Contemporary Women's Theatre*, ed. Lynda Hart (Ann Arbor: University of Michigan Press, 1989), 25–40; "Foodtalk in the Plays of Caryl Churchill and Joan Schenkar," in *The Theatre Annual* 40 (1985), 137–57; "Notes on Technique in Feminist Drama: Apple Pie and Signs of Life," in *Women & Performance, A Journal of Feminist Theory* 1, no. 2, 58–72; "Notes on Technique in Feminist Drama," in *Feminist Re-Visions: What Has Been and Might Be*, eds. Vivian Patraka and Louise A. Tilly (Ann Arbor: University of Michigan, 1983), 46–63.

CABIN FEVER

CABIN FEVER was first produced* in an early form at Studio 17, New York City in 1977, directed by Christopher McCann. The current version debuted at the Public Theater in New York City in 1978, directed by the author. It continues to be produced in many venues throughout North America, England, France, and Germany.

Characters
ONE
TWO
THREE

*__Author's Note:__ Plays, rather like the god Dionysius, are considered to be twice born: first on the page, and then on the stage. The "premiere" or "first production" or "first reading" of a new play is an important moment in its history and I have used as my yardstick the idea that the "premiere" of any play of mine is the first time I saw that play in a form I could recognize. I realize this rule of thumb is a peculiar one and, worse, that it relegates chronology to an approximate science. Chronology is an approximate science. The words, at least, are in the right order and as I wrote them.

Note: Since the characters never leave their chairs, the chairs must be regarded as part of the character's "character" and should be treated as such. That is, each chair should resemble and reflect the character who occupies it.

Any resemblance in the play to persons living or dead is purely coincidental: CABIN FEVER is entirely a work of the imagination.

Left to right: ONE, TWO, THREE. From the Theater for the New City production in New York City, 1983. (*Photo by Donna Gray*)

ONE: (*shuffles thru newspapers*) Wait a minute, I got it right here. (*reads*) Sixteen members of the Greene family assaulted the Mountain County Volunteer Fire Department at its annual covered dish supper late this afternoon. (*looks up*) That was . . . uh . . . spring before last. (*reads*) Milt Harrington died of injuries sustained when Davis Greene pushed a pickle dish down his throat. The dish, ironically, was the property of the deceased's wife.

CABIN FEVER

Three old things, ONE, TWO, and THREE, are sitting in their chairs on a farmhouse porch. It's a front porch with a low roof so that the ambiguity that passes for their faces is in specific shadow. When a face comes out of shadow by virtue of a rocker's forward motion, its distortions are apparent: a nose slightly misplaced, an alien eyelid, an oddly long upper lip. ONE and THREE are in rocking chairs, TWO is not. TWO has a hard time. Their bodies appear to be jointed in ways unknown to us. Movement of one extremity precipitates the movement of other, unrelated limbs. The whole performance is as uncomfortable and as choreographed as TWO and THREE's hard New England accents. ONE's diction is not regionally identifiable, though it is clearly "country." ONE is always played by a woman; TWO and THREE are more or less male. They are lit as for a comedy.

Number TWO takes out its bandana and mops its brow. Then ONE picks up a pile of old newspaper clippings, rifles it, sets it down. Then THREE snaps its suspenders, right and left. They repeat their motions out of order. Then ONE, TWO, and THREE begin to rock rapidly, then more slowly, as they lose all interest in self-propulsion. The rocking declines at different rates.

TWO: (*settling down*) Been quite a fall.

THREE: I <u>guess</u> so.

ONE: Uh-<u>huh</u>.

Pause

TWO: (*searching for another topic*) Hardest January I can remember.

4

THREE: (*agreeing*) Wilkes boys froze to death right in front a their <u>wood</u> stove.

ONE: (*shuddering*) Thank <u>god</u> for the thaw.

THREE: <u>Needed</u> a thaw to pry those Wilkes boys out a their rocking chairs.

Pause

ONE: Spring's a long ways off.

THREE: I <u>guess</u> so.

TWO: Don't close your eyes.

THREE: Y' might miss it.

TWO: Haw haw.

THREE: Hee hee.

Pause

TWO: <u>Awful</u> young to go, those Wilkeses.

THREE: Barely pushing eighty.

TWO: Wonder who's next?

THREE: Comes in threes, they say.

ONE: (*agitated*) <u>What</u> does, <u>what</u> comes in threes?

TWO: (*leans sideways and looks* ONE *as full in the face as possible*) <u>Death</u> does.

Slight pause

THREE: Wonder who's next?

Full pause

ONE: Thaw almost smells like spring.

TWO: (*quashing it*) Whole lot a <u>mud</u>, if y' ask me.

THREE: Ruts up the road something awful.

TWO: Thaw's no good for <u>anything</u>.

THREE: <u>That's</u> <u>right</u>. (*truculent*)

Pause

ONE: Do you . . . do you remember the winter of '47?

THREE: Nope.

TWO: Don't remember a thing.

THREE: (*to* TWO) Wasn't that the winter them Greene boys barbecued Pritchard's cow right on their front lawn?

TWO: (*laughs extravagantly*) Haw haw haw. (*stops short*) Nope it wasn't.

ONE: (*determined*) The winter of '47 wasn't <u>like</u> this winter.

TWO: <u>That</u> a <u>fact</u>.

THREE: Hard to be<u>lieve</u>.

TWO: <u>Ev</u>ery winter's like every other winter.

THREE: <u>Ay</u>-yuh. <u>Snow</u> and <u>mis</u>ery.

ONE: Well <u>this</u> winter was different.

TWO: (*flatly*) Don't remember it a<u>tall</u>.

ONE: (*story-teller's tone*) In the Winter of '47 the snow fell for 14 days and nights. And when it stopped the houses in the village were entirely covered and the people in the village could no longer remember what it was to see colors.

TWO: (*bored*) You don't say.

THREE: My my.

ONE: Barns couldn't be reached. Cows couldn't be milked and horses couldn't be fed. On the 15th day when the barn doors at last were opened, the people saw that the stalls and stanchions were running in blood. In their hunger the horses had eaten each other and in their agony the cows had strangled themselves in their ties.

Pause

TWO: (*shaking its head*) Spring's a long ways off.

THREE: No <u>call</u> to tell a story like <u>that</u>.

TWO: De-<u>press</u>ing.

THREE: Un-<u>nat</u>ural.

TWO: (*final judgment*) Entirely un-<u>nec</u>essary.

THREE: It's sitting around like this in the winter makes the mind turn to blood 'n gore.

ONE: <u>Cabin</u> fever.

THREE: (*cupping its ear*) What say?

TWO: That's what they <u>call</u> it.

Slight pause

THREE: Be real nice to have this thaw over with.

TWO: (*nods*) De-<u>press</u>ing.

THREE: Un-<u>nat</u>ural.

ONE: (*initiating*) Cabin fever's what happened to the Lillie girls this November.

THREE: Ruth and Margaret?

TWO: Believe I heard something about that.

ONE: You know they'd taken to drink since their daddy died.

THREE: Ay-yup. Old Fred.

TWO: Died purt near 20 years ago.

ONE: (*story-teller's tone*) Well things were pretty <u>bad</u> in November—<u>you</u> remember.

THREE: Nope.

TWO: Don't remember a thing.

ONE: Well they <u>were</u> bad. (*slowly*) And the wind howls around that Lillie house like 10,000 witches. . . . Things were real bad and the Lillie girls hadn't been to town for over a week. One night they were arguing like they always do after dinner and Margaret got so worked up she ripped out her false teeth and hit Ruth smack in the eye with them.

TWO: The <u>glass</u> eye?

ONE: That's right. Margaret knocked that glass eye right out of Ruth's head. And while they were kicking and clawing around on the floor there like they always do, one of them pushed the applejack into the kerosene heater and set the house on fire.

THREE: Always had a lot a <u>spunk</u>, them Lillies.

ONE: Well, the fire flared up quick as a cat and ate its way right through that old kitchen. As the blaze raged around them, Margaret got a strangle hold on Ruth, and Ruth set her teeth into Margaret's nose.

TWO: (*an aside*) Ruth still has all her teeth.

THREE: 'Magine that.

TWO: (*nodding*) All them teeth at seventy-three.

ONE: When the neighbors finally put the fire out and pulled the Lillie girls from the house, the county coroner had to cut three of Margaret's fingers from Ruth's neck.

TWO: Tough as <u>nails</u>, them girls.

Pause

THREE: (*sighs*) Spring's a long ways off.

TWO: <u>Dead</u> <u>right</u>.

Pause

THREE: <u>Terrible</u> story.

TWO: Don't like to think about it.

THREE: Don't blame you.

ONE: Wonder who's next.

TWO: They <u>do</u> say it happens in threes.

Pause. Sound.

THREE: Hear that?

TWO: Nope.

ONE: I'm not sure.

TWO: (*definitive*) Didn't hear a thing.

THREE: Well, it's a nor'easter.

TWO: How do <u>you</u> know.

THREE: Always starts by rattling the china closet.

ONE: That's true.

TWO: (*truculent*) How do <u>you</u> know?

Pause

TWO: <u>Can't</u> be a nor'easter. <u>Never</u> <u>happens</u> during thaw.

ONE: Well, it rattled that old closet.

THREE: That's so.

TWO: (*finally*) No such thing's a nor'easter during thaw.

Pause

THREE: Wonder if them Greene boys are out.

TWO: Y'mean now that hunting season's over.

THREE: <u>Ay</u>-Yup.

ONE: Haven't seen anything <u>dead</u>, have you?

TWO: (*ignores* ONE) They don't hunt during hunting season.

THREE: Nope. Too dangerous in the woods with all them out a state hunters, they say.

TWO: Haw haw haw. They hunt every day <u>but</u> hunting season.

THREE: <u>Mean</u>. Them Greene's were always <u>real</u> <u>mean</u>.

TWO: Remember the year they shot all the collies.

THREE: Nope.

TWO: <u>Ay</u>-Yup. Collie bit Harley Greene on the ankle and them Greenes dropped all the collies in the county. Got 57 of 'em before they stopped.

THREE: <u>Mean</u>. <u>Mean</u> boys.

Pause

THREE: Remember the spring they beat up the en-tire fire department?

TWO: <u>Who</u> did?

THREE: The <u>Greene</u> boys.

TWO: Nope. Don't remember a thing.

THREE: Well . . . (*tries, but can't*) Guess I don't remember either.

ONE: (*shuffles through newspapers*) Wait a minute, I got it right here. (*reads*) "Sixteen members of the Greene family assaulted the Mountain County Volunteer Fire Department at its annual covered dish supper late this afternoon." (*looks up*) That was . . . uh . . . spring before last. (*reads*) "Milt Harrington died of injuries sustained when Davis Greene pushed a pickle dish down his throat. The dish, ironically, was the property of the deceased's wife."

TWO: That's <u>three</u>! Comes in threes!

THREE: <u>What</u> does. What comes in threes!

TWO: (*leans and looks* THREE *in the face*) <u>Death</u> <u>does</u>.

ONE: Doesn't count. That was on last year's list.

TWO. Oh <u>hell</u>.

THREE: Too bad.

ONE: Came real close.

THREE: Better luck next time.

TWO: (*pouting*) <u>Hell</u>.

Pause

TWO: Spring's a long ways off.

Pause

ONE: There's that closet rattling again.

TWO: <u>Cab</u>in fever. You got it bad.

ONE: How do <u>you</u> know.

TWO: <u>Hear</u>ing things . . .

THREE: That's how it starts.

TWO: Then <u>see</u>ing things . . .

THREE: Carries on like that for a while . . .

TWO: <u>Do</u>ing things . . .

THREE: That's how it stops.

TWO: Better be careful.

THREE: Things could happen.

Pause

ONE: It's the sound of melting that bothers me so. Drip, drip, drip, drip. It's <u>aw</u>ful.

TWO: (*agrees*) De-<u>press</u>ing.

THREE: Un-<u>nat</u>ural.

ONE: I'd like to quit.

TWO: (*scandalized*) Nooooo.

THREE: What say?

ONE: I'd like to take a vacation. Go somewhere. Til spring comes.

TWO: Haw haw haw. Be a <u>real</u> <u>long</u> vacation.

THREE: <u>Ay</u>-yup. Spring's a long ways off.

Pause

TWO: (*a new topic*) S'pose it was those <u>Pratts</u> killed Gardiner's cat.

THREE: 'Magine so. They'd kill <u>any</u>thing.

TWO: <u>Ay</u>-yup. Janie found it nailed up near the old cellar hole. Blood just dripping out of it.

THREE: No call to do it <u>that</u> way.

TWO: Evil-minded, the whole family.

THREE: Always married their cousins.

ONE: (*musing*) I wonder what they'll get next.

TWO: (*an evil suggestion*) Seen the milk cow lately?

THREE: By the <u>Jesus</u>!

TWO: Wouldn't be <u>atall</u> surprised. Them Pratts'll kill <u>anything</u>.

THREE: (*half-rising*) I'll have the . . . Who's <u>con</u>stable this year?

TWO: (*with some satisfaction*) <u>Anson</u> <u>Pratt</u>.

THREE: (*disgusted*) By the <u>Jesus</u>.

ONE: You can't do a thing during thaw, anyway.

THREE: (*settling down*) That's so.

TWO: Can't do a thing in winter, neither.

THREE: That's so.

TWO: Come <u>spring</u> we'll get 'em.

THREE: (*satisfied*) <u>Hope</u> so.

ONE: If spring <u>comes</u>.

TWO: No <u>call</u> to say that.

THREE: Un-<u>nat</u>ural.

TWO: De-<u>press</u>ing.

ONE: Drip, drip, drip, drip. It's driving me crazy.

   Pause. Sound.

TWO: Was that a . . . ?

ONE: <u>What</u>, was that <u>what</u>.

THREE: Heard the closet rattle, didn't you.

TWO: (*stubborn*) Nope. Didn't hear a thing.

   Pause

ONE: (*baiting* TWO) Guess you know about the Palmer girl.

THREE: (*with satisfaction*) Terrible thing.

TWO: (*a bit of interest*) Haven't heard a word.

THREE: Took an axe to her baby brother last Wednesday.

TWO: (*excited*) She g<u>et</u> him? He's <u>dead</u>?

ONE: Missed him. Slipped and cut off her big toe.

THREE: (*explaining*) She's only ten. Her aim's still bad.

TWO: (*disappointed*) Thaw's a terrible thing.

ONE: Palmer family's been <u>in</u>sane for years. (*counting on its fingers*) First Gert beat Charlie to death with a poker . . .

THREE: (*chiming in*) Then Bud burnt up his children . . .

ONE: Now Billy can't stay away from Jepson's sheep . . .

THREE: And Annie . . .

TWO: (*interrupting*) Haven't heard a <u>thing</u> about it.

ONE: (*to* TWO) <u>You're</u> kin to the Palmers.

THREE: That's <u>so</u>.

ONE: You're kin to <u>everyone</u> around here.

THREE: That's so.

   Pause

TWO: So're you.

THREE: (*sadly*) That's so.

   Pause

ONE: Drip . . . drip . . . drip. Wonder what it's like in Florida?

TWO: Ex-<u>pen</u>sive.

THREE: Un-<u>seas</u>onable.

   Slight pause. Loud sound.

TWO: (*starts*)

ONE: <u>Heard</u> it, didn't you.

TWO: (*reluctantly*) Heard something.

THREE: <u>China</u> closet. That's how it starts.

ONE: (*story-teller's tone*) By tonight all this melt will be solid ice. The drips will freeze as they fall.

THREE: The wind . . .

ONE: And the wind will roar down off the mountain like a terrible revenge. There won't be a warm place in the house to hide.

TWO: The snow . . .

ONE: The snow will seem to come right out of the wind. But it will cover the ice so quickly that we will forget what the bare ground looks like. By morning it will be drifted almost to the porch roof. And by next week we won't remember what it is to see colors.

THREE: Don't remember much <u>any</u>ways.

TWO: <u>Nope</u>. Don't remember a <u>thing</u>.

Pause

THREE: Guess I'd better see to the stock.

TWO: No sense in <u>that</u>.

ONE: They're pastured over to Brown's.

TWO: Too far to go before the storm.

THREE: (*in frustration*) By the <u>Jesus</u>.

TWO: (*fatalistically*) 'Magine they'll freeze to death.

ONE: <u>Nothing</u> lives through a nor'easter.

THREE: (*agony*) By the <u>Jesus</u>.

TWO: Should've seen to 'em yesterday.

THREE: Yesterday was <u>thaw</u>.

Pause

ONE: Brown's boy's out with 'em.

THREE: That's a <u>high</u> pasture. No shelter there a<u>tall</u>.

TWO: 'Magine he'll freeze to death along with the stock. (*brightens*) <u>Say</u>. That makes <u>three</u>. <u>Three</u> of 'em. It <u>comes</u> in <u>threes</u>.

ONE: <u>What</u> does, <u>what</u> comes in threes?

TWO: <u>Death does</u>.

Pause

THREE: Boy hasn't froze <u>yet</u>.

ONE: The wind could <u>change</u>.

THREE: Ice could <u>melt</u>.

ONE: Things could <u>happen</u>.

THREE: Boy's still <u>alive</u>.

TWO: (terribly disappointed) Aw <u>hell</u>. <u>Hell</u>.

　　Pause. Rock. Rock.

THREE: Wouldn't mind a little supper.

TWO: (*disbelief*) You . . . <u>hungry</u>?

THREE: Wouldn't mind a little <u>something</u>.

ONE: I'll go see about boiling some turnips.

TWO: Don't bother.

THREE: No <u>sense</u> in it.

ONE: Why not?

TWO: Stove's out.

THREE: <u>Went</u> out two, three hours ago.

ONE: (*energetic*) Well I better kindle it right up. The nor'easter'll freeze the plumbing for sure.

TWO: <u>Can't</u> kindle it.

THREE: No more <u>wood</u>.

ONE: (*irritated*) Well then I'll <u>chop</u> some wood.

TWO: <u>Can't</u> chop any wood.

THREE: <u>Axe</u> handle's broke.

ONE: My <u>god</u> what will we do?

THREE: Wait til spring.

　　Slight pause

TWO: (deliberately) Spring's a long ways off.

　　Pause

ONE: This is . . . very bad.

THREE: Only the beginning.

TWO: <u>Ay</u>-yup. Thaw's barely over.

THREE: Got to pay for <u>everything</u>.

TWO: <u>That's</u> <u>right</u>. Had a <u>good</u> <u>thaw</u> and now we got to pay.

ONE: At least the dripping will stop. Drip, drip, drip, drip. It's driving me crazy.

Pause

TWO: (*evilly*) Well, now . . . <u>snow</u> makes a sound.

THREE: So it does. So it does.

ONE: <u>What</u> <u>are</u> <u>you</u> <u>saying</u>!

TWO: When the wind dies down, you can hear it.

THREE: Sssst. Sssst. Sssst. Like that.

TWO: Ay-yup. <u>Some</u>thing like that.

ONE: I can't stand it.

TWO: Why <u>sure</u> y' can.

THREE: You just <u>forgot</u>, that's all.

TWO: <u>Hard</u> to remember from winter to winter.

THREE: No <u>sense</u> in it.

TWO: You'll get used to it. Just like you did the dripping.

THREE: Sssst. Ssssst. Sssst.

Pause

ONE: (*experimentally*) I could . . . <u>kill</u> myself.

TWO: (*interested*) <u>There</u> now. That'd make three.

ONE: Or I could kill <u>you</u> or <u>you</u>.

THREE: Might better make up your mind.

TWO: Important thing like that.

ONE: (*musing*) Maybe I'll . . . burn the house down.

TWO: (*helpful*) No more kindling.

THREE: Believe we're out a matches.

Slight pause

ONE: (*a joyous inspiration*) I'll <u>shoot</u> the <u>dog</u>!

THREE: Too <u>late</u>.

TWO: The <u>Greene</u> boys got 'im yesterday.

Pause. Sound.

THREE: Listen to that.

TWO: Never heard it rattle like that before.

ONE: When does . . . when does the sound start.

THREE: (*cupping its ear*) What say?

ONE: (*louder*) The snow sound. When does it start.

THREE: Soon's the wind stops blowing.

TWO: (*cheerful*) Ay-yup. Lasts til spring.

THREE: 'Course spring's a long ways off.

TWO: Might better get yourself used to that sound.

THREE: (agreeing) Be hearing it for awhile.

Pause. ONE *leafs through the newspaper clippings.*

ONE: (a little frantic) Maybe there's something here about the sound. Some-thing . . . to help me stand it . . .

TWO: (*to* THREE) Cabin fever.

THREE: Worst case I ever saw.

TWO: Takes 'em just like that.

THREE: That so?

TWO: Ay-yup. One minute they're regular and then they're hearing things.

THREE: Or seeing things.

TWO: (*darkly*) Doing things.

ONE: Here it is. I found it right here. (*reads*) "Fran Lampman age fifty-two was removed from her home by the Mountain County rescue squad early yester-day morning in an hysterical condition. Constable Pratt's opinion is that it ap-pears to be a simple case of religious dementia but Miss Lampman's brother Lyman, who resides with her, testified at the inquiry this morning that Miss Lampman has been very upset by sounds of an undetermined nature which he has been unable to hear. Miss Lampman was judged incapable of testi-mony and remanded to the State Hospital for the Insane."

Pause

TWO: Not much help there.

THREE: My. My.

TWO: Old Fran. Known 'er since she was <u>born</u>.

THREE: Don't remember her, though.

TWO: Nope. Don't remember a <u>thing</u>.

Pause

ONE: What will I do.

TWO: Now now.

THREE: There there.

TWO: <u>Nerves</u>.

Slight pause

ONE: If the wind doesn't stop, the sound won't start. Isn't that right?

TWO: (*considering*) Seems to be.

THREE: (*more accommodating*) No doubt.

ONE: (*brightens*) <u>Well</u>, then. I won't need to worry til the wind stops.

TWO: <u>That's</u> the spirit. Wind's hardly <u>started</u>.

THREE: That's <u>so</u>.

TWO: Thaw's barely <u>over</u>.

THREE: (*agreeing*) <u>China</u> closet's real quiet.

TWO: (*acme of agreeableness*) Be a <u>long time</u> before the wind stops.

Pause

ONE: This is . . . not bad.

THREE: Calm before the storm.

TWO: That's what they <u>call</u> it.

THREE: Don't mind it a <u>bit</u>.

ONE: It's . . . <u>com</u>fortable . . . waiting.

TWO: (*quickly*) Well now, depends what you're <u>wait</u>ing for.

THREE: (*nods*) Hate to wait for <u>Christ</u>mas.

TWO: Or <u>spring</u>. <u>Hate</u> to wait for <u>spring</u>.

TWO *and* THREE *both look at* ONE *who hesitates then nods.*

ONE: Spring's a long ways off.

Sound. Pause. Sound. They ignore it.

THREE: Pretty <u>quiet</u> around here.

TWO: So it <u>is</u>.

THREE: 'Magine the Greene boys keep to home in weather like this.

TWO: <u>Brown</u> boy's out, though.

ONE: (*flatly*) So's his uncle.

TWO: (*scandalized*) Noooo.

THREE: (*shakes its head*) My my.

TWO: Old <u>Clar</u>ence. He'll never learn.

THREE: Last I heard he got 'lectrocuted crossing Pike's meadow.

TWO: (*leering*) He was sneaking through Maud Mason's bedroom window and lightening hit him on the hand.

THREE: Hee hee hee. Act a <u>god</u>.

TWO: He's in for it <u>this</u> time.

THREE: (*shaking its head in disbelief*) Out in a nor'<u>easter</u>.

TWO: Increases the odds. (*calculating*) Two Browns out in a storm—one of 'em's bound to get it.

ONE: Will that . . . <u>satisfy</u> you?

Pause

TWO: (*exasperated*) Got nothing to <u>do</u> with me. It comes in <u>threes</u>. Death's got to come in <u>threes</u>. Then <u>we'll</u> be safe.

THREE: (*unconcerned*) <u>Ay</u>-yup. For a while.

ONE: (*a little hysterical*) <u>We</u> come in threes too. There's <u>three</u> of <u>us</u>.

TWO: Now you just calm down.

THREE: Don't think a <u>thing</u> about it.

TWO: (*shakes its head*) Un-<u>nat</u>ural.

THREE: De-<u>press</u>ing.

TWO: Clear case a <u>cabin</u> <u>fever</u>.

Pause. Rock. Rock.

THREE: (*almost an afterthought*) Plenty a room at that State Hospital I hear.

TWO: <u>That</u> <u>so</u>?

THREE: <u>Ay</u>-yup. Built a nice new wing last summer.

TWO: 'Magine Fran Lampman'll miss her neighbors there all the same.

THREE: Always was a sociable woman.

TWO: (*a significant look*) No doubt she could <u>do</u> with a little company.

THREE: <u>Ay</u>-yup. Could be she'll <u>get</u> a little company.

TWO: Never can <u>tell</u>.

THREE: Nope. Y'can't.

   Pause. Absolute silence.

ONE: There it <u>goes</u> again!

TWO: Now now.

THREE: There there.

ONE: It's started al<u>ready</u>! Before the wind!

TWO: Here now. It's just the dripping. Pick up them newspaper clippings and find us something good about the neighbors.

THREE: It's all this sitting around turns the mind to blood 'n gore.

ONE: (*dully*) Cabin fever. (*then begins to rifle the newspapers*)

THREE: What <u>say</u>?

   Pause

TWO: Anything in there about them thieving Sumners? Haven't seen them in a <u>long</u> time.

THREE: Seems to me I heard something about the Sumners a while back.

TWO: Don't remember it, do you?

THREE: Nope. Don't remember a thing.

ONE: (*renewed interest*) Here it is. I have it right here (*reads*) "A strange case has been puzzling doctors in Mountain County as of late. May Sumner age 59, wife of George Sumner a well-known farmer here . . ."

TWO: (*interrupts*) Haw haw. <u>I'll</u> say he's well-known.

THREE: Sold that acre off'n his wood lot to three <u>different</u> people at the same time.

TWO: Wife's a good deal worse 'n <u>he</u> is.

ONE: (*resumes*) ". . . wife of a well-known farmer here, was taken with a fit of laughing upon receiving a letter announcing the death of her husband's mother Clara Everett Sumner age 92."

TWO: (*interrupts excitedly*) That's <u>it</u>! That's <u>three</u> of 'em!!

THREE: <u>Wrong</u> <u>county</u>. Old Clara was at the rest home over to <u>Heartwellville</u>.

TWO: By the <u>Jesus</u>.

ONE: (*resumes*) "The fit of laughter has continued without ceasing for three days and three nights and doctors are certain that unless it can be stopped, Mrs. Sumner will go to her reward. All are puzzled by the origin of Mrs. Sumner's illness as it is well known that she nursed her mother-in-law devotedly for twenty-five years."

THREE: Thaw's a terrible thing.

TWO: Well now, don't be too sure about that. (*counting on its fingers*) We got two Browns out in the elements and May Sumner laughing up a storm. Thaw's <u>just</u> <u>fine</u> with me.

Pause

ONE: (*shudders*) I'm . . . <u>cold</u>.

TWO: Stove's out.

THREE: (*helpful*) Need a <u>fire</u> to keep warm.

ONE: I'm . . . <u>hungry</u>.

TWO: Can't <u>cook</u> on a cold stove.

THREE: Raw turnips'll make y' <u>sick</u>.

ONE: The snow . . . is falling in my head.

TWO: (*looks at* THREE, *both shake their heads*)

ONE: Soon it will drift up past my eyes. I won't remember what it is to see colors. (*looks down at newspapers*) Black and white. All . . . black and white.

THREE: (*to* TWO *sotto voce*) Can't go see about that state hospital till the storm's over.

TWO: (*glumly*) Storm won't be over til <u>spring</u>. Can't go til <u>spring</u>.

THREE: (*a look at* ONE) Spring's a long ways off.

Slight pause

ONE: I'm so <u>lonely</u>.

TWO: (*hearty*) Plenty a company <u>right</u> <u>here</u>.

THREE: Real <u>good</u> company, if y' ask me.

TWO *and* THREE *guffaw,* ONE *is blank.*

TWO: (*sotto voce*) By the <u>Jesus</u>, hope it's not going to be one a them <u>violent</u> cases.

THREE: Doubt it. Always had a quiet nature.

TWO: Hope so. Hate to have to rassle 'er to the ground with all that ice out there.

THREE: Might slip and break your <u>neck</u>.

TWO: (*darkly*) <u>That'd</u> do it. <u>That'd</u> make the third.

THREE: No <u>sense</u> thinking like that. She <u>always</u> had a quiet nature. (*slight pause*) 'Course sometimes the quiet ones are the worst.

TWO: Think she meant what she said about killing <u>us</u>?

THREE: (*cool*) Never can tell.

TWO: By the Jesus, it's enough to give me the <u>willies</u>.

THREE: <u>Here</u> now. Don't <u>you</u> go around the corner.

TWO: Any minute that wind'll start up and bring the snow. And then she'll hear the sounds. God knows <u>what'll</u> come of it.

THREE: No <u>sense</u> talking like that. Believe she's a good deal calmer about it than <u>you</u> are.

TWO: (*settling down*) It's <u>got</u> <u>to</u> <u>come</u> <u>in</u> <u>threes</u>. Wish to <u>hell</u> somebody'd <u>die</u> so I could <u>re-lax</u>.

ONE: (*focusing at the word "die"*) I think . . . <u>I'm</u> dying.

TWO: (*utterly disgusted*) Aw <u>hell</u>.

THREE: Need a little <u>exercise</u> is all. All this sitting around turns the mind to blood 'n gore.

TWO: So it does. So it does. Might better step into the dooryard and bury the <u>dog</u>.

THREE: Ay-<u>yup</u>. The Greenes shot him right in front a the <u>kitchen</u>. Be nice to get him buried before the ground freezes.

TWO: Or before one a them Andrews comes along and <u>eats</u> him.

THREE: Those Andrews at it <u>again</u>?

TWO: Better <u>believe</u> it. Caught Henry eating a dead <u>cat</u> last week behind Gardiner's store. And the kids . . . <u>Say</u>. (*to* ONE) Wasn't there something in the paper about little Delores Andrews?

ONE: (*makes an effort*) Why . . . yes . . . I think you're right . . . just let me . . . (*rifles the newspapers*) . . .

TWO: (*to* THREE) Don't know who's <u>worse</u>. The Pratts or the Andrews.

THREE: I'd put money on the Pratts <u>any</u> day.

ONE: <u>Here</u> it is. I have it right here, I . . . think.

TWO *and* THREE *wait expectantly.* ONE *tries to read and fails.*

ONE: I . . . can't see to read. It's . . . snowing . . . so . . . hard . . . The drifts . . . are almost . . . up to my eyes.

TWO: (*violent*) By god you give me that paper or I'll put your eyes out myself!! (*snatches paper from* ONE)

THREE: <u>Here</u> now. No sense in <u>that</u> kind a talk.

TWO: <u>Where</u> is it?! WHERE?! There's no printing on this damn paper!! It's <u>blank</u>! It's <u>white</u>! It's <u>all</u> <u>white</u>!

ONE: (*calm*) It's the snow. The snow has drifted up past your eyes. Soon you won't remember what it is to see colors.

THREE: (*takes paper from* TWO, *shakes its head*) <u>I'm</u> no help <u>atall</u>. Never <u>did</u> learn to read right.

Pause. TWO *has covered its eyes in attitude of despair.* ONE *twists round grotesquely, apparently to catch a sound.*

ONE: (*dead voice*) The <u>SOUND</u>. I hear the sound of the snow!

Pause. ONE *freezes, its hands over its ears in attitude of despair.* THREE's *speech to go very slowly:*

THREE: <u>Well</u>. (*pause*) Look at <u>them</u>. (*pause*) Didn't hear a <u>thing</u>, myself. (*pause*) Wonder who's next? (*pause*) <u>Terrible</u> way to spend the winter. (*pause*) Mighty <u>quiet</u> around here. (*pause*)

THREE's *hands slowly, will-lessly come up to cover its mouth. Like* ONE *and* TWO, *it freezes in attitude of despair. Stage lights whiten unendurably.*

Blackout

Part II

It's spring now, an uncertain spring, and ONE, TWO, *and* THREE *are back and dozing on the kitchen porch of their farmhouse. Their weird collection of rag-bag farm clothes reflects the changed season: there is more of the torn T-shirt and safety pin influence and less of straps, hooks, buckles and overcoats.*

The country view front and back is the same but there is no longer a dog sleeping in the dooryard. Pots of draggled geraniums, lobelias, and ageratums droop from hooks on the underside of the porch roof and flats of unhealthy looking tomato plants surround the rocking chairs . . . It is clear that all the living things on stage are struggling to recover from some malefic fact of nature.

ONE, TWO, and THREE are struck, suddenly, by the weak sunlight of early spring. As usual no one moves, then, very slowly, as though awakening from a hundred-year hibernation, the three things begin small stretches and great yawns—and a series of uncomfortable shiftings on their inappropriate seats.

ONE: I feel old.

THREE: I feel tired.

TWO: (*feeling of its face*) My skin's real bad.

Pause

THREE: Terrible winter we had. Just terrible.

TWO: Don't remember a thing.

Pause

ONE: (*blinking its eyes*) I still can't hear too good.

TWO: (*cupping its ears with its hands and agreeing*) My eyes hurt something wicked.

THREE: Can't seem . . . t' clear my throat.

ONE: (nods) Winter's like that.

Pause

TWO: Had a good sleep, though.

THREE: Ay-yup. Longest I've slept in a while.

ONE: (*as though remembering*) I didn't sleep . . .

TWO: You didn't?

THREE: Thought you were sleeping.

TWO: (*suspicious*) What were y' doing?

ONE: I was . . . dreaming.

TWO: (*incredulous*) By the Jesus.

THREE: My my. Haven't had a dream in years, myself.

ONE: (*defensive*) Well . . . that's what I was doing.

TWO: (*slowly*) What's it like, t' dream?

THREE: Have t' talk much?

ONE: (*as though remembering*) No. The dream was quiet. And <u>white</u>. The dream was <u>snow-white</u>.

TWO: <u>T</u>errible thing.

THREE: Wouldn't <u>care</u> t' dream like that, myself.

TWO: Nope. Not a<u>tall</u>.

THREE: Hope it don't happen again.

TWO: A <u>bad</u> habit.

   Pause

THREE: (*ominous, to* ONE) Good thing y' don't re<u>mem</u>ber it.

ONE: But I . . .

TWO: (*quick*) <u>Never</u> <u>mind</u>.

THREE: Don't <u>like</u> t' know another person's dreams.

TWO: (*definitive*) Your own business en<u>tire</u>ly.

THREE: (*shaking its head*) A <u>bad</u> habit.

   Pause

ONE: (*an attempt*) Latest spring I can remember. (*pause*) Wouldn't you say.

THREE: Nope. Wouldn't say that.

TWO: Not a<u>tall</u>.

THREE: (*truculent*) <u>Ear</u>ly spring if y' ask me. Snow was all gone by the fourth a Ju<u>ly</u>.

TWO: Latest spring <u>we</u> ever had was the spring a '98. Remember the spring a '98?

THREE: Nope. Don't remember a <u>thing</u>.

TWO: Snowed right up through August. Had eighteen inches the morning a the 21st.

ONE: <u>No</u>.

THREE: Y' don't say.

TWO: Weeell . . . I <u>think</u> that's how 'twas.

THREE: Nothing like that <u>this</u> year.

ONE: My goodness no.

TWO: Might even get a few vegetables out a the ga<u>r</u>den . . . <u>this</u> year.

THREE: (*to* TWO) <u>Say</u>. When did you <u>plant</u> that garden anyhow?

TWO: <u>Me</u> plant? (*to* ONE) I thought 'twas <u>your</u> turn t' plant this year!

ONE: (*innocent*) Oh no.

TWO: By the <u>Jesus</u>. (*to* THREE) Then 'twas <u>your</u> turn. <u>You</u> were s'posed t' plant!

THREE: (*irrevocable logic*) I planted <u>last</u> year.

ONE: That's <u>so</u>. I remember the turnips.

THREE: Ay-<u>yup</u>. That's all we got outa that garden. Frost and bugs and wood-chucks took the rest. (*pause, resigned*) Like they always do.

TWO: (*twisting in its chair*) By the Jesus! Y' mean it was <u>my</u> turn t' plant the garden!

THREE: (*quietly*) That's what I said.

TWO: WELL I DIDN'T DO IT. I DIDN'T PLANT A THING.

Long pause

THREE: Now that's a pity.

ONE: A real shame.

THREE: 'Magine we won't have much to eat come winter.

ONE: Don't have much right now.

THREE: Looks like summer's going t' be even worse 'n winter was.

TWO: WHY DIDN'T YOU REMIND ME.

ONE: Never thought to.

THREE: Too busy.

ONE: Dreaming.

THREE: Sleeping.

Pause

ONE: (*placating*) Well well.

THREE: Now now.

ONE: Nothing to get ex<u>c</u>ited about.

THREE: That's right. Just tighten your belt a little.

TWO: Don't remember <u>ever</u> going without a garden.

THREE: Had t' happen sometime.

Pause

ONE: Course it . . . (*appears to consider*) didn't exactly have to happen right <u>now</u>.

THREE: Not the best <u>time</u> for it.

ONE: Could a waited til <u>next</u> year.

THREE: Ay-yup. Next year would have been much better.

ONE: We would a been pre<u>pared</u>.

THREE: That's right. Now we're caught short.

ONE: <u>Real</u> short.

ONE *and* THREE *stare at* TWO *who fiddles with its overalls.*

THREE: Well well we'll make the best of it.

ONE: (*parting shot*) <u>Have</u> to.

Pause

TWO: (*timorous*) Must be . . . <u>some</u>thing here we can eat.

THREE: Can't think of a <u>thing</u>.

TWO: (*gaining power, to* ONE) <u>You</u>, mebbe.

ONE: (*looks*)

TWO: (*elbows* THREE) Haw haw.

THREE: Hee hee.

TWO: (*jocular, to* ONE) Seems t' me you're the <u>young</u>est.

THREE: (*also jocular*) Ay-yup. <u>And</u> the tenderest.

TWO: Better than <u>coon</u>, they say.

ONE: <u>What's</u> better than coon.

TWO: <u>Hu</u>man meat.

THREE: Y'<u>don't</u> say.

TWO: Better than coon <u>and</u> possum.

THREE: Well now, possum's pretty good if y' cut the fat out of it.

TWO: Anyways that's what they <u>say</u>. Human meat's better 'n <u>all</u> of 'em.

ONE: <u>Who</u> says. Who <u>knows</u> around here.

TWO: Them Greene boys, for one.

THREE: (*helpful*) Ate up their nine year old cousin in March.

TWO: (*pondering*) Was it the girl or the boy they ate.

THREE: Believe it was the boy . . . Nope . . . <u>wait</u> a minute . . . they was twins. Ay-yup, twins. (*with satisfaction*) Ate 'em <u>both</u>.

TWO: Charlie Palmer's mighty sold on human meat.

THREE: Always had a big mouth, that Charlie.

TWO: <u>Claims</u> he ate part of his daughter's <u>leg</u> last Fall.

THREE: (*disgusted*) Them <u>Palmers</u>. Little Alice chopped off her toe taking a swing at her brother. Mrs. Palmer's so pore she must a fried it right up. <u>That's</u> how close Charlie <u>Palmer's</u> been t' <u>hum</u>an meat.

TWO: Never <u>could</u> trust them Palmers.

THREE: Run their mouths <u>night</u> and <u>day</u>.

Pause. Subject exhausted.

ONE: (*coming out of trance*) I had no . . . idea . . . people were doing that . . . <u>here</u>.

TWO: By the <u>Jesus</u> where you <u>been</u>.

THREE: Been going <u>on</u> here since I was a <u>kid</u>.

ONE: (*still tranced*) I heard . . . rumours about it happening in other towns . . .

TWO: Ay-<u>yup</u>. <u>Heart</u>wellville. Board a selectman barbecued the postmaster in Heartwellville this fourth a <u>July</u>. Must have been quite a sight. That postmaster weighed over 300 pounds.

THREE: And over to Shaftesbury. Did y' hear what they're stuffing their turkeys with over to <u>Shaftes</u>bury?

TWO: (*grim*) <u>I</u> heard. Haw haw.

ONE: (*shudders*) I thought . . . I mean . . . I hoped . . . (*incredulous*) <u>right</u> <u>here</u> <u>in</u> <u>Mountain</u> <u>County</u>?!

TWO: (*evil*) Well, now, that must a been quite a dream you were dreaming.

THREE: Reckon it lasted a lot longer than this <u>winter</u>. Haw haw.

TWO: Hee hee. (*pause, then starts again*) Guess you didn't hear about Harry <u>Briggs</u>' little baby.

THREE: Guess I <u>did</u> hear.

ONE: What. Hear <u>what</u>?

THREE: Baby fell right through the floor a that Ford truck Harry's been driving. Rusted right <u>out</u> on him. Ford trucks never <u>were</u> any good.

TWO: Guess you didn't hear what happened after <u>that</u>.

THREE: Nope I didn't. Harry was so busy cursing that <u>Ford</u> out he didn't ever finish <u>tell</u>ing what happened to the <u>ba</u>by.

ONE: (*tremulous*) What . . . <u>did</u> happen.

TWO: (*story-teller's tone*) Well now . . . Them Briggs didn't notice right off the baby was gone.

THREE: (*explains to* ONE) Got eleven kids, y' know. <u>Bound</u> t' lose one or two of 'em from time t' time.

TWO: (*resumes*) Anyways, by the time they counted up the kids and found the baby <u>was</u> gone, they were a good long ways from where they dropped it.

THREE: (*expressionless*) That a fact.

TWO: (*resumes*) Well they got turned around quick enough and started back, but no sign a that baby. Then all t' once Harry Jr., gives a big holler.

THREE: (*aside to* ONE) Reckon Harry, Jr.'s fourteen, fifteen by now. Little slow in the head, but he's got good lungs.

TWO: (*resumes*) Harry Jr. gives a holler because he's seen one a them no good Gardners sitting on the side a the road, picking at her teeth.

ONE: (*horrified realization*) My god, <u>no</u>.

TWO: (*satisfaction*) Ay-<u>yup</u>. And Harry Jr. knows them Gardners don't clean <u>nothing</u> unless there's a mighty good reason. So Harry Jr. jumps outa the truck, rastles that Gardner kid t' the ground—<u>Janie</u> Gardner it was—and squeezes something outa her hand. Guess you all know what <u>that</u> was.

THREE *and* ONE, *spellbound, indicate by awkward gestures that they'd rather be told.*

TWO: <u>Finger</u> bones. <u>That's</u> what. <u>Baby's</u> finger bones. That little imp a hell was cleaning her teeth with the Briggs baby's <u>fing</u>er bones.

THREE: (*deadpan*) Y' <u>don't</u> say.

ONE: (*covers face*)

TWO: <u>Amaz</u>ing is what I call it. Them Briggs hadn't lost that baby for more 'n twenty minutes.

THREE: Quick as a cat, that Janie Gardner.

TWO: Ay-yup. Her third infant this week.

ONE: Where . . . is . . . she . . . now?

TWO: (*elaborately casual*) Janie? 'Magine she's weeding her mother's garden. A course she was down two, three days with an <u>up</u>-set stomach.

ONE: No one . . . <u>did</u> anything?

THREE: Didn't catch 'er in the act.

TWO: Got t' have a <u>corpse</u> t' prove a <u>murder</u>.

ONE: But the finger . . . (*can't say it*). Those <u>things</u> she was cleaning her teeth with . . .

TWO: Well, now, she might a picked <u>them</u> up anywheres.

THREE: Don't 'magine them Briggs were any too sorry t' be relieved of another <u>mouth</u> t' feed.

TWO: Don't 'magine they were.

Pause. Some rocking and resettling.

THREE: (*brightly*) It <u>does</u> feel good t' be in the <u>sun</u> again.

TWO: Ay-<u>yup</u>. Sure <u>does</u>.

TWO *and* THREE *look at* ONE, *coercing a confirmation.* ONE *starts to rally, then sinks.*

ONE: It's not . . . <u>much</u> of a sun.

THREE: (*brightly*) All we got.

TWO: (*pugnacious*) <u>Glad</u> t' see it.

Pause

THREE: (*reviving the subject*) Guess if y' like <u>hu</u>man meat y' don't <u>need</u> t' worry about your garden.

TWO: That's so.

THREE: If y' like <u>hu</u>man meat, all y' need to worry about is your neighbors.

TWO: Haw haw. (*serious*) Whether or not they taste good.

THREE: Hee hee. (*serious*) Whether or not <u>they</u> like human meat.

Pause

ONE: (*rouses*) We <u>got</u> any neighbors?

TWO: Don't remember.

THREE: There's the Lillie girls . . . wait a minute . . . Nope. They're <u>dead</u>.

TWO: How 'bout the Browns?

THREE: Over to South Stream Road? You don't remember a <u>thing</u>. Brown boy <u>froze</u> t' death up in his uncle's pasture this winter. Browns are <u>all</u> dead . . . <u>Now</u>.

ONE: Guess we <u>don't</u> have any neighbors.

THREE: Nothing to worry about then.

TWO: <u>That's</u> so.

Pause.

ONE: (*experimentally*) In the old days, neighbors around here used to hunt each other like deer.

THREE: (*bored*) My my.

TWO: (*also bored*) Y' don't say.

ONE: But they only hunted at certain times.

THREE: When was <u>that</u>.

ONE: (*casual*) Oh . . . right about . . . <u>now</u>, in the middle of the summer. They only hunted at certain times and in special places.

TWO: (*slight interest*) <u>What</u> places.

ONE: (*casual*) Oh . . . places like <u>this</u> one . . . mountain farms.

Pause. TWO *and* THREE *shift a little.*

ONE: Yessir, those hunting seasons in the old days were just like <u>carnivals</u>. The people would dress up every morning in the colors a blood and go out to stalk their neighbors.

THREE: (*slight shudder*) Believe I felt some rain.

TWO: <u>Know</u> y' did. Can smell it coming on.

ONE: (*insistent*) They'd take down their guns and they'd <u>creep</u> into their wood-lots and they'd <u>crouch</u> in their barns. And pretty soon a neighbor'd come along doing the same thing, and then you'd hear the sound a the bullets . . .

THREE: What's the <u>purpose</u>.

TWO: Downright <u>fool</u>ish if y' ask me.

ONE: Believe it had something t' do with . . . uh . . . blooding the soil. That's what they <u>called</u> it. The old people used t' think it made the crops grow better.

TWO: By the Jesus, I never heard <u>that</u>.

THREE: Me neither. Never heard a thing <u>about</u> it.

Pause

ONE: Maybe I dreamt it.

Pause

THREE: (*mean*) Thought you dreamt in <u>white</u>.

TWO: <u>That's</u> <u>so</u>.

ONE: I <u>did</u> say that . . . It must have been the <u>winter</u> hunting I dreamt about.

TWO: (*suspicious*) They did that in <u>win</u>ter-time?

ONE: Ay-yup. And ate the bodies same as they did in summer.

Pause

TWO: (*snif snif*) Could a <u>sworn</u> I was smelling rain. (*snif snif*) But 'tain't exactly <u>like</u> rain . . .

THREE: (*snif snif; to* ONE) You got something on the stove?

ONE: There's no food in the house.

TWO: It's a real . . . <u>heavy</u> smell . . .

THREE: (*quickly*) Don't think a <u>thing</u> about it.

Pause

ONE: (*slowly*) Well . . . well.

TWO: My . . . my.

THREE: Here we <u>are</u>.

Pause

TWO: Ay-<u>yup</u>.

Pause

ONE: (*softly*) It seems like there was more good will back then.

TWO: What're you <u>talk</u>ing about?

THREE: Can't hear a <u>word</u>.

ONE: (*a little louder*) I mean in the <u>old</u> days. When the neighbors went hunting. There was nothing . . . <u>mean</u> about it. They always had their reasons.

TWO: Haw haw. Got their reasons <u>now</u>, by the Jesus.

THREE: Hee hee. That <u>so</u>? What are they.

TWO: Human meat's the tastiest meat around. That's the reason pure and simple.

THREE: Can't beat that for a reason.

TWO: Nope. Y' can't.

Slight pause

ONE: Well, in the old days it was for the <u>crops</u>. They hunted to make the <u>corn</u> grow. That's what they said. And everybody got a fair chance to shoot. (*shudders*) Not like what . . . Janie <u>Gard</u>ner did.

THREE: <u>Hell</u> that's <u>noth</u>ing compared to what <u>some</u> of 'em do 'round here.

TWO: Better believe it. Mighty rough crowd up on <u>this</u> mountain.

THREE: Always <u>was</u>.

TWO: (*with satisfaction*) Ay-<u>yup</u>.

Pause

ONE: (*insistent*) And in the old days, everybody got a chance to <u>speak</u>. To say their last words before they died. And the words were taken down and buried with 'em.

TWO: By the Jesus y' wouldn't get far with something like that in <u>this</u> town.

THREE: By god <u>no</u>. People dying too fast in <u>this</u> neighborhood. No <u>time</u> t' take dictation.

TWO: Haw haw.

THREE: Lucky if someone digs a hole and throws the body <u>in</u> it.

TWO: Lucky if there's anything left a the body t' <u>throw</u> in the hole.

THREE: Hee hee. <u>That's</u> the truth.

ONE: (*shakes its head*) Terrible thing not to have your say before you die.

TWO: Ohhhh I dunno.

THREE: Time t' <u>have</u> it is when y'r <u>alive</u>.

Pause

TWO: Mighty <u>quiet</u>.

THREE: <u>Too</u> quiet.

Pause

ONE: (*quietly*) It seems . . . <u>awful</u> to me.

TWO: <u>What</u>'s awful.

THREE: Can't hear a <u>thing</u>.

ONE: To pass . . . silently out of the world . . . On bad days, it's what I . . . <u>dream</u> about.

TWO: (*sharply*) Now <u>now</u>.

THREE: (*warning*) There <u>there</u>.

TWO: (*finally*) <u>No</u> <u>dreaming</u>.

THREE: A bad habit.

Pause

TWO: (*snif snif*)

Pause

ONE: I . . . <u>smell</u> something.

THREE: <u>No</u> y' don't.

TWO: Not at<u>all</u>.

THREE: It's the <u>rain</u> coming on.

ONE: No it's . . . <u>thicker</u> than rain. (*snif snif*) It's got a heaviness to it . . . it's (*snif*) it's kind of a . . .

THREE: (*throws up its arms and coughs loudly*) Cough cough cough

TWO: (*hits* THREE *awkwardly on the back*)

THREE: Can't clear my throat at<u>all</u>.

TWO: Must a been something you <u>ate</u>.

> TWO *and* THREE *exchange looks.* ONE *puzzles over the smell. Pause.*

TWO: By god I'm getting hungry my<u>self</u>.

ONE: Snif snif.

THREE: (*a little sour*) Should a planted that <u>gar</u>den.

> *Pause.* TWO *looks at* THREE.

THREE: (*amends*) Course vegetables are kinda hard t' take day in and day out.

TWO: <u>Boring</u>. Real <u>boring</u>.

ONE: (*snif snif*) It's kind of a . . . <u>red</u> smell . . .

TWO: <u>Here</u> now.

THREE: Don't care t' listen to <u>that</u> kind a talk.

ONE: But I . . . almost recogni . . .

TWO: (*sharply*) You just <u>hush</u> yourself.

THREE: Don't think a <u>thing</u> about it.

TWO: Almost time t' take a <u>nap</u>.

ONE: WHAT nap.

TWO: After<u>noon</u> nap.

THREE: Got t' get your rest.

TWO: Never <u>know</u> when you're going t' need your <u>strength</u>.

THREE: <u>That's right</u>.

   They subside, glumly.

TWO: <u>Aw</u>ful quiet.

THREE: Haven't heard a bird or a cricket yet.

ONE: (*slowly*) I wonder . . . where . . . the small animals are.

TWO: De-<u>pressing</u>.

THREE: (*shaking its head*) Un-<u>nat</u>ural.

ONE: I haven't seen a fox . . . or a skunk . . . or a rabbit . . .

THREE: <u>Ay</u>-yup. Even the woodchucks're gone.

ONE: (*slowly*) I wonder . . . what . . . <u>happened</u>.

THREE: Well y' won't hear no <u>yard</u> animals, that's for <u>sure</u>.

TWO: Greene boys got 'em all last <u>Fall</u>.

THREE: <u>Ay</u>-yup. Shot purt near every house-dog in the county.

TWO: And the nor'easter froze up most a the stock this winter . . .

THREE: By the <u>J</u>esus. No <u>wonder</u> it's quiet.

TWO: 'Bout all that's around is a few hens.

ONE: And the neighbors.

THREE: Don't <u>have</u> no more neighbors.

ONE: The other <u>people</u>, I mean.

   Pause

TWO: Wonder which a them is <u>left</u>?

THREE: You can bet money those Pratts're still around.

TWO: Don't doubt it. Pratts always had the sharpest teeth in town.

THREE: Heard old man Pratt didn't saw a single board for that sap house a his.

TWO: Y' don't <u>say</u>.

THREE: That's <u>right</u>. <u>Son</u>ny Pratt chewed right through 'em. Neatest job y'ever saw.

ONE: (*sceptical*) When did you see it.

THREE: Didn't see it. <u>Heard</u> about it.

TWO: Anyways them Pratts're still around for <u>sure</u>.

Pause

TWO: Who else?

They think.

THREE: Well there's little Janie Gardner. <u>She's</u> a tough one.

TWO: 'Magine Harry Briggs Jr.'s got t' her by now.

THREE: (*agrees*) Takes things hard, young Harry.

TWO: Course if Harry Jr. got little Janie, y' know what <u>that</u> means.

THREE: Sure do.

TWO: Ay-yup. Happens that way every time.

ONE: <u>What</u> does. <u>What</u> happens.

TWO: Re-venge. <u>That's</u> what happens. 'Magine Janie's dad's dismembering Harry Sr. 'long about now . . .

THREE: And Harry Sr.'s wife is hacking away at Janie's mom.

TWO: Ay-<u>yup</u>. that's how it goes.

THREE: Got t' pay for <u>every</u>thing.

TWO: (*the capper*) Got t' <u>fin</u>ish what y' start.

THREE: Ay-yup. Clean your plate. That's what my maw always said.

TWO: Haw haw.

THREE: Hee hee.

Pause

ONE: Wonder if there'll be a town picnic this year.

TWO: (*evil*) No lack a <u>main</u> <u>courses</u>.

THREE: <u>That's</u> so.

TWO: Might have a little problem with attendance, though.

THREE: Hee hee. Population's getting smaller every year.

   Slight pause

ONE: The town picnic was always like . . . a family supper.

TWO: <u>Is</u> a family supper.

THREE: <u>Everybody's</u> kin around here.

   TWO *and* THREE *look at* ONE.

TWO: (amends) <u>Most</u> everybody.

   Pause

ONE: (*afresh*) In the old days, the town picnics were called hunting feasts.

TWO: (*ritual boredom*) My my.

THREE: (*the same*) Y' don't say.

ONE: They had them twice a year—once for the summer blooding and once for the winter one—and both times they'd last for weeks.

TWO: Do tell.

THREE: (*sniffs, starts to speak, then relapses*).

ONE: (*persists*) It was all done according to rules that everybody knew about. There were times to eat and times not to. Times to say certain words and times to be silent. Everybody knew <u>what</u> they were s'posed to do and <u>when</u>.

TWO: (*false interest*) Glad t' hear it.

THREE: Ay-yup. (*snif snif*)

   TWO *and* THREE *continue sniffing.*

ONE: And when the feasting was over, and before the graves were closed for good, the survivors always held a reading of the last words said by their departed neighbors.

THREE: (*snif snif*) By the Jesus don't know's I can stand that smell.

TWO: (*agrees*) It <u>is</u> getting thicker.

THREE: Wonder what in hell it is.

ONE: (*relentlessly*) The last words of the departed were always written down in an ink made from the blood of . . .

TWO: (*with finality*) <u>That's</u> <u>it</u>.

Pause

THREE: (*slowly*) By the Jesus, b'lieve you're right . . .

ONE: (*snif snif*) A thick red smell . . .

TWO: (*snif snif*) Heavy and sweet . . .

A gradual crescendo

THREE: Sticks in my <u>throat</u>.

TWO: Can't seem t' clear it out a my <u>eyes</u>.

ONE: I hear it pounding in my <u>ears!</u>

Pause

TWO: (*embarrassed*) Well, now.

THREE: (*the same*) No <u>need</u> t' get excited.

Slight pause

ONE: It won't go <u>away</u>! It won't ever <u>go</u> <u>away</u>!

TWO: <u>Course</u> it will.

THREE: Going away <u>now</u>.

TWO: (*sniff snif*) Can't smell a <u>thing</u>.

THREE: Hardly a<u>tall</u>.

Pause

TWO: (*to* ONE) You calm down.

THREE: Don't think a <u>thing</u> about it.

TWO: (*ominous*) Smell's all gone.

Pause

THREE: Might better finish up that story.

TWO: Ay-yup. (*prompts*) Feasting in the old days . . .

ONE *is silent*

THREE: I wonder, did they <u>cook</u> that human meat.

TWO: Cooked or raw, it's still the best eating around.

THREE: How do <u>you</u> know.

TWO: Just <u>do</u>, that's all.

ONE: (*starts suddenly*) How <u>do</u> you know.

Pause

TWO: Had some myself.

THREE: (*admiring*) Why you old <u>dog</u>!

ONE: (*shudders*) Brrrrr.

THREE: (*again*) My, my, y' never said a thing <u>about</u> it.

TWO: (*satisfied*) Never needed to. (*pause, a look at* THREE) 'Magine I'm not the only one around here who's had a taste a human.

ONE: What do you mean.

THREE: (*hurriedly*) How'd it happen. When did y' <u>do</u> it.

TWO: (*casual, story-teller's tone*) Ohhh . . . Musta been two, three years ago. B'lieve it was <u>your</u> turn (*to* ONE) t' plant the garden. Course it was so dry that year nothing came up. (*to* THREE) You remember how it was . . .

THREE: Nope. Don't remember a <u>thing</u>.

TWO: Well it <u>was</u> dry . . . Anyways, I was setting over on the front porch one afternoon—towards sunset it was—just looking at that dry patch a garden ground. And old Miz Overstreet was over on the far meadow filling up her skirt with herbs . . .

ONE: They say she can heal anything.

THREE: <u>Used</u> t' heal. Old lady hasn't been <u>seen</u> in two, three years.

TWO: I sat there looking at Miz Overstreet and my belly was as empty as that garden patch. Couldn't hardly stand it so I stood right up and pitched a rock square at the back a Miz Overstreet's head. (*pauses impressively*) Dropped her without a sound.

ONE: <u>Nothing</u>? She said . . . nothing?

TWO: Didn't have the opportunity.

Pause

THREE: Have t' be real hungry t' go after old Miz <u>Over</u>street. Uh . . . How <u>was</u> she?

TWO: Tough. <u>Real</u> tough. (*pause*) But tasty.

Pause

ONE: So . . . many people dead.

THREE: (*contemptuously to* ONE) Well what'd you <u>think</u>.

TWO: <u>Winter</u> got 'em? Haw haw.

THREE: They drowned in Barber's <u>Pond</u>? Hee hee.

Impressive pause, then slowly

TWO: They got <u>eaten</u>.

THREE: <u>Every</u> <u>one</u>.

Impressive pause, then nastily

TWO: T'wasn't the nor'easter got the <u>Brown</u> boy.

THREE: No <u>sir</u>. It was Milt Harrington.

TWO: Wasn't lightening that got his uncle Clarence, neither.

THREE: Never did figure out who ate old Clarence Brown.

TWO: 'Magine it was <u>Mrs.</u> Brown.

THREE: (*to* ONE) Y'didn't <u>really</u> think Fran Lampman died in the state asylum, did you?

ONE: <u>Fran</u>? But they said . . .

TWO: (*firmly*) Them no-good attendants finished her off in the ambulance.

THREE: Chewed her right down to the fingernails.

TWO: Didn't even wait t' check her in.

THREE: <u>So</u>ciable woman, Fran. Known 'er all my life.

TWO: Don't remember her though.

THREE: Nope. Don't remember a <u>thing</u>.

Pause

TWO: (*stretching a bit*) Ay-yup. Lost a lot a people in this town.

THREE: Some of 'um more'n once.

ONE: What do you mean?

TWO: Guess you can tell the story . . . <u>now</u>.

THREE: Don't know as it's safe.

TWO: Nobody left t' make it <u>un</u>safe.

THREE: (*brightens*) That's true. (*pause*) <u>Well</u>. (*story-teller's tone*) 'Member that girl who bought the old Pike Place?

ONE: The one who fell down the cellar hole?

THREE: Ay-yup. Married that Baptist minister.

TWO: Used t' hang her by her heels outa the upstairs parlour window.

THREE: Ay-yup. That's the one. Anyways the Baptists said she fell down that cellar hole and <u>died</u>.

TWO: <u>Pushed</u> in, if y' ask me.

THREE: (*persists*) Afternoon of her funeral—oh two, three years ago it was, I was passing the Baptist cemetery. 'Member how <u>wet</u> that spring was?

TWO: Nope. Don't remember a thing.

THREE: Well it <u>was</u> wet. Couldn't get a thing t' grow that year. Brown boy claimed he saw brook trout swimming around the green beans. Anyways it was so wet the Baptists hadn't even filled in the grave-hole.

TWO: Careless, them Baptists.

THREE: Well I stood there in all that mud and my belly was as empty as the grave-hole. So I got down on my knees and dug that coffin right up.

ONE: My . . . <u>god</u>.

TWO: (*approving*) Y' <u>don't</u> say.

THREE: Ay-<u>yup</u>. Dug it right up and pried it open. (*pauses*) And there she was, big as life. (*pauses, dreamy*) Strangest thing, though. She was . . . part turned over and her right hand was stuck up in her mouth.

TWO: (*to* ONE) Here's the <u>good</u> part.

THREE: Near as I can make out, them no-good Baptists must a buried her alive. Looked like she'd bitten right through her fingers when she woke up in that coffin. (*pause, shakes head*)

TWO: We got any a them Baptists left?

THREE: Nope, not a one. They were the first t' go. No stamina a<u>tall</u>.

ONE: The <u>girl</u>. What happened to the <u>girl</u>?

THREE: Oh <u>her</u>. (*slight pause*) I ate her. (*considers*) Well <u>most</u> of her.

TWO: How <u>was</u> she.

THREE: Mighty damp. But <u>tasty</u>. Real <u>tasty</u>.

ONE: (*struggling with revulsion*) Did she . . . were there any <u>last</u> <u>words</u>? Anything in the coffin?

THREE: Well. (*considers*) She didn't say anything t' <u>me</u>. Haw haw.

TWO: Hee hee.

ONE: (*desperate*) A piece of <u>paper</u>. Something written <u>down</u>.

THREE: Don't remember seeing a <u>thing</u>. Course it was pretty wet down there.

TWO: 'Magine it was pretty messy too.

THREE: Wasn't the neatest meal I ever had. Haw haw.

TWO: Hee hee. 'Magine if there <u>was</u> a piece of paper y' might've overlooked it.

THREE: That's so. You're right there.

ONE: God, god, another one going silent out of the world . . .

TWO: (*crudely*) All this talk's making me hungry.

THREE: Could do with a bite my<u>self</u>.

   Slight pause

TWO: Got no vegetables left.

THREE: Not a one.

TWO: (*significant look*) Guess we'll have t' start elsewhere.

THREE: Ay-yup. Got t' do the best we <u>can</u>.

TWO: Might not be as easy as you think.

THREE: (*a look at* ONE) We've known 'er a good, long time.

TWO: Don't remember much <u>about</u> 'er though.

THREE: Don't remember a <u>thing</u>.

   Pause

TWO: 'Magine that'll make it easier.

   Pause. ONE *is silent, trance-like, as though in a dream.*

THREE: Can't seem t' work myself <u>up</u> to it.

TWO: Guess I can take care of it. (*pause*) If I <u>have</u> to.

THREE: Think about being hungry.

TWO: Don't have t' think. I <u>am</u> hungry.

THREE: Think about how tasty she'll be.

TWO: She'll be . . . tough. Real tough. Like the rest of them.

   TWO *begins to blink rapidly and* THREE *starts pulling at its collar.*

THREE: This is no way t' carry on.

TWO: You're right there. Soon's I can open my eyes I'll get down to it.

THREE: If I get my throat clear, I'll beat y' to it.

(TWO *works on its eyes with its fists, scrubbing and punching awkwardly.* THREE *grabs its throat with both hands, trying to force its adam's apple into a more comfortable position.*

Meanwhile, ONE *removes a pencil and paper from the pouch of its coveralls.*)

ONE: Where was I? Oh yes, the Burial. (*story-teller's tone*) After the hunting feast was over, and before the lids of the coffins were nailed down, the last words of the departed were always written in red and laid right in on the bodies. (*amends*) On what was <u>left</u> a the bodies. Then all the townspeople gathered around the gravesite and . . . and . . . (*breaks off, looks at* TWO, *then at* THREE) Hmmm. Don't imagine it's too late to do a little work on that garden. I could get in a second sowing a lettuce. I could (*figures*) put in some wax beans and some a that New Zealand spinach. Wouldn't hurt to try a little winter wheat. Too <u>bad</u> about the corn. Corn's what they <u>always</u> used t' plant. Well, well, have t' do what I can. That soil's going t' need a lot a <u>bone</u> and <u>blood</u>meal. (*looks at* TWO *and* THREE, *still struggling with their eyes and throat*) Heh heh. <u>That's</u> no problem a<u>tall</u>. (*poises pencil above paper*) Let's see now, what were those words? Ahhh. (*writes and reads slowly*) "Soon's I can open my eyes I'll get down to it." That's one. And the other was . . . uh . . . "If . . . I get my throat clear I'll beat y' to it." Hmmm. Not too interesting. (*pause*) But . . . (*philosophical*) there you are. Folks never really know what their last words are going to be. If <u>they'd</u> known, (*a gesture towards* TWO *and* THREE) I'm sure they could a done better. (*Looks again at* TWO *and* THREE; *the lights begin to redden.*) Snif snif. Don't know <u>why</u> they said that smell was going away. It's coming on stronger than ever. (*pause*) Well, might better get on with it. Got to get that garden in before Fall.

(ONE *elaborately removes from the front pouch of her coveralls a knife and fork.* TWO *and* THREE *turn to stare at* ONE *as the lights redden so acutely that the stage appears to be running in blood. An infrared freeze of the three things, then . . .*)
Blackout

SIGNS OF LIFE

To the ladies

SIGNS OF LIFE premiered at The Women's Project at The American Place Theatre, New York City, in 1979, directed by Esther (Izbitsky) Herbst. Since then it has had more than 150 productions in North America and throughout the world. These photographs are from the premiere at The American Place and from The Horizon Theatre production in Washington, D.C., 1985.

Characters

P. T. BARNUM
DR. SIMON SLOPER
THE MOTHER/THE NURSE
HENRY JAMES
KATHERINE PEABODY LORING
THE WARDEN
JANE MERRITT
ALICE JAMES
THE FREAKS: WORKHOUSE INMATES/THE BLIND

Note to the actors: It might be helpful to imagine the characters in this play as each an aspect of a *shared* consciousness, rather than each an exponent of a *separate* consciousness. They do have in common certain prejudices and inclinations which make even the most opposed characters seem to share—however stealthily—a kind of identity. The effect this identity (or these identities) should have on the audience is a constant and nervous recollection of familiarity; a shudder of recognition in the most incongruous places. The actors must do everything possible to increase the audience's discomfort in this respect.

Author's Note: Art made from extreme situations can often find its "facts" (i.e., the hinges upon which certain of its circumstances swing) in history. Thus, the Uterine Guillotine expertly wielded by Dr. Sloper in *Signs of Life* was invented and named by the founder of American gynecology, Dr. J. Marion Sims—a man who "performed" countless clitoridectomies and referred to himself in writing as "the architect of the vagina." Thus, too, Alice James's "companion" really was Katherine Loring; Jane Merritt, the Elephant Woman, had a male counterpart in the narrative of the Elephant Man by Sir Frederick Treves; and Henry James's burning of his sister's journal happened just as it does in *Signs of Life*.

Left to right: DR. SLOPER, HENRY JAMES. (*Photo by Martha Holmes*)

DOCTOR: And with these hands I have opened all the organs of the female pelvis . . .

HENRY: (*Warning*) Doctor . . .

DOCTOR: Picked the rare flowers of a lady's garden: the polyps, the fibroids, the cysts . . .

HENRY: Let me warm your cup . . .

Left to right: THE ELEPHANT WOMAN, P. T. BARNUM. (*Photo by Martha Holmes*)

BARNUM: Freaks. I never had one yet that didn't dream. Life's a terrible thing. Sometime's it's a terrible thing.

Left to right: DR. SLOPER, THE MOTHER, P. T. BARNUM, KATHERINE LORING, HENRY JAMES. (*Photo by Martha Holmes*)

DOCTOR: Alice James was the most accomplished neurasthenic I have ever treated. Her fits were <u>marvel</u> of patient orchestration. She had a genius for the well-timed disease. A real genius. What a performer she would have made.

Left to right: DR. SLOPER, ALICE JAMES.

DOCTOR: Then we could move on to a simple ovariotomy. It's taken me hundreds of attempts to perfect that one. I wish we could keep you conscious for it. You would so appreciate the precision.

ALICE: I have a certain . . . <u>attachment</u> to my organs, doctor.

SIGNS OF LIFE

The Lobby

An actor in the costume of P. T. BARNUM *struts and frets and twirls a cane beside the ticket booth. As the audience buys its tickets,* BARNUM'S *voice is amplified throughout the lobby. His spiel continues—improvised, syncopated, outrageously hokey—until every person has entered the house. The actor who speaks* BARNUM'S *part can address individual members of the audience by, for instance, what they wear—"Mr. Red Shirt, Miss Brown Bag"—but he must never be abrasive or accosting. Good-humoured lubricity is the tone to take. Here are some of the things* MR. BARNUM *might say:*

BARNUM: Ladies and gentlemen, gentlemen and ladies, welcome to P. T. Barnum's American Museum! Please have your money ready. We have a fascinating bit of exotica here for you tonight. The lady you've all heard so much about is with us at last! That's right, folks, it's Elephant Woman! Queen of the Curiosities! Empress of the Awful! <u>The</u> most extraordinary female freak of the decade, just returned from a triumphant tour of Western Europe!

Ladies and gentlemen! Elephant Woman <u>walks</u>, she <u>talks</u>, she even <u>laughs</u> like a human being, but due to a dreadful accident of birth she appears to be part pachyderm. That's what I said, Madam, the lady looks just like an elephant. She's got an arm the size of an oak tree! A nose like an elephant's trunk! And other features too horrible to mention!

Come on in sir, don't hesitate. Line forms to the right. You <u>know</u> P. T. Barnum wants to please the people.

Folks, I've combed the world to bring back attractions the American people want to see! Remember Mme. Clofullia, the Bearded Lady from Belgium? I know you <u>do</u>, Ma'am. The in-credible Chang and Eng—the Siamese siblings who couldn't bear to be separated? <u>You</u> were here on their opening night, Sir. I remember your face. How about the famous Mermaid from Feegee? The renowned Gen. Tom Thumb? All these and many more have made their debuts right here in P. T. Barnum's American Museum.

But I tell you, ladies and gentlemen, there's never been anything here like the young lady you're about to see tonight. Those of you with conditions of the heart—I'd advise you to have your glycerin tablets ready. Ladies, if you're subject to fainting fits, reach for your smelling salts now. We have a physician in attendance, but he can't be everywhere at once.

That's right, friends, move right along. Have your money ready. P. T. Barnum guarantees you'll never have an experience like this one again. Believe me folks, it's the best bargain in the solar system! Etc., etc., etc.

The Apron

As the seats begin to fill and until the house lights go down, the following scene is played on the stage apron over the sounds of an arriving audience. The scene must be repeated continuously (with, perhaps, certain attitudinal changes) until the last person to arrive has seen it at least once through:

At a tea table, STAGE LEFT, HENRY JAMES, DR. SLOPER, KATHERINE LORING, *and* JANE ELIZABETH MERRITT (*the* MOTHER) *are serving each other in an abstracted and ritualistic way.* BARNUM *comes from the lobby to join them. The table must be very small, so that the characters are at some pains to avoid touching each other. The scene should induce in those members of the audience who actually listened to* BARNUM's *spiel and therefore expected something salacious, a sharp feeling of disappointment. If it puts them in an unreceptive mood—so much the better. The actors will only have to work harder at seduction. As each character speaks, she/he turns from the tea ceremony and addresses the audience.*

BARNUM: (*Elegiac.*) In the middle of the hottest summer I can remember, the summer of 1864, the summer I began my American Museum, a female child was born to Jane Elizabeth Merritt of the city of New York. That child made almost as much money for me as General Tom Thumb did.

DOCTOR: (*Clinical and breezy.*) The child was born a monster and that's the simple truth of it. Clinically, she suffered from an extreme form of a disorder diagnosed by me twenty-four years after her birth. The name of the disorder is multiple neurofibromatosis. The name of the child was Jane Merritt. It was not until Mr. Barnum discovered her, that she became known as . . . um . . . (*Distastefully.*) the Elephant Woman.

MOTHER: (*A sense of wonder and protest.*) <u>Joan</u>, I named her Joan, after . . . someone. At birth, her skin was only a little roughened, only a little thick. When she smiled at me she was like any happy child. Her mouth moved a little . . . strangely, that was all. (*Slowly.*) She <u>was</u> slow to walk. Very slow. (*Quickly.*) But there was no reason to imagine what she would become . . .

HENRY: I saw what she became. I saw it only once. Of course, I never told Dr. Sloper what I saw. Why take the story out of a good man's mouth? At any rate, one autumn afternoon in 1889, while temporarily eluding the febrile demands of my sister Alice, I walked into Mr. Barnum's American Museum. And there she was, the Elephant Woman. Surrounded, it seemed to me then, like any youthful heiress, by a small, but significant circle of admirers who blocked her face from my view. It was not until I'd made my way to the front of the crowd, that I saw the tears on her . . . terrible cheeks.

(*Pause. A general muttering of tea service language.*)

"Won't you have more?"

"Will you have a little?"

"One lump or two?"

"No thank you."

"Yes I believe I will."

"Petit fours are so bad for the figure."

"An unusual day."

"A most unusual day."

(*Pause.*)

BARNUM: The year that I was clerking in a drygoods store in Bridgeport, Conn. — 1851 it would have been — the four sons of Henry and Mary James were treated to an awful surprise. A girl child came into the James family. A baby sister. In her Newport, Rhode Island home, Mary James produced a healthy daughter, Alice by name. (*Sits back, amused.*) I understand the James boys never forgave her.

HENRY: (*Disgusted.*) A daughter? A sister for William, Wilkie, Robertson and me? What an indignity. Girls didn't have much of a chance in our family, I'm afraid. Alice became a life-long invalid.

KATHERINE: (*Tenderly.*) I took her to my bosom as though she were my own child. We were the same age, but I saw the damage they had done to Alice as clearly as I saw the color of her eyes, which were, incidentally, slate blue. She had beautiful eyes. I loved her eyes.

DOCTOR: Alice James was the most accomplished neurasthenic I have ever treated. Her fits were a marvel of patient orchestration. She had a genius for the well-timed disease. A real genius. What a performer she would have made.

(*The characters look at each other, relinquish their grip on the tea service, and*

KATHERINE, MOTHER *and* BARNUM *rise and move off stage;* BARNUM *allowing the ladies to rise first and trailing huckster's phrases; good-naturedly, experimentally, almost to himself:*)

BARNUM: That's right, ladies and gentlemen. You heard what I said. The Elephant Woman. A gen-u-wine, home grown, American freak.

(HENRY JAMES *and his protagonist from the novel* Washington Square *are left alone at tea. Their actions are precisely those of two late-Victorian gentlemen at a tea table; that is, murderously banal. The actors' voices must be intimate and possessive when discussing facts and feelings, and bored and correct when asking for butter or more tea.*)

HENRY: A pleasure to see you again, Dr. Sloper.

DOCTOR: It must be five years since we've taken tea together, Mr. James.

HENRY: Surely not that long, sir.

DOCTOR: Five years, Mr. James and I still remember where our conversation left off.

HENRY: Let me see. I believe I had just said that the similarities between my sister Alice and your . . . um . . . <u>patient</u> Jane Merritt were striking.

DOCTOR: And then the Spanish-American War was declared.

HENRY: (*A little confused.*) Oh yes, of course. The war. (*He begins to resettle the tea things and he and* DR. SLOPER *both rearrange themselves in the attitudes of their conversation of five years ago.*)

HENRY: (*Energetically.*) It <u>is</u> a striking coincidence, doctor.

DOCTOR: Both women being my patients, you mean.

HENRY: I mean both of them being what they <u>were</u>. So . . . limited.

DOCTOR: My dear Mr. James. How can you compare <u>your</u> brilliant sister with <u>my</u> freak of nature? More tea?

HENRY: No, no more thank you. My brilliant sister, dear doctor, spent twenty years in bed and produced nothing more than a cancer of the breast. If <u>that</u> isn't freakish . . . (*Shrugs, drinks tea.*) The <u>butter</u>, Dr. Sloper.

DOCTOR: Certainly, Mr. James. (*Forgets it.*) And my poor <u>freak</u>, Jane Merritt . . . in <u>her</u> twenty years, I suppose you could say she produced nothing more than <u>me</u>. It was those experiments on (*corrects himself.*) uh . . . <u>with</u> the Elephant Woman that made me famous, you know. (*Butters a scone energetically.*) She was to me what most humans spend their <u>lives</u> seeking out. My perfect <u>subject</u>, my sublime <u>object</u>, my . . . inspi<u>ration</u>! (*Decrescendo.*) Uh . . . sugar, Mr. James?

HENRY: Thank you doctor, I never take sugar.

DOCTOR: In the whole of my association with Jane Merritt, I could never <u>bear</u> to take my eyes from her. The attractions of such repulsiveness . . .

HENRY: (*Visibly irritated.*) The . . . <u>but</u>ter, Dr. Sloper.

DOCTOR: Certainly, Mr. James.

(*Slight pause. Sounds of butter transferred to scones and other tea table business.*)

HENRY: Well, doctor, I couldn't say that Alice had a <u>repulsive</u> physiognomy, but she <u>did</u> come into the world with her Mother's architectural forehead and her Father's flamboyant chin. (*Pause, shakes his head.*) A discouraging combination. (*Pause.*) I could scarcely . . . tolerate the sight of her. (*Sighs.*)

(*Pause. They muse.*)

DOCTOR: (*Suddenly a toast.*) The ladies, Mr. James?

HENRY: (*Roused, raises his cup.*) Indeed, Dr. Sloper.

(*Pause. Again tea sounds. The moment the* DOCTOR *begins to speak,* HENRY *begins to sleep, nodding precariously into the scones.*)

DOCTOR: More hot water? Faces <u>do</u> have a terrible effect on us Mr. James. Careful, these scones are <u>piping</u> hot. I've often wondered what it was in Jane Merritt's expression that moved me to explore the secrets of her bones.

HENRY: (*Awakens abruptly.*) Doctor, doctor, life's cup is <u>brim</u>ming with imponderables. (*Holds his cup up.*) I <u>will</u> have a touch more water, if you don't mind. My own dear Alice presented <u>me</u> with a similar question. (*Drinks his tea.*)

DOCTOR: Go on, Mr. James.

HENRY: Well . . . I've always wondered what it was in Alice's eyes that drove me to pursue the secrets of her journal. She wanted that journal published, you know. Released into the world from the miasmal swamp of her opinions. (*Examines a toasted scone.*) Naturally, I . . . burnt it to a crisp.

DOCTOR: Hmmmm.

HENRY: Yes.

(*Pause. They muse.*)

DOCTOR: (*The toast.*) Ahh, the ladies, Mr. James.

HENRY: (*Raises his cup.*) Indeed, Dr. Sloper.

(*An appreciative pause. They both lean back. Then they both lean forward.*)

HENRY: Strong tea, doctor.

DOCTOR: I send to England for it.

HENRY: It has a distinctive . . . <u>taste</u>, doctor.

DOCTOR: <u>Does</u> it, Mr. James.

HENRY: A peculiar . . . <u>color</u> as well.

DOCTOR: Everyone says that.

HENRY: A certain . . . cloying consistency.

DOCTOR: Ummmm.

HENRY: One might say an almost . . . sacra<u>men</u>tal quality.

DOCTOR: (*As though paying a compliment.*) The quality is in your imagination.

(*Pause.*)

HENRY: I believe I'll take a biscuit.

DOCTOR: Please do, Mr. James.

HENRY: What a dry taste.

DOCTOR: Really.

HENRY: Dusty, a dusty sort of dough.

DOCTOR: They're made in my kitchen, Mr. James.

HENRY: It tastes . . . ossified, it tastes . . . god help us . . . it tastes like <u>bone</u>.

DOCTOR: Impossible, Mr. James.

HENRY: (*A rising panic.*) Dr. Sloper. There is blood in my cup. And there is bone in my biscuit.

DOCTOR: <u>Just</u> <u>deserts</u>, Mr. James.

HENRY: (*Calming.*) Ahhh yes. Quite right, doctor.

(*Pause. He muses majestically.*)

DOCTOR: (*The toast.*) The ladies, Mr. James.

HENRY: (*Remembering.*) Ah yes, the <u>ladies</u>, Dr. Sloper.

(*They raise their cups. The house lights go down. They lower their cups. The stage lights come up. They remain at tea throughout the play, moving in and out of the action as indicated.*)

The Stage

Any set you like so long as it is mostly vacant, clearly confining, and entirely out of the light. A few objects are possible, but they must be innocent ones: broken and/or remnants of other, wholler objects. What is present throughout the play is a bed, a sort of chiffonier (its mirror is covered when it's JANE MERRITT's *chiffonier, uncovered when it's* ALICE JAMES's) *and a bedside chair. These props are seen from one angle when they are in* JANE MERRITT's *room and from another angle when they are in* ALICE JAMES's *room. It's always the same room, the arrangement is always the same; it is merely our axis of vision that must appear to change. In the American Place Theatre production, the stage was split;* ALICE JAMES's *room and* JANE MERRITT's *room faced and reflected each other. And the tea-table was cranked by cable from* JANE MERRITT's *area in the first act to* ALICE JAMES's *area in the second act.*

All the scenes centering on JANE *are played in her room; all the scenes centered on* ALICE *are played in her room.*

Jane Merritt's Room in the Workhouse

Stage lights come up on JANE's *room in the Workhouse.* JANE's MOTHER *and the* WARDEN—*a large and imposing southern woman—are* UPSTAGE RIGHT, *in close conversation. An earlier* JANE (*earlier than we see through the rest of the play*) *is* CENTER STAGE, *hidden from view by a cluster of Workhouse inmates. An ancient hag, a pair of idiots, a deformed young man, a stammerer, a spasmodic adolescent all crowd around her staring and pointing, lifting her garments, removing her cloak. She remains hidden until the* WARDEN *ends the following scene, each of whose lines can be randomly assigned:*

"It's a monster."

"A real monster."

"Did you . . . did . . . did . . . did . . . didyou . . . didyou . . . did you see the <u>skin</u>?"

"That's not <u>skin</u>."

"It's <u>tree</u> trunk."

"It's <u>ele</u>phant hide."

"Touch it go ahead."

"I dare you."

"How does it <u>stand</u> with legs like that."

"Never mind standing, how does it <u>eat</u>."

"The mouth looks sewed shut."

"Nobody's gonna make me sit next to that thing."

"It's a <u>her</u>, it's a <u>her</u>, look at the chest!"

"It's an elephant woman."

(*One of the idiots takes what appears to be a hat and mask from* JANE, *puts them on and capers around the stage.*)

"Can she <u>walk</u>?"

"Poor thing."

"Can she <u>hear</u>?"

"Poor <u>thing</u>."

"Can she <u>speak</u>?"

"The <u>poor</u> <u>thing</u>."

(*More punching and poking of the unseen* JANE: *the inmates are having a wonderful time.*)

"I hear they're going t' set 'er up in a room here."

"Haw haw. I'd set 'er up in a jar of formaldehyde, that's what <u>I'd</u> do."

"Ohhh Christ, hush your mouths, here comes Warden."

"Ssssh, ssssh, she'll beat us."

"Quick, quick <u>dress</u> the thing."

"Put her cloak on. <u>Hurry</u>."

"Sssh for gawd's sake."

"The <u>hat</u>. Get the <u>hat</u>."

"It's <u>Warden</u>."

(WARDEN *and* MOTHER *move toward the cluster of freaks,* MOTHER *in mid-conversation.*)

MOTHER: And I named her after that woman who led the army in France. I thought, when I saw . . . what she was, I thought she would need a strong name.

WARDEN: Back! Stand back you motherless children or I'll beat you black and blue! (*As the* DOCTOR *speaks, she charges the crowd, swatting indiscriminately.*)

DOCTOR: (*At tea, to* HENRY.) Jane, of course was her name. Elephant Woman came later. I often imagined that plain name was the source of her attraction for the novels of that other Jane, Miss Austen. Can you believe it, Mr. James? That misbegotten, deformed creature fancied herself the heroine of an Austen novel, sitting in some sunlit corner of a rectory garden, embroidering antimacassars for her father, the vicar! As if those horrible hands could hold a needle!

(WARDEN *subsides, breathing heavily. The inmates are strewn about the stage, momentarily subdued. The figure of* JANE MERRITT *draped in dark cloth is exposed; an icon* CENTER STAGE.)

MOTHER: (*To* WARDEN, *to everyone.*) At birth her skin was only a little roughened, only a little thick, it was . . . there was no reason to imagine what she would become. She smiled at me like any baby, she smiled frequently. She loved bright bits of color and she would . . . always have me by her.

(*The inmates regroup, a skirmish is imminent.*)

WARDEN: (*To* MOTHER *as she terrorizes the freaks into a corner.*) You just keep talkin', honey, while I take care a my children here.

DOCTOR: Bright bits of color. Oh yes indeed. Mother's <u>rouge</u> pots. The mother was a common whore, the child born a monster, and that's the simple truth of it.

WARDEN: (*Mopping her brow.*) Now you all calm down, all a you! (*To* MOTHER.) They just silly little children and they got to be treated as such.

MOTHER: Oh I knew something wasn't right about her mouth. I'm a seamstress and I know what it is to make a good fit. Her mouth didn't fit right. There was an extra piece on it, a flap of skin, that just grew and grew until she couldn't nurse or cry or even smile. So I sewed the cape and mask and we made a game of it. Hiding from the light, we called it. And now my . . . customers won't come for their fittings as long as that "monster" is there. And that monster is my only child and we are starving together . . . Life is a terrible thing, Warden. Sometimes it's a terrible thing.

WARDEN: (*To* JANE, *ignoring* MOTHER.) And <u>this</u> here's mah new child. Well, darlin', let's have a look at you.

MOTHER: (*Moves in front of* JANE.) Warden, it's <u>too</u> <u>soon</u>. She <u>shrinks</u> from the eyes of . . . other people. In all her life, she's hardly . . . been in the light.

WARDEN: (*Hands on hips.*) Lady, this here's the Workhouse. You leavin' your daughter here, you got to leave <u>all</u> of her. Now move yourself on outa here. And let me do mah duty. We're holdin' a class today. You just git along and leave her to me.

(JANE *stands stolidly until her mother embraces her, then the one good arm, the left one, comes up and touches the* MOTHER's *face.*)

WARDEN: Here now let's have a look at you.

(WARDEN *takes off* JANE's *cloak. Then her hat and mask.*)

WARDEN: Oooooo mah <u>gawd</u>. Is that a human <u>bein</u>'?

(*Everyone on stage freezes; an awe-full moment.*)

MOTHER: (*As though in explanation.*) She was born at a carnival. I was at a carnival . . . standing near the Elephant. He turned towards me, I began to bleed . . . and she was . . . born <u>right</u> <u>there</u> in the . . . sawdust.

WARDEN: (*Transfixed, gentler.*) Go 'long now Miz Merritt. It's gonna take quite a while to get her integrated in with the rest of 'em. It'll be easier if you go along.

MOTHER: (*A list.*) They <u>stone</u> her, they <u>shout</u> at her, they knock her down, and now a <u>carnival</u> wants to <u>buy</u> her from me. (*Shudders.*) I am her mother and I cannot stand the sight of her. <u>Some</u>one has to protect her . . .

DOCTOR: Jane Merritt was abandoned to a workhouse when she was very young. I presume her mother's lovers couldn't tolerate the sight of their mistress's little monster.

MOTHER: (*Takes a miniature of herself from her reticule and puts it in* JANE's *good hand.*) Try to keep this longer than I've kept you. (*Exits quickly.*)

(JANE *releases one horrible wail. It is literally released—like a bird from a cage—and is as suddenly gone.* WARDEN *and* JANE *face each other,* WARDEN *still transfixed, as we are, by what* JANE *looks like.*)

WARDEN: (*Loudly, to break the horror.*) Alright, the rest of you get on ovah here, we gon' have a class. We gon' have a class in lookin' and seein' and (*Another look at* JANE.) bein' a freak. Cause you all freaks and you might bettah learn to be what you are. Now pick up them books. (*Inmates stoop to a pile of tattered periodicals.*) You now (*To* JANE.), <u>what</u> did she say yo' name was. <u>Jane</u>. You, Jane Merritt, you stand here. Least you can do is learn to <u>hold</u> a book.

(*The inmates assemble in front of* WARDEN, *weaving, bobbing, slobbering, some with their books upside down. Throughout* WARDEN's *monologue they listen as intently as their various handicaps allow them to, and respond to her commands as well as they can. The staging here is surreal: a parody of all parodies.*)

WARDEN: Now the first thing you want to learn in this class is HOW TO LOOK. You bettah know you all look <u>real</u> disgusting. Ready now? The lesson is HOW TO LOOK. Look to the side. Keep your head straight. Not up in the air. When you look to the side see what's there. Just see what's there. To the <u>side</u>, to the <u>side</u>, to the <u>side</u>. (JANE *looks down.*) In a freak class there's no reason to look <u>down</u>. Everybody in the <u>world</u> already down on <u>you</u>. Just look to the side and <u>see</u>. See. <u>See</u> that bastard sneakin' <u>up</u> on you. <u>See</u> his knife. Be AWARE. See that nice lady gon' give you some money. <u>See</u> her look. She just <u>waiting</u> t' see you smile. <u>Limp</u> on up to her now and hold out your hand. Good. Look to the side, to the side, to the side, to the side. <u>See</u>. In a freak class you got to be awake. You in training for your life. If you're <u>real</u> <u>lucky</u>, one a them carnivals yo' Mama was talking about might pick up on you.

(JANE *might seem to register the word "Mama."*)

Now the last thing you got to learn in this class is how to laugh accordin' to an audience. Most a you gonna end up bein' looked at by a lot a people, and you got to learn to laugh real big so people think you're happy. Nobody's gonna pay to see you if you can't be happy for 'em. C'mon now. Let's show her how to laugh.

(FREAKS *and* WARDEN *laugh.*)

AH HA HA HA HA HA HA HA HA HA HA HA HA HA.

(*The laughter degenerates into scuffles among the inmates and* WARDEN *moves in to swat them.*)

"It's <u>her</u>, Warden. It turns my stomach standing in front of her." (*Points to* JANE.)

"She smells terrible."

"She looks awful."

"She's a real <u>freak</u>."

WARDEN: Hush yo mouths now. We gon' have Dr. Sloper in to look at her. She's some kind of a scientific curiosity.

"Dr. Sloper!"

"He's no doctor."

"He's a <u>ghoul</u>."

"A <u>grave</u>-robber."

"A <u>butcher</u>."

"He's always bringing those knives around."

"Lost his own little girl on the operating table."

"Stomach-trouble, I heard."

"Appendicitis."

"Whatever <u>that</u> is."

"He's the . . . he's the . . . he's . . . he's . . . <u>he's</u> the <u>freak</u>!"

DOCTOR: (*His most urbane, organ-like tone.*) I love all swelling things, Mr. James. Buds in spring, women's bellies before they come to term, the waxing moon, and yes, one of my . . . specialties, the vermiform appendix before it bursts.

(WARDEN *herds the inmates offstage with cuffs and threats:* "Classtime! Get a move on monsters! Let's go! Classtime!" *etc., etc., and* JANE *is left alone. She limps toward the bed, examines it, pulls herself up on it, seems content.*)

JANE: (*With great difficulty, the mouth is virtually sealed.*) This, my home. I have it. (*Takes out* MOTHER'*s miniature.*) This, my mother. I . . . lose her. No mother . . . no home. Now I . . . have . . . nothing. (*And the wail flies again like a bird from her throat.*)

DOCTOR: (*Largely.*) Well, Mr. James, Jane had <u>everything</u>. One short examination of her disordered body and the weight of all my interests amassed a gigantic precipitation and rained down a shower of gold into her lap. (HENRY *yawns hugely.*) She was the <u>real</u> <u>thing</u>, an anatomist's <u>dream</u>, <u>a</u> <u>true</u> <u>case</u> of congenital deformity! My first examination of her was a scientific reve<u>lation</u> . . .

(*And the* DOCTOR *moves from his tea table into* JANE's *room, carrying a satchel filled with scalpels.*)

DOCTOR: (*His most patronizing and mellifluous tone to* JANE.) Now my dear, I'm going to speak very gently, I know you don't understand me, but the sound of my voice will calm you as it calms all my patients. (*Seeing her see his scalpels.*) No, no, don't worry, I bring these with me as a matter of course. There will be no cutting, certainly not yet. I simply wish to examine you for a greater cause. Um . . . Mother Science, my dear, Mother Science.

(*As he examines* JANE, *he speaks to* HENRY *as though he were an entire anatomy class taking notes. The lights come up very bright.*)

The subject of this disorder is a woman aged twenty-four. The disorder concerns both the cutaneous and the osseous systems of her body. With the curious exception of the . . . um . . . genitalia and the left arm and hand, the subject has tubercles covering the whole of her integument. The subcutaneous tissue has greatly increased in amount and density; the surface of the integument itself shows a papillomatous condition, particularly exuberant over the dorsal region and the gluteal districts. The entire bone structure is enormously hypertrophied. Huge dewlaps hang from her outsize skull; bands of connective tissue seal off her mouth and left ear. Are there any questions so far?

HENRY: Can she speak, doctor?

DOCTOR: Her power of speech, if she had it, would be totally impaired.

HENRY: How does she move?

DOCTOR: Articulation of all joints (*He moves her right knee, she jerks away.*)— oops, sorry my dear—is extremely difficult. There appears to be an old injury to the right hip which has resulted in a painful (*He touches her hip, she jerks away.*)—tch, sorry again, <u>very</u> painful and extremely restrictive displasia.

HENRY: (*Reaching for a biscuit.*) And eating. What about eating?

DOCTOR: A liquid diet is . . . barely possible. (*Carelessly.*) More than likely we'll run a tube down her nasal passage and feed her that way. It's easier on the staff.

HENRY: What about . . . evacuation?

DOCTOR: (*A little professional laugh.*) What <u>about</u> it?

HENRY: (*Embarrassed.*) How does she do it?

DOCTOR: As best she can, sir, as best she can.

HENRY: (*Changing the subject.*) What is your prognosis, doctor?

DOCTOR: Death at an early age, I'm afraid. Though, certainly, it's far too soon to rule out the possibility of a surgical cure. I have great faith in my little knives gentlemen, <u>great</u> <u>faith</u>.

HENRY: You intend to operate, then?

DOCTOR: I intend to examine the subject (*Ominous.*) <u>much</u> <u>more</u> <u>thoroughly</u>. And <u>then</u> make my decision. No further questions? (*Pause.*) In sum, then, the subject before us can barely walk, eat, speak, or eliminate, and it is to be profoundly hoped that the god who invested her with this condition, also withheld from her the power to perceive it. Thank you very much, gentlemen. (*To* JANE.) And now, my dear, a few daguerrotypes for Mother Science. I want you to hold very still, yes, very good, that's right. I know you can't understand me, but there will be a flash of light . . .

(JANE *registers horror at the word "light," the light when it comes is blinding, there is a blackout, and the* DOCTOR *is back at the tea table.*)

DOCTOR: She was a world, I tell you Mr. James she was an entire universe . . .

Jane Merritt's Room in the American Museum

BARNUM: (*Offstage, picking up where he left off in the lobby.*) "That's right, folks, she's the best bargain in the solar system."

(*The lights come up on* JANE, *now dressed for display as Elephant Woman, sitting on her bed, looking at the miniature of her mother. As* BARNUM *enters, she hides the picture.*)

BARNUM: Bargain! The joke's on Phineas T., my dear! You're a bargain for everyone but me. Elephant Woman costs more to keep than a whole <u>herd</u> of elephants. (*Goes to a liquor bottle on the chiffonier, pours a drink.*) That gilt cage of yours alone took six weeks profits right out of my pocket. (*Starts to smell the liquor.*) My god! What a stench! You're beginning to smell the way you look. (*Drinks.*)

HENRY: (*Extremely irritated.*) The <u>butter</u>, doctor.

DOCTOR: Oh certainly, certainly.

(BARNUM *drinks again. Sounds of satisfaction.*)

JANE: (*With difficulty, but clearer than before.*) I'm . . . hungry.

BARNUM: Now Jane, you know you can't eat before a show. You'll spoil the performance. (*Regards the bottle.*) Expensive brand. But worth it. Well worth it. (*He drinks.*)

JANE: I'm . . . cold.

BARNUM: The admiration of the crowd will warm you, my dear. (*Regards the bottle.*) Nothing like a little refresher in the middle of a day. (*Pause.*) Or at the beginning of a day. (*Pause.*) Or at the end of a day. (*Pause.*) For that matter drinking all night long is a wonderful experience.

JANE: The light . . . bothers my eyes.

BARNUM: The light is for the people. The people <u>like</u> to see what they're paying for. (*Holds bottle up to the light.*) Shines just like gold . . . (*Raises bottle to his mouth.*)

JANE: My mouth is bleeding again.

BARNUM: (*Stops cold.*) What! Blast that doctor! We can't have <u>blood</u> for the performance! The people won't put up with <u>blood</u>! He guar<u>anteed</u> there'd be no blood!

JANE: The knives he used . . . were not clean.

BARNUM: <u>Damn</u> the fool! I'll have his diploma. <u>Doctors</u>. Licensed scoundrels! <u>That's</u> what they are. Legal murderers! (*Calming.*) How's your speech. Any better?

JANE: As you hear it.

BARNUM: (*As though noticing it for the first time.*) It <u>is</u> better, <u>much</u> better. Before he cut that flap back all you could do was slobber. There's an improvement, alright.

JANE: It's . . . easier to speak. When I want to.

BARNUM: (*Anxious.*) And you can laugh? Can you laugh yet?

JANE: (*Patiently.*) He made me try. I can laugh a little.

BARNUM: (*Relieved.*) Good, good, people love to see a freak laugh. (*Pause.*) God knows why. Well, we'll just have to put up with the bleeding for a while. Maybe the crowd won't notice it.

JANE: There . . . <u>is</u> no crowd.

BARNUM: (*Self-important.*) There will be, my dear. This is P. T. Barnum's Museum. There are <u>always</u> crowds here.

JANE: There were five people in the audience this afternoon . . .

BARNUM: Afternoons are slow . . .

JANE: . . . but their eyes were awful. One man especially . . .

BARNUM: (*Definitively.*) There will be an enormous crowd here tonight. I can promise you that. The name of P. T. Barnum does not produce dead houses, my dear.

(*Slight pause.*)

JANE: I think . . . I'm dead.

(*Pause.*)

BARNUM: (*Breaks it, malevolently.*) You had better not be, my dear. You have a show to do in ten minutes.

JANE: I mean . . . I think I'm dying. When I look into the eyes of the people I think I'm dying. You never look at me anymore, but they . . .

BARNUM: (*His speech becomes more inebriated, coarse, and colloquial; he drinks throughout.*) They better be looking at you, by God, that's what they're here for! Ach! The fools! They live with their eyes sewed shut and they come to P. T. Barnum to clip the stitches for 'em. And when I show 'em something it has to be so shocking that it'll last 'em til the next time they come to me to show 'em something—because they won't see a thing til I SHOW IT TO 'EM. NOT ONE THING. ME! I HAVE TO DO IT! P. T. BARNUM! I HAVE TO SHOW ONE HALF OF THE WORLD TO THE OTHER (*Drinks.*) half. God what a responsibility. (*Drinks, subsides slowly, notices that* JANE *has put her mask on. Speaks quietly.*) And what are you doing?

JANE: I'm . . . dreaming.

BARNUM: (*Drunken dignity.*) Y' don't say.

JANE: I'm dreaming I'm with people whose eyes are in their hands.

BARNUM: (*Drunken largesse.*) Go right ahead, m' dear.

JANE: The hands are touching me in every part of my body. There are hands on the bones of my feet. Now I feel them melting the muscles of my upper arms. They are rubbing the nerves of my throat. There is a hand inside my stomach. There are hands reaching for my kidneys. Fingers are straightening my ribcage. There is a hand holding my heart. Hands are between my thighs. Wait. Something has happened. The hands are . . . (*Stops.*)

(*Pause.*)

BARNUM: (*Coarsely.*) Hands? On your body? Hah! That's no dream, that's a nightmare. Haw haw haw. (*Stops.*) Freaks. (*Dejected.*) I never had one yet that didn't dream. (*Pauses, bottle in hand.*) Life's a terrible thing. Sometimes it's a terrible thing. (*Drinks.*)

JANE: (*Takes mask off.*) What happened to your other freaks? The ones you tell the stories about?

(Slight pause.)

BARNUM: *(Bluster.)* Why they all went on to illustrious retirements my dear, just as
you will. *(Pause. He drinks. A grim litany.)* Mme. Clofullia, the Bearded Lady,
lost her beard. Some kind of gland disease. She cut her throat in Schenectady,
the year I took you out of the Workhouse. The Siamese Twins hated each other
so much, they hunted up some phony doctor in Tennessee to cut 'em apart.
They died on the operating table. Tables, I should say. They insisted upon separate operating tables . . . Let's see. Tom Thumb. Poor Tom Thumb. He fell in
love with a large lady from Louisville who took his money and ran a toy sword
right through his little heart. What a loss that was. That boy was the biggest
money-maker I ever had. The Mermaid from FeeGee was nothing but a papier-
mache doll . . . As to the rest of 'em . . . *(Pause.)* . . . I really don't remember.

(Pause.)

JANE: *(Slowly.)* Life must be a terrible thing.

(Noise.)

BARNUM: Shh! Listen! Do I hear people?! *(Excited.)* There are people out there.
What do y' know. I told you, P. T. Barnum always produces. We're going to
have a real show tonight, by God. I've got to get out there and work that
crowd. *(Turns back, ominous.)* Now listen, my dear, I want a big laugh out of
you when we bring the lights up. Do you understand? A very big laugh. That's
what the people want and that's what they're going to get! We're not here to
disappoint the people! *(Exits. Offstage we hear him:* "Ladies and gentlemen.
We have a fascinating bit of exotica here for you tonight.")

(As soon as BARNUM's *voice dies away, the Blind people of* JANE's *dream enter.
There should be seven of them, as in the story the Persian poet Rumi tells about the
seven blind people confronting an elephant. They all move slowly towards* JANE,
*groping the air in front of them. One of them begins a modal hum—in, say, the
mixolydian mode—and the others take it up, with variations always in the mode of
the theme, until* JANE *is surrounded by the Blind and surrounded by the sounds of
the Blind. Each of the Blind concentrates on touching a different area of what
passes for* JANE's *body. The movement of the hands of the Blind must be precisely
choreographed so that the icon becomes one of Elephant Woman being created as
a sculpture by the hands of the Blind. The music, the modalities, should seem to
come out of what the hands are touching. A real effort must be made by the actors
to receive and transmit the vibrational frequencies of Elephant Woman's body. At
the moment the icon is complete, that is, at the moment the Blind have created a
sculpture of sound to enclose the sculptured form of Elephant Woman—they must
seem to vanish from her room. Lights dim to darkness.)*

DOCTOR: After that first examination at the Workhouse, Jane Merritt passed completely from my life. (HENRY JAMES *is soundly sleeping.*) Mr. James, forgive me,

but your elbow is in the creamer. (DOCTOR *shakes* HENRY *who wakes, startled and mumbling*: "I wasn't asleep, I wasn't asleep.") Oh, I'd hear of creatures like her, here and there, exhibited in small towns on the Chattaqua Circuit— Mme. Monster this and Elephant Woman that—but I could never be sure it was my freak they were talking about. Only if I heard that Mme. Monster could not bear the light, or that the famous Elephant Woman was remarked by the crowds who viewed her to have had tears running down her terrible cheeks—only then was I certain that this was the creature I'd examined in the Workhouse on that fateful day. For that poor, stunned specimen displayed the most painful aversion to any form of light . . . She broke down completely during the last series of daguerrotypes. I have treasured a few prints that show her tears. See here and here Mr. James—imagine tears from such a creature!

HENRY: (*A brave show of wakefulness and response.*) Tch tch shocking. Perfectly shocking. (*Snoozes immediately.*)

DOCTOR: Yes, yes it was shocking. Something about the blinding flash of the gunpowder . . . terrified the life out of her . . .

Jane Merritt's Room Inside Her Mother

Lights come up slowly on JANE, *alone in her room. She is remembering what it was like to be inside her mother and, remembering, speaks about it:*

JANE: It is dark in here. I am crowded by walls of flesh not my own. My eyes— shut. My ears—useless. Folded tight against my head. My thick skin is wrinkled. My tusks are little buds. My trunk is rolled up. Every part of me is curved or curled against every other part. I am in a prison to grow. But I grow strangely. I can feel it.

Suddenly I hear my father's voice, speaking from another place. He is loudly calling my Elephant name. The soft clotted blood on which I rest is sucked away. Flesh not my own begins to press and release me. I am in a terrible pain of pressing back. I push past this pain to other pain. Flesh not my own closes around me. I give up. I am renewed. I push again. Flesh closes around me again. I give up again. I am little. I do not move. Then I push again. In a river of liquids not my own, I push out into blinding light. Now the walls are not the walls I know. I hear my father calling my Elephant name nearby. The light is like a loud noise. Something . . . has happened. (*With wonder.*) My . . . trunk is gone. The buds of my tusks . . . retreated. My large ears . . . no more. In their place, lumps of bone, strings of flesh. I am . . . not what I was. Something has happened. I am not what I am supposed to be. My mother sees me between her thighs. She knows something has happened. When she sees me, her scream . . . is as loud as the light.

(*Blackout and back to the* DOCTOR *and the drowsy* HENRY. *Before the lights come up fully on the tea table,* HENRY's *voice issues defensively from the darkness*: "I'm not asleep. Doctor. I heard every word you were saying.")

DOCTOR: Well, I found her again of course. I couldn't let a prize like that escape me. I installed her right here in my hospital. Under my protection. In sight of me, always in sight of me. Naturally, she was a trifle . . . reluctant to expose herself to science at first. Just the . . . tiniest bit inclined to refuse certain . . . necessary treatments. But I was very convincing and, of course, she had no place else to go . . .

Jane Merritt's Room in the Hospital

A pile of books is on the floor. DOCTOR SLOPER *sits in the bedside chair, examining and writing. His knives are with him, gleaming sedately in their box.* JANE *is asleep sitting up, her back propped by pillows, her heavy head resting on her knees. When she wakes, she speaks more clearly than she has before.*

JANE: It's always the same dream.

DOCTOR: The Blind again, eh? Turn just a little to the right, please.

JANE: The dream of people whose eyes are in their hands.

DOCTOR: (*Pleased.*) Really, Jane, your articulation is superb. How is the lip this morning?

JANE: It won't stop bleeding. I think you shouldn't have cut it again.

DOCTOR: Don't be ridiculous, my dear. You know you're much happier speaking.

JANE: I spoke before. You couldn't understand me.

DOCTOR: And now I can. That's important, my dear. Head up now. By God, we'll have you smiling yet. Now if we could only get you to sleep lying down like other people . . .

JANE: I could try. I would love to try.

DOCTOR: But of course we know that's not possible. Your head is far too heavy. If you were even to lie back for a moment, your windpipe would snap like a straw. (*Visualizes it.*) Just like a straw.

JANE: I have thought of it that way many times.

DOCTOR: Don't bother to, my dear. We have enough pillows here to keep you propped up forever. (*Pause, writes.*) You've finished all your books, I see.

JANE: Miss Austen is my favorite. She fits things together so . . . nicely.

DOCTOR: (*Busy with writing.*) A peculiar taste for you.

JANE: Oh I <u>like</u> a good fit.

DOCTOR: Odd that you should . . . I have another patient with tastes like yours. The sister of a famous novelist. (*Musing.*) She's been dying for years . . .

JANE: (*Suddenly.*) Life must be a terrible thing.

DOCTOR: (*Abstracted.*) So it is, my dear, so it is. (*Pause while he checks a list.*) Now we're going to palpate that hip.

JANE: (*Speaking over the pain of the examination.*) I'd like to read more of the Brontë sisters. Sometimes I think I can hear my father in their books, calling my Elephant name across the moors.

DOCTOR: (*Not listening.*) What? Oh anything you like Jane. Shift your weight a little, please.

JANE: And sometimes I see him in Miss Austen's parlor scenes, swinging his trunk back and forth, just as he did the day I was born.

DOCTOR: Good, Jane. Hold that position.

JANE: Then often he comes to me when I read Miss Emily Dickinson. She only describes an inch of him in each of her poems. But that inch is enough.

DOCTOR: (*Irritated.*) Hold <u>still</u>, Jane. How can I examine you if you <u>move</u> every minute?

JANE: (*Experimentally.*) This morning he spoke to me directly for the first time. (*Imitates him.*) "Come to me, daughter," he said. "My thick skin will protect you, my heavy legs will shelter you, my trunk reaches out to embrace you, my memory will conserve you — come to me and be healed."

DOCTOR: (*Ignoring her and looking at his watch.*) Well, we'll have to suspend the usual examination this afternoon. I have an engagement for tea and (*Looks at his watch.*) I see that I'm already late. Tomorrow at the same time, my dear.

(*JANE slowly sinks into her sleeping position. DOCTOR exits in a hurry to the tea table. Sits down with a thump. HENRY seems to waken.*)

HENRY: Dr. Sloper?

DOCTOR: Mr. James?

(*HENRY starts to sleep again, but pulls himself awake.*)

HENRY: Did I understand you to say that you annexed that poor creature for your own purposes?

DOCTOR: Never in this world, Mr. James.

HENRY: I'm relieved, Dr. Sloper.

DOCTOR: I'm delighted, Mr. James.

(*Pause. HENRY begins again to sleep, than rouses briefly.*)

HENRY: Doctor?

DOCTOR: Sir.

HENRY: Whose purposes <u>were</u> they?

DOCTOR: Mother Science's, Mr. James, Mother Science's.

(HENRY *nods, then rouses again. They muse.*)

DOCTOR: (*The toast.*) Shall we drink to the ladies, Mr. James?

HENRY: (*Roused.*) Ah yes. Of course. The ladies.

(*Cups are raised, complete blackout on both sets.*)

Alice James's Room in Henry's House

The lights come up on ALICE JAMES's *room. The mirror on the chiffonier is now uncovered.* ALICE, *who does indeed have her mother's architectural forehead, is reclining on her bed-chaise, propped with five pillows and blanketed with three shawls. She is rifling the pages of her journal irritatedly.*

ALICE: Damn! Where is it? It's bad enough keeping a journal without losing track of what you've written in it. (*Reads a passage mockingly.*) "Anyone who spends her life as an appendage to five cushions and three shawls is justified in committing the sloppiest kind of suicide at a moment's notice." Hmmm. Not very cheerful, are we? Ahhh, I remember <u>this</u> one " . . . it used to seem to me that the only difference between me and the insane was that I had not only all the horrors and suffering of insanity but the duties of doctor, nurse and straight-jacket imposed on me too." Oh Alice, Alice, what an inhospitable temperament. Ahhh, <u>here</u> we are. (*Reads slowly as though experiencing it.*)

    "On the morning of my thirteenth birthday, and I remember still how sudden the impulse was, I walked into my brother Harry's bathroom, and I carefully removed his razor from its box, and I carefully stropped it back and forth as I'd seen him do so many times, and I carefully shaved off every hair on my body except the hairs growing on the top of my head. I was so careful that although it was the first time I had used a razor <u>in that way</u>, I did not experience a single cut. Every morning for months after that I would walk into Harry's bathroom and repeat the same performance before his mirror. Fear and embarrassment made me careless, and each morning fresh cuts followed the razor over my skin. I was able to stanch the cuts on my face with small pieces of lambswool which I wet under the faucet as I had seen Harry do. Until it dried, the wool blended nicely with my skin. The cuts on my arms were deeper, somehow, and harder to stop from bleeding. There is something in the conformation of an arm that does not . . . lend itself to the razor. The most I could do with these cuts was to conceal them under the awful, long-sleeved middy blouses that Aunt Kate so persistently sewed for me. At odd moments during the school day, I would look down to see the white sleeves of my middy dotted and stained with blood from the cuts on my arms. I began to develop complicated rituals that kept my arms below the level of the school desk . . . so that I would not have to see what my brother's razor had done to me."

(HENRY *moves from the tea table into* ALICE's *room and stands at her bedside. She quickly closes the journal.*)

ALICE: (*Surprised, it's a first meeting.*) Harry. You're so . . . sneaky.

HENRY: My dear. How are you.

ALICE: (*Cheerfully.*) Dying, as usual.

HENRY: Alice, I wish you would concentrate more on cheerfulness.

ALICE: Ah Harry. What does it matter. I'm here at last, with you and Katherine to care for me. (*Ominous.*) Until the end.

HENRY: (*Uncomfortable.*) You don't . . . plan to go back to the old house in Cambridge, then?

ALICE: My dear, you should have <u>seen</u> them dragging my carcass between Boston and New York! I'll never have the courage to attempt <u>that</u> trip again. Really, if it hadn't been <u>my</u> body bumping around in that railway car, I would have enjoyed the spectacle immensely. As it was, (*Ominous.*) I had an attack.

HENRY: Oh good god. Not again.

ALICE: (*Cheerfully.*) Again <u>and</u> again. I had two of them, actually. The one in Grand Central Station was the most interesting. (*Coyly.*) Several old friends of the family happened to be catching trains at just that moment, and so were able to watch me thrashing about on the floor of the grand concourse.

HENRY: Alice, Alice! And the sentence. I suppose you couldn't have an attack without saying that sentence.

ALICE: Katherine tells me I was in full voice. She never heard me articulate it so clearly, she said. Although Mary Cabot insisted that <u>she</u> missed the last two words.

HENRY: (*Horrified.*) Mary <u>Cabot</u> was there!

ALICE: (*Happy as a clam.*) And Bay Lodge. Who complimented me on my performance.

HENRY: If the James family has a social position left, Alice, it's no thanks to you. I suppose you were examined by a physician?

ALICE: They called in that Dr. Sloper again. You know. The one who operated on his own daughter and killed her. (*Admiring.*) He has such an . . . <u>extensive</u> collection of scalpels.

HENRY: Well, Alice. What is it this time? Neurasthenia? Hyperaesthenia? Nervous prostration? You always inspire doctors to such impressive diagnoses.

ALICE: (*Dimpling as for a compliment.*) Nothing of the kind, Harry. Dr. Sloper said I was quite strong enough to go on having attacks for years if I wanted to. He made me very happy. He <u>did</u> want to examine a little further a lump he found on my right breast.

HENRY: On your right b . . . . delicacy was never your strong point, Alice. How did Dr. Sloper manage to find a <u>lump</u> on your <u>chest</u> in the middle of the Grand Central Station!

ALICE: Well, <u>naturally</u> I was carried to the ladies' room. They stretched me out on the cosmetics counter. And the doctor noticed the blood stain on my . . . um . . . <u>bodice</u>. Katherine said I was quite a sight laid out amongst the powder puffs and the eau de colognes.

HENRY: And where <u>is</u> the redoubtable Miss Loring? She's usually not more than two inches from your right elbow.

ALICE: Katherine's gone to Barnum's Museum. You know her taste for curiosities.

HENRY: And is she come to stay here forever also?

ALICE: You know, Harry, that Katherine is <u>devoted</u> to me.

HENRY: I see. It <u>is</u> forever then.

ALICE: Take comfort, brother. I may not last the year.

HENRY: Alice. If I have one certainty in this diseased and distracted world, it is the strength of your constitution. You've survived the constant treatment of at least ten reputable physicians. It's quite a testimonial.

ALICE: I won't need much in the way of attention, brother. Your devotion, all of Miss Austen's books—I haven't read her in at least a year—and some of the Brontës', will do me very nicely.

HENRY: (*Pouting.*) Alice, it's plain to see you prefer the books of those scribbling females to mine. You haven't asked after the new novel at all.

ALICE: Nonsense, Harry. I like your novels enormously. Especially the ones you steal from me.

HENRY: (*Stiffly.*) I have no idea what you're referring to.

ALICE: Brother. Year after year you have entered my sickrooms armed with paper and pencil or with your prodigious memory and you have taken careful note of my valetudinarian ramblings. And then six months, eight months, a year later, I find embedded in your narratives the subjects we've turned over.

HENRY: Oh that. Perfectly justifiable, sister. It's all in the family.

ALICE: Certainly, Harry. Certainly. And if I ever turn my hand to writing, I'll feel as free to use you as a resource.

HENRY: (*Pompously.*) I think I'm quite safe on the score.

ALICE: Ah! I hear Katherine in the foyer. Leave me brother. I'd like to greet her alone.

(*Blackout on stage, lights up on the tea table.* HENRY *now sits in the host's seat.*)

HENRY: Alice was the most severe trial of my entire life, Dr. Sloper. And yet, she fascinated me, utterly fascinated me. I believe the tea is ready now.

DOCTOR: Thank you, I never take tea at this hour. It has a desperate effect on my sense of time.

HENRY: (*Not at all interested.*) Really? Have some marmalade then, the biscuits are pure poison without it. Well, as I say, my sister Alice nearly drove me mad. (DOCTOR *consults his timepiece.*) First she resisted getting sick. Then she resisted getting well. Then she resisted dying. God how she resisted dying. The family used to say it was your diagnosis that killed her, not the tumour. Your diagnosis . . . and the scalpels. (*Slyly.*)

DOCTOR: (*Shakes his watch.*) I . . . (*Shake, shake.*) . . . never had the occasion to use any of my instruments in treating your sister, Mr. James. It was a great disappointment to me. (*Shake, shake.*)

HENRY: I meant her obsession with scalpels, of course, doctor. Any physician in the Adams Nervous Asylum can tell you about the hundreds of butter knives and nail scissors Alice had secreted in her dresser drawers—and the pages of comparisons between the pains in her body and the kinds of cuts different blades can inflict. (*Grim.*) I saw them all before they were incinerated.

DOCTOR: What is this nonsense about my scalpels, then? And do you have the time, Mr. James?

HENRY: It's tea time, Dr. Sloper. Have another biscuit. Well it seems that when Alice first saw your scalpels in that railway station, it set the seal on her obsession. She had never seen anything quite like them before. And to make matters worse—will you have some tea now, doctor?

DOCTOR: (*Shaking his timepiece.*) Thank you, it's not time yet.

HENRY: To make matters worse she began to insert the word "scalpel" into that disgusting sentence she used to say when she was having her attacks.

DOCTOR: Oh yes, you mean . . .

HENRY: (*Quickly.*) Never mind, doctor, I heard quite enough of that phrase while Alice was alive. The family calculated once, that from the time she was nineteen, Alice averaged five major attacks per month, day in and day out, good weather or bad, until her demise. That is to say, by conservative estimate, my gently reared and modest sister Alice spewed out that horrible sentence of hers at least seventy times a year. Seventy times!

DOCTOR: (*Still shaking the watch.*) Tea-time.

HENRY: I beg your pardon?

DOCTOR: Tea-time. Alice was always "taken" during tea-time. She always had an attack between the hours of four and six in the afternoon.

HENRY: Yes . . . yes . . . I think you're right. I'm <u>sure</u> you're right. She loved to catch those dowagers with their hands on their tea cozies.

DOCTOR: (*Stretches complacently.*) I <u>will</u> take some marmalade. These biscuits are disgusting.

HENRY: (*Hand on marmalade.*) I can't hold it back any longer!

DOCTOR: (*Hopefully.*) The marmalade?

HENRY: No, no doctor, the <u>truth</u>. The truth is that Alice <u>was</u> a great trial to me, but not the greatest one.

DOCTOR: (*Dully.*) The marmalade, Mr. James.

HENRY: (*Hand on the marmalade again.*) The greatest trial of my life was Katherine Peabody Loring.

DOCTOR: (*Brightens.*) Ah, I remember, the Amazon.

HENRY: Amazon? The colossus. The skyscraper. The <u>mon</u>onument. The moment Alice met that woman, she took to her bed prostrate with love. She was so fond of Miss Loring's <u>nursing</u> that I—her own brother—was treated entirely as a superfluous appendage.

DOCTOR: You <u>were</u> superfluous, Mr. James. You certainly were superfluous.

(*They muse.*)

DOCTOR: (*Sighs, reaches for the marmalade, raises it.*) The ladies, Mr. James.

HENRY: Ah yes. The ladies. (*Deeply depressed.*)

Alice's Room in Henry's House

Dimout on the tea table. Lights up on ALICE *and* KATHERINE, *who is competently arranging flowers in a vase.* KATHERINE *moves constantly throughout the play; a woman of intense, palpable vitality.*

KATHERINE: There you are, my dear. Some signs of life.

ALICE: Harry does keep a dismal house.

KATHERINE: Sepulchral. Positively sepulchral.

ALICE: He keeps a dismal house because he was a dismal child. The only way I could stir him up was to have a nervous attack in some public place.

KATHERINE: I hope you made the most of your opportunities.

ALICE: Oh, I did reasonably well.

KATHERINE: (*Smiling in remembrance.*) You should have seen Mary Cabot's face this morning after you delivered your sentence.

ALICE: It does seem to be what they call a real "showstopper." The last thing I remember is Miss Cabot's tiny red eyes fixed on me in horror. (*Smiling in remembrance.*)

KATHERINE: Is it always like that Alice?

ALICE: Always. (*As though it's happening.*) Someone's eyes in a crowd catch mine, I feel the . . . censure or the disgust, or I invent it, I abandon a certain portion of my consciousness and as I fall, I speak . . .

KATHERINE: Always the same sentence?

ALICE: Ever since I can remember.

KATHERINE: (*Admiring.*) What an exhibitionist you are, my love.

ALICE: It used to drive the family insane. (*With some satisfaction.*) Father spent years dragging me from eminent nerve doctor to eminent nerve doctor. And they all told him the same thing.

KATHERINE: That you would either die or recover.

ALICE: Exactly. Well, I've been at this for the last twenty years or so, and I am neither dead nor recovered.

KATHERINE: (*To the bed, carrying a counterpane, smiling.*) It's a miracle we met, Alice.

ALICE: (*A hand on* KATHERINE.) A miracle?! I spent months arranging it.

(*Embrace. Release.*)

(*Pause. The mood recedes.*)

ALICE: It's peculiar about that doctor, don't you think.

KATHERINE: The one who treated you this morning.

ALICE: Yes that one. Dr. Sloper.

KATHERINE: He reminds me of Harry.

ALICE: It's peculiar about those knives of his.

KATHERINE: Well you know, dear, physicians are not the most balanced class of people.

ALICE: But to carry them everywhere like that . . . in a little leather box . . .

KATHERINE: Rather unsanitary, if you ask me. You ought to show him your collection of nail scissors and hat pins, my love. That would quiet him down.

ALICE: (*The staged equivalent of a blush.*) Umm . . . Where are they?

KATHERINE: I put them in the drawer there (*Points to chiffonier.*) so that we'd be spared Harry's reaction. The last time you came to visit he found the pen knives.

ALICE: (*Laughing.*) I'll never forget his face when he saw my sketchbook.

KATHERINE: And I'll never forget his actions. Three month's commitment to the Adams Nervous Asylum.

ALICE: (*Nonchalant.*) It was comfortable. And they gave me all the drawing paper I wanted . . . (*Inconsequently.*) Massachusetts has more mad houses than any state in the union. (*Pause.*) I ought to know.

KATHERINE: (*Definitively.*) Harry's a monster.

(*Pause.*)

ALICE: Katherine.

KATHERINE: What is it, love.

ALICE: (*Tentatively.*) Do you really suppose Harry thinks I don't know what a terrible life he leads?

KATHERINE: A brain surgeon might be able to uncover your brother's thoughts, Alice. I'm not qualified.

ALICE: Guilty exchanges on docks. That vast sensibility of his brought to bear on the bodies of adolescent sailors. (*Laughs a little.*) How surprised they must be if he talks to them.

KATHERINE: And how bored.

ALICE: Poor fellow. At least I've retired into the kind of friendship the world is still forced to support. (*To* KATHERINE.) The Woman's Home Companion. (*Reaches for her, and we have the sexual connection for the first time powerfully.*) With your breast still spotted red from my love-making.

KATHERINE: (*Intimate.*) I want you well Alice.

ALICE: I've never been well, Katherine.

KATHERINE: Then I just . . . <u>want</u> you.

ALICE: Ah! That's different.

KATHERINE: But when you <u>are</u> well, we'll go to the country.

ALICE: (*Taking it up.*) And the sun will warm our bodies.

KATHERINE: (*Slyly.*) And the wind will cool our ardour.

ALICE: (*Glumly.*) And then Harry will appear.

KATHERINE: He always does, doesn't he?

(*Pause.*)

ALICE: (*Experimentally.*) We might . . . poison him.

KATHERINE: With the tea <u>he</u> serves, he must be immune to everything by now.

ALICE: Well, I <u>could</u> have another attack.

KATHERINE: That would kill him on the spot. (*Grimly.*)

ALICE: (*Musing.*) What a carnival . . .

KATHERINE: Life, you mean.

ALICE: (*Purposefully.*) I had my first attack at a carnival. Did you know that?

KATHERINE: At a carnival! Oh, Alice, what a performer you are.

ALICE: It <u>was</u> a carnival. They had taken me to a carnival for my thirteenth birth-day. (*As though experiencing it.*) I was standing near the largest Elephant, watching him. Suddenly he turned and seemed to come straight at me, trumpeting wildly and swinging his trunk like an ax. The woman next to me fell to the floor of the tent and began to bleed between her legs. The last thing I remember is her horrified eyes on my face . . . (*Pause.*) When I woke up, I found that I had suffered the fit, said the sentence, and nothing was in its proper place.

(*Pause.*)

(*Ascendant.*) And ever since that summer, I have dreamt constantly of monsters; inhuman shapes, all hung with lumps of bone and strings of flesh . . . And ever since that summer, I have yearned to watch the blood of my father and all my brothers run a red river through the halls of our childhood home.

(*Pause. No one moves for a while.*)

KATHERINE: (*Slowly.*) You write these things in your journal, Alice?

ALICE: Everything is in my journal.

KATHERINE: Everything about Harry?

ALICE: Everything I can think of.

(*Pause.* KATHERINE *considers.*)

KATHERINE: We had better put it in a safe place.

(*Lights dim on the stage.* ALICE *and* KATHERINE *on the bed, barely visible. The twining of their fingers produces on the wall behind the bed an image like an elephant moving. The elephant must absolutely seem to be the shadow of their shadows—no matter how awkward the image is. As* HARRY *and the* DOCTOR *begin to speak the shadow world deepens to black, all lights on the stage are extinguished . . . Lights up on the tea table.*)

HENRY: Yes I burnt Alice's journal, but I couldn't burn Alice's friend.

DOCTOR: You should have given her to me, Mr. James. I would have found a use for her.

HENRY: I never thought of it. What a pity she wasn't mine to give.

DOCTOR: So many times I had to visit the cemeteries to carry on my researches . . .

HENRY: Well, I can't say that Miss Loring was in any condition to be researched, doctor.

DOCTOR: I thought she was in perfect condition. I <u>will</u> have some tea now, if you don't mind.

HENRY: Ahh, at last. I think you'll find this to your taste . . . I meant that Miss Loring was <u>alive</u>. You don't generally . . . um . . . experiment on the living, do you doctor?

DOCTOR: Not . . . generally. (*Changing the subject.*) And yourself, sir?

HENRY: <u>Only</u> on the living. Though there are certain publishing scoundrels— critics I mean—who would deny it. Well, well, the house of fiction has many windows. Hasn't it. Doctor, what's the matter?

DOCTOR: (*Sputtering into his tea.*) What have you done to the tea?

HENRY: Done to the tea?

DOCTOR: Ptui! It tastes like old medical journals!

HENRY: Old . . . literary reviews.

DOCTOR: What did you say? Ptui.

HENRY: Not medical journals, Dr. Sloper. Literary magazines. I have them ground and roasted.

DOCTOR: (*Disgusted.*) Good god.

HENRY: Then I brew them up. (*Some satisfaction.*) And <u>then</u> I drink them. An old family custom. Alice was devoted to it.

DOCTOR: (*Back to shaking his watch.*) De-votion. That's what they give us, Mr. James. Devotion.

HENRY: Who does, Doctor?

DOCTOR: The <u>ladies</u>, Mr. James.

HENRY: (*Rousing himself.*) Ah yes, of course, the <u>ladies</u>, Dr. Sloper.

(*Blackout.*)

Alice James's Room in Henry's House

KATHERINE *reclines, unrecognizable, on* ALICE's *bed. She's covered with* ALICE's *shawls, propped by* ALICE's *pillows, and she looks just like* ALICE *until she moves.* HENRY *bursts in from the tea table.*

HENRY: Alice, damn you Alice, there isn't a butter knife left in the whole house! How can I offer people biscuits without butter knives? What did you do with them <u>this</u> time! Oh! Miss Loring. (*Embarrassed docility, nervous laugh.*) Wherever is Alice?

KATHERINE: She had another fit this afternoon. (*Bitterly.*) Dr. Sloper took her to the hospital.

HENRY: (*Exasperated.*) God, what an inconvenience. (*Collects himself.*) I mean, how is she? Is she . . . recovering?

KATHERINE: She always recovers, Mr. James. No thanks to the doctor. She never would have gone to the hospital if she'd been conscious. She can't <u>bear</u> waking up in a white room.

HENRY: (*Nods.*) Yes, I understand. It's . . . too much like death.

KATHERINE: (*Bitterly.*) I couldn't stop him from taking her. He insisted upon his medical rights. (*Burst out.*) Medical rights, when all my darling needs is to be held and spoken softly to! (*Pause.*) But he was adamant. (*Pause.*) I think . . . I did manage to . . . scratch him a bit, though.

HENRY: Miss Loring, you're joking.

KATHERINE: And just possibly, the tip of my right boot came into rather painful contact with the middle portion of his left shin.

HENRY: (*Horrified.*) A brawl? Here in my house? With my honored friend? Over the prostrate form of my sister? (*Looks like he's going to faint.*)

KATHERINE: Here, Mr. James, why don't you lie down. I'm sure that Alice, if she were <u>here</u> and not in some <u>horrible hospital</u>, would invite you to use the chaise.

(HENRY *staggers to the chaise, muttering,* "This is too much, really this is too much," *etc.* KATHERINE, *with an evil intent, begins to settle him on the pillows and cover him with the shawls so that, finally, he looks very much like* ALICE.)

KATHERINE: (*An evil intention.*) That's <u>fine</u>, Mr. James. You just rest here awhile. <u>Alice</u> won't mind. <u>She's</u> probably still unconscious, anyway. I'll go into the kitchen and fix you a cup of chamomile tea. I'll make sure it's chamomile and not that dry tea you've been serving lately. Alice and I haven't enjoyed <u>that</u> tea a bit.

(KATHERINE *exits.* HENRY *wriggles around trying to get comfortable, there is a clanking sound behind him and he reaches under the pillow and draws out an entire set of butter knives tied up with a ribbon. He holds them up in disbelief. Blackout.*)

(*Lights dim on stage; tableau of* NURSE *massaging* ALICE *in* DR. SLOPER'S *hospital, during the following scene between* HENRY *and the* DOCTOR. *Lights up on the tea table.*)

HENRY: I've been thinking very hard about hands, Dr. Sloper.

DOCTOR: Have you, Mr. James.

HENRY: I've been thinking . . . without hands, what would we have?

DOCTOR: (*Dourly.*) A nation of double amputees, no doubt. Please pass the butter.

HENRY: (*Unstoppable.*) If we have no hands, then we have no art. If we have no art, then, certainly, we have no life. Think of it. (*Pause.*) . . . The natural cause of <u>death</u>. Well sir?

DOCTOR: (*Finally lured into it.*) Death <u>has</u> no natural causes, Mr. James.

HENRY: I hoped you'd say that, doctor. More tea?

DOCTOR: (*Unstoppable.*) Death, Mr. James, is almost always the result of an unnecessary exploration. <u>This</u> gentleman, seeking the pleasures of youth, pushed his heart too hard. <u>That</u> one, pursuing wealth, worked his only son into the grave. <u>That</u> lady's compensatory drinking exhausted her liver; <u>this</u> one's consumption of tonics destroyed her bladder. (*Pause.*) Etcetera.

HENRY: (*Slyly.*) <u>This</u> doctor, seeking fame, cut too deeply into the deformities of a friend . . .

DOCTOR: (*Immediately.*) <u>That</u> writer, pursuing immortality, drew too painfully upon the life of a sister . . .

(*Pause. They regard each other.*)

HENRY: Ahh! What would we do without the ladies?

DOCTOR: I haven't the slightest idea.

(*Pause. A new rhythm.*)

HENRY: I think I'll order more tea.

DOCTOR: A fine idea.

HENRY: Something a little less dry.

DOCTOR: What about a Japanese tea.

HENRY: I have one right here, doctor. Just let me reach it for you.

DOCTOR: (*Uncertainly.*) Tea makes everything . . . clearer.

HENRY: Here we are, doctor. Japanese tea.

DOCTOR: Ummm. It smells very fine.

HENRY: (*Beaming.*) Doesn't it. Nothing like a good Japanese tea—made from the subjects of the Emperor Hirohito.

(*Pause. They drink a kind of agreement.*)

DOCTOR: (*Looking at his hands.*) This is the hand that invented the Sloper speculum . . .

HENRY: Really, doctor.

DOCTOR: And this one fashioned the Sloper scalpel . . .

HENRY: A famous instrument.

DOCTOR: In this hand, my daughter's appendix burst like a bag of water . . .

HENRY: I wish you wouldn't.

DOCTOR: And with these hands I have opened all the organs of the female pelvis . . .

HENRY: (*Warning.*) Doctor.

DOCTOR: Picked the rare flowers of a lady's garden: the polyps, the fibroids, the cysts . . .

HENRY: Let me warm your cup.

DOCTOR: (*Magisterial.*) Scooped up ovaries without question, extracted uteri without number. Ahh, Mr. James. The signs of life are closer to the bone than you imagine. And when you find them, there's no stopping until you're covered with blood . . .

(*Slight pause.*)

HENRY: One sugar or two?

DOCTOR: (*Impassioned.*) Two please. When you find them you must cut and cut . . . (*Tastes the tea, calms instantly.*) Ummm, a very good tea indeed. Your health, sir.

HENRY: Thank you doctor. This is the finger that poked Alice's right eye all through our childhood.

DOCTOR: You don't say.

HENRY: And this is the hand that stopped her mouth the second time she said her sentence.

DOCTOR: My my.

HENRY: This one signed her commitment papers to the Adams Nervous Asylum . . .

DOCTOR: A noble sacrifice.

HENRY: And this one plunged the pen deep into her bosom and produced life with her heart's blood.

DOCTOR: Well <u>done</u>, sir.

(*Pause.*)

HENRY: It <u>is</u> an excellent tea, doctor. Is it time for the toast yet?

DOCTOR: Goodness yes, it <u>is</u> time. (<u>Raises the cup</u>.)

HENRY: (*Enthusiastically.*) To the <u>ladies</u>, Dr. Sloper.

(*Blackout on the tea table and the stage.*)

Alice's Room in the Hospital, again

DR. SLOPER *stands by* ALICE's *bedside, showing his scalpels to* ALICE, *who is propped up with pillows.*

DOCTOR: And this one here is so light, it can slip through the gluteus maximus virtually without resistance.

ALICE: God knows why you'd want to do <u>that</u>. (*Placatingly.*) But it <u>is</u> an amazing instrument. I have nothing in <u>my</u> collection to match it.

DOCTOR: (*Horribly disappointed.*) Oh? I didn't know you had a . . . collection.

ALICE: (*Self-deprecatingly.*) A . . . small one. Penknives, poignards, stilettos, hat-pins, razor-blades—<u>house</u>hold items. Nothing <u>serious</u>. Nothing like <u>yours</u>, doctor.

DOCTOR: (*Visibly relieved.*) Well. In that case, let me just show you the latest of the Sloper scalpels. The one I hope to be remembered for. (*Pulls out a horrible, three-pronged instrument of torture.*)

ALICE: I'll certainly remember you for it.

DOCTOR: It's the Uterine Guillotine. I designed it to separate the organs of the female pelvis from their moorings. No rending, no tearing, no post-operative oozings. Just a quick cut and it's all over.

ALICE. For the woman.

DOCTOR: (*Dismissing it.*) In a manner of speaking. (*Pause. A sly look.*) Uh . . . Miss James. Have you . . . ever considered . . . having the operation?

ALICE: The tumour is in my breast, doctor. Not below it.

DOCTOR: It's an operation every woman should have at your time in life.

ALICE: I think . . . not, Dr. Sloper.

DOCTOR: (*Inspired.*) We could begin with the vesico-vaginal fistula operation. Quite unnecessary, in your case, but a beautiful operation, nonetheless. It collapses the vagina and makes those . . . monthly infirmities you women suffer entirely unnecessary.

ALICE: I haven't menstruated in years.

DOCTOR: Then we could move on to a simple ovariotomy. It's taken me hundreds of attempts to perfect that one. I wish we could keep you conscious for it. You would so appreciate the precision.

ALICE: I have a certain . . . attachment to my organs, doctor.

DOCTOR: Then, of course, if you're willing—and so many of my female patients are—we could (*Dramatic tone.*) strike at the root of the evil. We could cut everything out. We could have a FULL HYSTERECTOMY. (*Appreciative pause by the* DOCTOR) What do you say, Miss James.

ALICE: I say . . . CERTAINLY NOT. What about my breast tumour. Isn't that what I'm here for?

DOCTOR: Oh that. It's completely inoperable. If I cut you for that, you'd bleed to death in twenty minutes.

ALICE: (*A little smile.*) Now you're beginning to tempt me.

DOCTOR: (*Horrified.*) Miss James! I'm a physician, not a murderer.

ALICE: (*Mock-surprise.*) Ohhh. Well . . . (*Considers.*) since I'm so clearly about to leave this life, I think I'd like to go out more or less intact. Female organs, tumour and all. (*Looks at her breast.*) Ahhh the stain. Do you see the stain?

Funny how . . . it begins to bleed whenever you come near me. (*Looks up at him.*)

(*Pause. An exchange of hard looks.*)

ALICE: Who are you hiding upstairs. Doctor.

DOCTOR: What do you mean?

ALICE: And how long has she been there?

DOCTOR: How do you know it's a "she."

ALICE: I saw the nurse carrying the works of Jane Austen into her room. The only male in America who reads Jane Austen is my brother Henry. And <u>he</u> does it for competitive reasons.

DOCTOR: The woman upstairs is being treated for an incurable disorder.

ALICE: How is she being treated?

DOCTOR: <u>Surg</u>ically, Miss James.

ALICE: I'd like to speak to her.

DOCTOR: That's impossible. She can't speak without bleeding.

ALICE: I'd like to see her then.

DOCTOR: That's out of the question. You can't move without fainting.

(*Pause.*)

ALICE: What is the woman's name, doctor.

DOCTOR: She's called . . . Jane Merritt.

(*Pause.*)

ALICE: (*A long sigh.*) I think I'd like to read now, doctor.

DOCTOR: I'll speak to Nurse about it. We're here to make you . . . comfortable, Miss James. I hope you remember that.

(*An incredulous look from* ALICE, *then the* DOCTOR *exits.* ALICE, *alone, shifts uncomfortably, looks around. Each group of sentences, after the first one, should be spoken with a different voice as though coming from different parts of her body.*)

ALICE: Such . . . a . . . white room.

(*Pause.*)

From just behind the eyes, my head feels like a dense jungle into which no ray of light has ever penetrated.

(*Pause.*)

This unholy granite substance in my breast enlarges daily, consuming cell by cell, all the living tissue that surrounds it. I can feel its appetite increasing.

(*Pause.*)

Sometimes when Katherine is out of the room, or always when the doctor approaches, I feel every pointed instrument I own turning its blade against me. And then this uninvited lodger in my breast begins to leak and seep.

(*Pause.*)

I feel . . . (*Stops, then in her normal, acerbic tone.*) I feel that one has a greater sense of intellectual degradation after an interview with a doctor than from any other human experience.

(*Blackout. A match strikes at the darkened tea table, two cigars are lit, then the lights come up.*)

HENRY: (*Puffing importantly.*) I have always thought that Alice's tragic health was, in a manner of speaking, the only solution to the problem of her life.

DOCTOR: (*Puffing reflexively.*) The only solution we could accept . . . Mr. James.

(*Blackout.*)

The Apron

It is later than it was, both at the tea table and on the main stage, but tea-table time is much *later than main-stage time.* P. T. BARNUM *stands alone in a circle of light,* STAGE LEFT. *He leans against the proscenium, bottle in hand.* HENRY *and the* DOCTOR, *dimly visible* STAGE RIGHT, *are still at tea, but their exchange has lessened—now it's a breath or two faster than what a slow motion camera might record. As* BARNUM *begins to speak, he makes short, staggering forays in and out of the circle of light. He might describe circles with his movements or he might describe ellipses. Whatever shape his choreography takes, there must be a clear literal and metaphoric play between* MR. BARNUM, *the dark and the light. The words he speaks are a half-drunken reminiscence, his style much more careless now, in the manner of one who sinks into "himself" when unobserved.*

BARNUM: Well she's dead, poor freak. What's her name's dead. My old Elephant Woman. I heard it on the street this morning. Or was it . . . yesterday morning? Strangled to death in her sleep, they say. (*Drinks.*) Poor freak. I didn't make a dime off her. (*Shakes head. Drinks.*) Wonder what happened to that gilt cage of hers. (*Examines his frayed cuffs.*) It cost me six weeks' take. (*Examines his bottle, then straight to the audience.*) Life's a terrible thing. You know that? You know that. Sometimes it's a terrible thing.

(*Blackout on* BARNUM.)

Jane Merritt's Room in the Hospital

Same set, the mirror still covered, the tea table very dim. JANE *is standing slightly off center,* CENTER STAGE. *Her diction will be clearer than ever and her form much less in focus as a thing of horror. She is dressed as a Victorian lady, and stands quite straight.* JANE *is in a circle of light, a cone of light if possible. In her good hand she holds the small picture of her mother which she looks into as though it were a mirror.*

JANE: I am looking at my face in the mirror—a thing the doctor has forbidden—and I do not believe what I see. The sight of my own skin makes me scream. (*A scream begins and stops.*) I look at my body, and it's . . . a costume, a bad fit, the hide of some animal that will live a long time. I cannot live a long time. I cannot hold this heavy head up any longer. (*Pause.*) Every night in my dreams I lie down with the blind. (*Pause.*) Every day my lip bleeds in a new place. (*Pause.*) No matter how often I look at myself, I still do not know what I really see.

(*As* JANE *speaks the next line, she shrinks into what she was at the play's beginning.*)

The image blurs, the ugliness fades, and the face of a woman my mind can live with covers my own face. (Looks, long pause.) I read somewhere . . . that Charlotte Brontë was a very small and plain lady. And I think Nurse told me that George Eliot was the ugliest woman in England.

(*Blackout on* JANE MERRITT. *Lights up on the tea table.* BARNUM, *hair white and carrying, once again, his cane, has joined* HENRY *and the* DOCTOR. BARNUM's *diction in company is precise and "observed."*)

BARNUM: Well, gentlemen, that's how it's always been with me. Profit and loss, profit and loss.

HENRY: Some tea, Mr. Barnum?

DOCTOR: Do have a biscuit. They're made in Mr. James's kitchen.

BARNUM: (*Horrified.*) I never drink . . . tea, thank you. Tans the stomach. (*Counting on his fingers.*) Yes . . . Tom Thumb, Mme. Clofullia, Chang and Eng. I lost 'em all and I mourned 'em all. (*Looks at his bottle.*) In my fashion. (*Slight pause.*) But the worst of it—gentlemen (*Calls to* HENRY *and the* DOCTOR *who are separately musing.*), the worst of my losses was Jumbo, the Elephant. You remember Jumbo.

DOCTOR: I don't believe I recall him . . .

HENRY: I don't think I ever saw him . . .

BARNUM: (*The showman, now.*) Why gentlemen, Jumbo was the most expensive pachyderm in the en-tire world. He created an e-normous sensation wherever

I exhibited him. Frightened the ladies into fits. (*Chuckles comfortably.*) Anyways I lost Jumbo just before your dear sister died, Mr. James. Remember how hot that month was?

HENRY: I do not.

DOCTOR: I thought it was unusually cool.

BARNUM: Well, it <u>was</u> a hot month and Jumbo stepped up on a railroad track to get a little air just as the four-forty from Chicago was pulling in. It was a terrible meeting. Poor Jumbo had to be shot in the head. A three thousand dollar elephant. (*Shakes head and drinks.*) I cried like a baby. Three thousand dollars. (*Pause.*) I think they cut him up for cat food. (*Pauses, drinks, looks at bottle, drinks.*)

(*Pause.* HENRY *and the* DOCTOR *ignore* BARNUM.)

HENRY: You know, doctor, I've been thinking.

DOCTOR: Marvelous exercise, Mr. James. I prescribe it whenever possible.

HENRY: I've been thinking of making a play out of certain . . . um . . . past events.

DOCTOR: Ah, Mr. James. To make a play. That <u>would</u> be the distinguished thing.

BARNUM: Seems to me I once owned a theatre somewhere. . . . St. Louis, was it? Birmingham? (*Drinks largely.*)

HENRY: (*Irritated.*) I've been thinking of making a play about <u>Alice</u>, Doctor.

BARNUM: Ah! your dear sister. Wonderful idea, Mr. James. (*Slight pause.*) I saw quite a bit of her . . . um companion in those last months.

HENRY: (*Surprised.*) <u>Did</u> you, Mr. Barnum.

DOCTOR: How . . . un<u>usual</u>.

BARNUM: Oh yes indeed. Why she used to . . . (*Pause.*) Whatever happened to Miss Loring? (*Pause.* BARNUM *embarrassed at the silence.*) I mean after Miss James's . . . uh demise. Where did she go?

DOCTOR: I haven't the slightest idea.

HENRY: I can't remember.

BARNUM: (*Trying to cover the chill.*) I thought I heard she was trying to get a manuscript published. (*Muses.*) Could it have been something of Miss James's?

DOCTOR: (*Quickly.*) Highly unlikely.

HENRY: (*Finally.*) Utterly impossible. (*Pause,* softer.) My dear sister could scarcely put a sentence together. She never wrote a word in her life.

DOCTOR: She was a <u>collector</u>, Mr. Barnum, not a <u>writer</u>.

HENRY: (*Firmly.*) She had a <u>large</u> collection of <u>small</u> household items.

(*Pause. The subject is sealed.*)

BARNUM: I . . .

DOCTOR: <u>Do</u> have some biscuits, Mr. Barnum.

HENRY: A glass of milk, perhaps.

BARNUM: No, no . . . (Trails off.)

(*Pause.*)

DOCTOR: In this . . . play you will write, Mr. James, what will you do with Miss Loring? How would you treat a character like Miss Loring?

HENRY: An early death, I think. Somewhere in the first act.

(*Smiles of satisfaction by both gentlemen.* BARNUM *is ignored, asleep or befuddled.*)

HENRY: More tea, doctor?

DOCTOR: More <u>sugar</u>, Mr. James.

(*Freeze and blackout. Lights up on* ALICE *and* KATHERINE.)

Alice's Room in Henry's House

ALICE *is on her bed-lounge reading from a newspaper;* KATHERINE *is near the chiffonnier.*

ALICE: "And the old couple, poverty stricken, homeless, without hope, was found bound together, with stones in their pockets, at the bottom of the Hudson River early this morning." (*Admiring pause.*) What a <u>beautiful</u> story.

KATHERINE: Alice, you're a ghoul.

ALICE: (*Carefully cutting out the article.*) It runs in the family. Put it in the journal, will you darling?

KATHERINE: (*Grimly.*) Right next to the story of the woman who took poison on the eve of her marriage to the mail clerk.

ALICE: She certainly made the better choice. (*Slight pause. Realizing something.*) You know I've kept that journal ever since I had my first attack.

KATHERINE: (*Obliging, indulgent, but fatigued.*) You have the most unusual hobbies, Alice.

(*Pause.*)

ALICE: (*Looks at* KATHERINE, *a cold, indifferent tone.*) Aren't you ever tired of my hobbies?

KATHERINE: (*Looks, stops.*) Certainly, I am.

ALICE: And aren't you sometimes bored by my symptoms? Disgusted by my brother? Drained of your vital energy by my demands?

KATHERINE: (*Dead serious.*) Continually, my dearest.

(*Pause.*)

ALICE: (*Satisfied, more alive.*) I thought so. You've been a nurse too long, Katherine.

(*Pause.*)

KATHERINE: All my life, I have moved from the illness of one woman to the illness of another. My mother's long disease, my sister's unending complaints, your own unusual symptoms . . . (*Back to whatever normal is.*) Life is a terrible thing Alice. (*A patient pause.*) Why don't you go on reading, it will calm you.

ALICE: (*Numbly takes the paper and begins to read.*) Here's something . . . This one. What a sad story. The largest Elephant in Mr. Barnum's Museum— Jumbo the Giant—was run over by a railroad train. It says here that he died in agony, over a period of eighteen hours. "The animal was finally dispatched amid cries of terrible suffering by a well-placed bullet in the brain. Prior to the shooting of the elephant, Mr. P. T. Barnum, owner and exhibitor of the animal, was observed to be selling sarsparilla and collecting coins from the large and raucous crowd that had gathered to watch the death-throes of its favorite circus star."

(*Blackout on* ALICE's *room. Just in back of the tea table,* STAGE RIGHT, *we see a corner of* **Jane Merritt's Room in Dr. Sloper's Hospital.** NURSE *and* DR. SLOPER *are lighted in consultation.*)

DOCTOR: She's . . . dead! Jane's gone! I don't believe it! We were going to operate again tonight!

NURSE: There'll be no more cuttings on that body, doctor. It's gone beyond all of us.

DOCTOR: It's impossible that this could have happened now! She made a complete recovery from the last operation. I examined her myself! She's in perfect health!

NURSE: That's right. doctor. Perfect health. And she's lying there dead as a dormouse.

DOCTOR: Lying. What do you mean lying there! Jane Merritt does not lie down!

NURSE: You haven't seen her? You didn't go in?

DOCTOR: Of course not. I . . . the sight of a newly dead body is . . . disturbing to me.

NURSE: Well she's lying there, the poor thing, flat on her back. I heard this awful sound coming from her room. Like someone blowing on a trumpet for the first time. I rushed right in and all her pillows were on the floor—can you imagine—and there she was lying flat on her back, her windpipe snapped like a straw. Just like a straw in the wind.

DOCTOR: (*Furious.*) One more operation! One more cutting and she would have been able to look in a mirror like other people!

NURSE: She looked in mirrors all the time, she told me so.

DOCTOR: One more operation and she could have laughed like other people.

NURSE: Go and look at her laid out on that bed, doctor. There's a smile on her face that's nearly splitting it.

(*Instant blackout. Lights up on the tea table.* HENRY *and the* DOCTOR *are present.* MR. BARNUM *is absent, but represented by his cane which is hung over the back of his chair. It's later than it was.*)

HENRY: (*In mid-sentence.*) . . . and the writing of this play has taken over my entire life.

DOCTOR: (*Buttering and pouring.*) Is that a fact, sir?

HENRY: It's more than a fact, doctor. It's virtually an obsession. There <u>was</u> a time when my evenings were spent in healthful promenades along the docks of New York . . .

DOCTOR: (*Looks up sharply at* HENRY, *who continues obliviously.*)

HENRY. . . . . stopping, now and then, to have a chat with a sturdy young seaman, or an occasional glass of hock with a naval officer.

DOCTOR: Really, Mr. James. I never would have thought you had any interest in the <u>navy</u>. I always assumed that Herman <u>Mel</u>ville had exhausted <u>that</u> subject.

HENRY: (*The subject is uncomfortable.*) In any case, doctor, my evenings now are consumed entirely by dreadful dreams. Even the act of writing has become a kind of constriction on my impulses.

DOCTOR: Nerves, Mr. James, nerves. The use of the chamomile flower brewed in a tea is very effective in these instances. Just let me put up a cup for you . . .

HENRY: All I imagine now are the eyes of this hideous audience fastened upon me as though my writing were a kind of performance. Front row, center, amongst the hundreds of pairs of undistinguished irises, are the unwavering orbs of my sister Alice, trained upon me the way a gun is trained upon a target in the moment before it is fired. I tell you doctor, I see my death in those eyes! My own death!

DOCTOR: Chamomile, Mr. James. Chamomile. Let us drink to your tranquility. (*Raises cup.*)

HENRY: (*Correcting.*) To the <u>ladies</u>, Dr. Sloper. We must always drink to the <u>ladies</u>.

(*Blackout on the tea table. Lights up on . . .*)

Alice James's Room in Henry's House

ALICE *lies back, noticeably weaker.* KATHERINE *in silhouette, her back to Alice.* ALICE *is writing in her journal.*

KATHERINE: They were at tea again together yesterday. Thick as thieves.

ALICE: I overheard them, I'm sorry to say. Henry was advancing that repulsive theory of his that Emily Dickinson had a distant passion for William Wordsworth.

KATHERINE: Wordsworth! Good god, Alice. Have you ever seen a <u>picture</u> of Wordsworth?

ALICE: I have, yes, unfortunately. He had a <u>very</u> short neck.

KATHERINE: Wordsworth! Your brother had better look to the tattered remnants of his <u>own</u> love life.

ALICE: I'm afraid he is, my darling. Haven't you noticed how . . . um . . . <u>lengthy</u> his evening absences have become?

KATHERINE: I was too relieved with his going to count the hours. (*Slight pause.*) Though now that I think of it, Mr. Barnum mentioned to me that Henry is often seen . . . perambulating the docks of lower New York.

ALICE: My, my. It must be a fairly public perambulation for Mr. Barnum to know about it.

KATHERINE: Not necessarily. Mr. Barnum has quite a talent for acquiring bizarre bits of knowledge.

ALICE: And so do you, my dear. I've noticed how your visits to Mr. Barnum's establishment have lengthened as the predictions for my life span have shortened.

KATHERINE: Even a nurse needs comfort, Alice. Those oddities in Barnum's Museum help to remind me that your early death is not the only freakish and terrible thing in this world.

ALICE: Katherine, my love. When will you remember that it's <u>life</u> that is the terrible thing! Life is such a tragedy, that it <u>requires</u> a happy end. And mine, thank god, is coming soon.

KATHERINE: (*Picking up Alice's journal.*) When I think of what you might have written . . .

ALICE: (*Disgusted.*) Oh good god Katherine! I might have written what Harry writes. Novels like dry deserts! Endless <u>Saharas</u> of insinuation and inference with scarcely an oasis or a sign of life in them. At least I have the satisfaction of knowing that I never put anything parched and dead into the world.

KATHERINE: But Alice, to die away from <u>me</u>! What will I do without you?

ALICE: Oh, you'll mourn me very prettily for a while. And then I imagine you'll find another selfish and interesting woman with a sentence to say.

KATHERINE: Never.

ALICE: Of course you will, Katherine. It's your fate. (*Pause.*) You know, my love, the only thing I regret about dying is that the experience will occur in New York City.

KATHERINE: (*Recovering herself.*) You're not serious.

ALICE: No, really. I'd <u>love</u> to die in New England. Those flinty faces, the granite inflections, the stone-cold eyes. Why Katherine, being in New England is the next best thing to being dead. I'd hardly notice the transition.

(*Blackout. Lights up on a corner of . . .*)

Jane Merritt's Room in the Hospital

We see only DOCTOR SLOPER's *back, in its white surgical coat slightly on-stage as he performs an autopsy on the off-stage body of* JANE MERRITT. NURSE *is behind him handing him instruments from a surgical tray.*

DOCTOR: <u>What</u> did you say? Dammit, hand me another surgical clip. Oh Jane, Jane. Alive, you were a wonder. Dead, you're miraculous! Where are those clips, dammit!

NURSE: (*Craning her neck to see.*) Why do you cut her so deeply? I thought you already knew everything there was to know about her.

DOCTOR: Ah so did I, Nurse. And maybe I do, maybe I do. But this dissection will tell me for sure, for certain. Oh my god, look at that! Just look at that!

(*Blackout. Lights up on the tea table.* HENRY *is yawning uncontrollably.*)

DOCTOR: It used to be, Mr. James, that you could understand how a thing worked by looking at it. A locomotive, a steam shovel, Theodore Roosevelt— none of <u>them</u> hid anything from the mind. But Jane Merritt!

HENRY: (*Bitterly.*) Jane Merritt and my sister Alice have their place in love's darkest night, doctor—way down in the bottom of the sandman's bag. They're what gets sprinkled in your eyes along with the sweeter dreams.

DOCTOR: (*Reaching for the creamer.*) You're having bad dreams again?

HENRY: I am. I write monstrous things in the day and dream dreadful ones at night.

DOCTOR: A good way to lose your audience, sir. I threw your last novel across the room three times before I'd finished the first chapter.

HENRY: (*Glumly.*) I must say you're in the company of every critic in America with that opinion. (*Brightly, with malice.*) Now your monograph on Jane Merritt's disorder . . . That business about the poor creature's . . . um . . . private parts was revoltingly unnecessary.

DOCTOR: (*A cautionary finger.*) Ah, but she <u>was</u> amorous. Yes, Mr. James, Jane was amorous. She would have liked to have been a lover. The signs were unmistakable. I saw great significance in the fact that the skin of her vulva was virtually the only area of her body untouched by the disorder.

HENRY: (*Choking slightly on his tea.*) A disgusting piece of work, doctor.

DOCTOR: I had to do it, Mr. James. Mother Science required it. It was certainly no choice of mine. God knows, if there's anything I hate, it's exploring the organs of the female pelvis.

HENRY: (*Genuinely shocked.*) My <u>god</u>, sir. You're a <u>woman's</u> <u>doctor</u>.

DOCTOR: (*Raises his cup.*) Let's have a toast to the ladies, Mr. James. <u>This</u> one is for the ladies.

HENRY: (*Raises cup glumly, sighs profoundly.*)

(*Blackout. Lights dimly up on* KATHERINE *and* ALICE. ALICE, *much weaker now, and supported by many pillows.* KATHERINE *sits by her, holding her hand and head. There is a spot on* ALICE'*s mouth, so that it is outlined, accentuated; its movements providing the only "action" in this short scene. Beginning with* ALICE'*s monologue and continuing through the* DOCTOR'*s and* HENRY'*s monologues, whatever is said should be spoken very fast as though to disintegrate the forms surrounding it.* ALICE'*s monologue must be a tableau with only* ALICE'*s mouth moving—almost a Pieta.*)

ALICE: I saw the most beautiful thing last night, Katherine. I saw a slender, perfect arm, white as lambswool, rising up from a rotted lump of flesh. (*Her body is taken by pain, she contracts sharply; the next few words are in stentorian voice.*) Katherine, Katherine, give me that morphine! I cannot bear the pain! It leaks and seeps into every corner of my life! (*Again, a spasm.*) I yearn for my death but I haven't the strength to go to it alone. Katherine! I beg you, give me that drug! You did it for your mother! (*Accusing and very loud.*) You did it for your mother!

(*Blackout. Lights up on that corner of* ALICE'*s room in* HENRY'*s house which rep-*

resents the **Operating Room.** *The* DOCTOR *in his white coat is still performing the autopsy on the body of* JANE MERRITT. *The* NURSE *is not present.*)

DOCTOR: (*Back still to us.*) Oh Jesus Christ! What a thing to witness! Oh horror, horror, horror! Who is the god that could leak life into such a form! Look at her ovaries! Look at her stomach! (*Calls in horror.*) Nurse, Nurse, for godssake Nurse come here and look at her breast!

(*Instant blackout. Lights up on* HENRY *who is pacing the stage in . . .*)

Alice's Room in Henry's House

HENRY: She followed me for spite, pure spite. I know very well she wanted to die in New England. (*Pause.*) But how my writing soared when she was with me. All the eyes at all the windows in my house of fiction were open wide. (*Pause, a shudder.*) Ugh! That forehead! The eyes underneath! (*Pause.*) Every night I dream lumps of bone and strands of flesh. Every day I struggle to disentangle the meaning of what I write from what I am writing. (*Pause.*) I can't go on without Alice. I know that now. (*Pause.*) I wonder . . . how I ever thought I could?

(*Blackout. Lights up again dimly on* KATHERINE *and* ALICE. ALICE'*s body is almost gone, now, but the voice is still alive and speaking.* KATHERINE *is taking dictation.*)

KATHERINE: Alice, darling . . . will you speak louder. I can scarcely hear you.

ALICE: (*Broken speech, the words constantly intersected by pain.*) This . . . block of stone in my breast . . . has moved to fill my throat, Kath . . . I cannot push the words past it . . . very well.

KATHERINE: Try . . . Alice . . . oh can't you try. I'll write everything down, every-thing . . . everything.

ALICE: It is . . . too late to expect anything . . . important of me, now, my darling . . . Just let me say my sentence once for you. I cannot . . . hold my head up any longer.

KATHERINE: Say it, Alice, speak it to me. It will be the last thing I write in your journal.

ALICE: (*Raises herself up with her arms around* KATHERINE'*s neck and speaks her sentence in* KATHERINE'*s ear.* KATHERINE'*s face in great pain,* ALICE *falls back smiling, and speaks with great difficulty.*) Remember me to Mr. Barnum.

(*Lights quickly down on* ALICE *and* KATHERINE, *then up for a moment very bright and blinding on the corner of the hospital where* JANE MERRITT'*s autopsy is being performed; the* DOCTOR'*s white jacket is now entirely covered with blood.* NURSE *is present, but mute and stationary. She holds the Uterine Guillotine in one hand.*)

DOCTOR: (*In an ecstasy.*) The blood, the <u>blood</u>, the <u>blood</u> <u>covers</u> me!! Oh it's red, it's <u>human's</u> blood! I've found the thing I needed to know. Nurse, Nurse, who would have thought it. <u>Joan</u> Merritt, <u>Jane</u> Merritt, the <u>Elephant</u> <u>Woman</u> . . . has blood . . . as red . . . as <u>yours</u>! !

(Instant blackout. Quick return to the tea table where HENRY *and the* DOCTOR *sit.* MR. BARNUM's *cane hangs casually over the middle chair. They are whiter, older, more crotchety. Parts of the tea service are missing, now, from the table. The characters' interaction with the missing parts should be a silent one.* HENRY *might reach for the creamer and register its lack; the* DOCTOR *could begin to pour tea into an absent cup; some one of them might turn to ask* MR. BARNUM *again if he could tolerate a biscuit. The charade must gradually run down and* HENRY *and the* DOC-TOR *should be left facing each other for a moment. A silence in which each one in turn leans forward to begin something, gives it up, and drops back in his chair.* HENRY *pulls himself together first.)*

HENRY: Alice wasn't buried until a full week after she died. It took the railroad five days to carry her body from New York to Cambridge. The train was struck by a horse cart in New York State, derailed in Western Massachusetts, and stopped for half a day in Brookline when it ran out of coal. The railway conductor told me that he had never in his life had such a journey. *(Pause, slowly.)* During all that time Katherine Loring sat up with Alice's body in the baggage car. She sat dry-eyed and stony-faced, she spoke to no one, she seemed, from time to time, to be writing sentences in a small black book. *(Pause.)* When the train finally reached Boston and Alice was . . . um . . . unloaded and carried to the platform, a careless porter set her down clumsily and the lid of her coffin sprang open. Katherine Loring had walked on ahead, so no one with sufficient authority was present to push down the coffin lid. And so Alice remained there on the platform of the second largest railway station in the Northeastern United States for quite a while . . .

DOCTOR: Her last public performance, you might say.

HENRY: It seems that a large crowd gathered—how often, after all, is such an exhibition presented in a public place? I was told that before Miss Loring returned, a man in a tattered coat began to offer refreshments for sale and even to sell tickets for what he promised were further revelations about the dead woman. My sister, Alice. *(Pause.)* The ticket seller was later driven from the railway station by Katherine Loring who seemed to recognize him.

DOCTOR: *(A look at* BARNUM's *empty chair.)* Mr. Barnum left his cane here.

HENRY: *(Carefully.)* I noticed that he had.

(Pause.)

DOCTOR: *(A fresh energy.)* Of course all I heard about your dear sister's death were the medical rumours. That, in her coffin, her fingernails were observed to have grown an inch.

HENRY: (*Nods.*) They did grow. It was a most amazing thing. Alice's last collection of pointed instruments. You might say . . . that she was buried . . . armed to the teeth.

(*Slight chuckles from both men. Pause.*)

DOCTOR: (*Tasting.*) The tea is quite cold.

HENRY: (*Tasting.*) The biscuits are . . . <u>very</u> dry. (*Glumly.*) The butter is gone.

DOCTOR: (*Irritated.*) Where's my . . . tea cup?

HENRY: (*Testily.*) I could have <u>sworn</u> I had a saucer . . .

(*Pause.*)

DOCTOR: You know . . . (*Stops.*) . . . I haven't really performed a successful operation since Jane Merritt's autopsy.

HENRY: My books have sunk like stones in still water since Alice died.

DOCTOR: (*Ostentatiously checking his watch.*) Face it, my dear sir. Life is far too crowded an experience to have in it a room for your happiness. (*Slight pause.*) Or mine, for that matter.

HENRY: (*Sighs heavily.*) I'd better ring for more tea things. Let me see, we need a saucer, another cup, the jam, the cream and (*Looks around the table.*) hmmm . . . everything else.

DOCTOR: Don't bother ringing, Mr. James. I've lost my appetite.

(*Suddenly* P. T. BARNUM *sticks his head into* **Alice's Room.**)

BARNUM: Ladies and Gentlemen, Gentlemen and Ladies, welcome to P. T. Barnum's street museum. Please have your money ready. That's right, folks. A whole new concept in the presentation of curiosities. See the cucumber man, see the human frankfurter from Fiji, see the incredible contortionist from the Carolinas. And make sure you see the most fascinating bit of exotica we have. Yes, that's correct, she's just behind the curtain. The child you've all heard so much about is with us at last! That's right, folks, it's Rhinoceros Woman. <u>The</u> most extraordinary female freak of the decade. Her elder sister cut quite a figure here and abroad a few years ago, but she was nothing compared to this little girl. <u>This</u> little girl is a <u>real</u> freak. That's right, folks, line forms to the right. Rhinoceros Woman walks, she talks, she even laughs like a human being, but due to a dreadful accident of birth she appears to be part rhino. That's what I said, Madam, the girl looks just like a little Rhinoceros.

(*A long, long laugh from* BARNUM *and his head disappears. Pause. During* BARNUM's *spiel* HENRY *has found his way back to his seat at the tea table and he and the* DOCTOR *have twisted around to look at* BARNUM. *In the pause between the end of* BARNUM's *spiel and the regrouping of the tea ceremony, much is indicated, noth-*

ing said. Then HENRY *and the* DOCTOR *resume, as though nothing has intervened since their last complaints at the missing parts of the tea set.*)

DOCTOR: I was sure you said your saucer was missing.

HENRY: It <u>is</u> missing, doctor, and I'm not happy about it.

DOCTOR: Oh, well, <u>hap</u>piness . . .

HENRY: Why that's odd.

DOCTOR: <u>What's</u> odd. Could you hand me whatever's left of those biscuits. My appetite seems to be returning.

HENRY: That's <u>very</u> odd. The butter-knives are gone. Every . . . damned . . . one of them.

DOCTOR: (*With some asperity.*) My, my. Is there anyone <u>else</u> in your household who collects pointed instruments? <u>Please</u> pass the biscuits, Mr. James.

(HENRY *has taken the plate of biscuits in hand and continues to hold them.*)

HENRY: This is most upsetting, doctor. (*Gets up with plate of biscuits which the* DOCTOR *is now grabbing for, and begins to pace.*) I can tolerate <u>bone</u> in my biscuits. I can put up with <u>blood</u> in my cup. But, doctor, I warn you, I will not do without my butter-knife. No sir, I will <u>not</u> do without my butter-knife.

DOCTOR: Dammit, Mr. James, give me those biscuits immediately! I don't care <u>what</u> you've ground up in them—book reviews, Japanese citizens, give them here, sir! They're <u>mine</u>! Give them <u>here</u>!

(DOCTOR *and* HENRY *both on their feet now. They begin to struggle trance-like over the plate, come out of their separate reveries and relapse into horribly embarrassed, self-exculpatory chuckles.*)

HENRY: Heee heee heee.

DOCTOR: Aha ha ha.

HENRY: After <u>you</u>, sir.

DOCTOR: No <u>no</u>, after <u>you</u>.

HENRY: I insist.

DOCTOR: (*Angry.*) Be <u>seated</u>, Mr. James.

HENRY: (*Vicious.*) You <u>first</u>, doctor.

DOCTOR: <u>I will not</u>.

(*Pause. They look at each other and begin the embarrassed laughing again.*)

HENRY: (*Conciliatory.*) I think we might sit down together, doctor.

DOCTOR: What a good idea, Mr. James.

(*Plunk. The sit down exactly together.*)

HENRY: Well, sir, I see we have only one cup between us.

DOCTOR: That's all we need for the <u>toast</u>, Mr. James. We certainly don't need more than one cup for the <u>toast</u>.

HENRY: Quite right, doctor. (*Slight pause.*) Which toast is that?

DOCTOR: (*Slightly puzzled.*) Why . . . our <u>usual</u> toast, Mr. James: (*Raises his cup high.*) To Jane Merrit and Alice James and all ladies everywhere. (*Ringing tones.*)

HENRY: (*Raises his hand, tentatively, and puts it on the cup also, slowly.*) To the ladies, doctor. Who would have thought their blood . . . could be . . . so . . . red.

(*Freeze. Instant blackout.*)

FULFILLING KOCH'S POSTULATE

FULFILLING KOCH'S POSTULATE was first produced at Theater for the New City, New York City, in 1986, directed by the author. Subsequent productions have been staged in London at the Gate Theater, in Berlin at the Theater am Halleschen Ufer, and at theatre festivals throughout North America. These photographs are from the premiere at Theater for the New City and the Gate Theater production in London.

Characters

MARY

MAID

ASST.

KOCH

Left to right: TYPHOID MARY, THE MAID. (*Photo by Gail Fischer*)

MARY: Oh, you know how it is. People die. (*pause*) And so forth.

MAID: Twenty families <u>die</u>! You work for twenty families and they all <u>die</u>?!

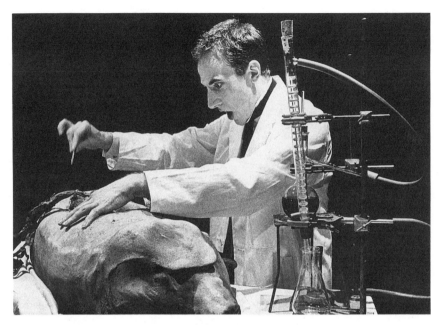

Left to right: PIG, DR. KOCH. (*Photo by Sheila Burnett*)

KOCH: It is exactly like peeling an onion (*pause*) Did you hear what I said? Exactly like an onion. You cut and cut and peel and peel and what you have left when you finish is something that will make you cry. (*sobs as he speaks*) Did you hear what I said?

FULFILLING KOCH'S POSTULATE

Part I

Proscenium stage, bicameral, both sides dimly lit. Audience STAGE LEFT: *a* KITCHEN, *expressionist style. Table, stove, very forced perspective. Audience* STAGE RIGHT: *a* LABORATORY, *expressionist style. Table, armchair, very forced perspective.* UPSTAGE CENTER: *two doors, side by side.* STAGE LEFT *door is the* MAID's *and gives on to the* KITCHEN. STAGE RIGHT *door is the* ASSISTANT's *and gives on to the* LAB.

MARY *in* KITCHEN, *chef's hat, very busy.* KOCH *in* LAB, *microscope, very busy. Both are fat, flat, crude, very Katzenjammer. They move and speak in Katzenjammer style. The* MAID *and* ASSISTANT *do the same with the added quality of insolence. All language must sound badly translated from the Bavarian—the diction displaced so that our attention to it is fully concentrated.*

Blackout. Lights up on KITCHEN.

KITCHEN: MARY *alone.*

MARY: (*singing, not the words, but something* like *the words*)

> When the pie is open
> The birds begin to sing
> Isn't that a tasty dish
> To set before a king.

Another day, another dish. Tum de dum de dum dum. Another day, another dish. (*considers*) Isn't that <u>poetry</u>? Isn't that something <u>like</u> poetry? Another day, another dish? No no. That's not poetry. I'm the <u>cook</u>. Dum de dum. (*sorts thru the dishes*) Oh my. This is not a cooking dish. This is a <u>laboratory</u> dish. This is a <u>petri</u> dish. Oh <u>my</u>. That's wrong. That is <u>completely</u> wrong. (*intake of breath*)

Why, there is something <u>in</u> the petri dish. It's alive! It's alive! No wait . . . (*inspects, then laughs heartily*) It's not. (*slight pause*) Every day I count the dishes in the kitchen. No no. That's wrong. I don't <u>count</u> the dishes. I'm the <u>cook</u>. I <u>cook</u> the dishes. (*begins again*) Every day I <u>cook</u> the dishes in the kitchen. A dish a day, a new dish <u>every</u> day. Oh it takes a strong mind to cook a dish a day. (*big smile*) It takes a <u>cook's</u> mind. But cooking is its own reward. That is what I <u>always</u> say. It is written in my book of cooking. My cook book. I keep a book for other cooks. (*pause*) If there <u>are</u> other cooks. (*pause*) I have never met another cook. (*pause*) I have the impression that I am alone in my work. Nevertheless, I keep a book for other cooks to look at. (*pause*) If there <u>are</u> any.

(*finds a smudge on a dish*) Oh my. Look at <u>this</u>. <u>White</u> <u>flour</u>. Oh cooking requires such courage. (*finds another smudge*) Oh <u>my</u>. <u>Confectioner's</u> <u>sugar</u>. Cooking requires such <u>strength</u>. The cook must experiment. Test. Taste. Review. In extreme cases fry. And roast. Oh cooking is its own reward. That is what I <u>always</u> say. (*big smile*) The <u>big</u> thing is cooking. The <u>best</u> thing is cooking. The important thing is . . . <u>just</u> . . . <u>to</u> . . . keep . . . <u>on</u> . . . <u>cooking</u>.

Blackout. Lights up on KITCHEN.

KITCHEN: MARY *in chef's hat.* MAID *enters chewing.*

MARY: What are you doing.

MAID: I'm tasting.

MARY: What are you doing.

MAID: I'm chewing.

MARY: What are you doing.

MAID: Eating. I'm eating.

MARY: (*broad grin*) She's eating. <u>What</u> are you eating.

MAID: Cookies.

MARY: She's eating cookies. Cookies from <u>cooking</u>? Cookies from the <u>cook</u>?

MAID: (*pointing finger*) Are <u>you</u> the cook?

MARY: (*cheerfully*) They're my cookies. I cooked them.

MAID: (*accusing*) You <u>are</u> the cook.

MARY: I cooked them. I <u>love</u> to cook.

MAID: (*horrified*) <u>You're</u> the <u>cook</u>! Splargh! Ptui! (*she spits out what's in her mouth, throws plate to floor, runs out of kitchen*) Ugh!!

MARY: (*shrugs*) Too much baking powder.

Blackout. Lights up on LAB.

LABORATORY: KOCH *holding test tube,* ASST. *enters.*

KOCH: Did you bring the dish.

ASST: Here's the dish.

KOCH: I asked for a <u>petri</u> dish. I have a postulate to test.

ASST: Ohhhh. I thought you said <u>cookie</u> dish.

KOCH: No no. Surely you didn't think that.

ASST: You don't like <u>cookies</u>?

KOCH: Cookies. Cookies. I don't remember if I like cookies.

ASST: <u>Here's</u> a cookie.

KOCH: (*brightening*) A cookie. (*reaches then draws back*) No no. I have already washed. Lister would never forgive me. I have a postulate to test.

ASST: (*accusingly*) You don't like cookies.

KOCH: Koch's Postulate. I am testing Koch's Postulate.

ASST: (*cups his ear*) Cook's what? Cook's <u>what</u>?

KOCH: I am isolating a bacillus which I suspect of causing typhoid fever in humans. (*sweetly*) I can't have a cookie now.

ASST: I'm telling you, Mr. Doctor. You'll be sorry if you don't take this cookie.

KOCH: (*busy at test tubes*) Go away and bring me a petri dish. What are they <u>teaching</u> them in medical school?

ASST: You'll be <u>really</u> sorry, Mr. Doctor. (*crashes plate to floor, runs out of* LAB)

Blackout. Lights up on KITCHEN.

KITCHEN: MARY *and* MAID *looking in oven.*

MAID: That's <u>disgusting</u>.

MARY: I agree it looks bad.

MAID: It's all <u>burned</u> and <u>black</u> and <u>twisted</u>.

MARY: The timing was a little off. That's all. I mistook the timing.

MAID: What is timing?

MARY: How long you cook a thing.

MAID: Oh. (*back to oven*) It's so . . . <u>small</u>.

MARY: That's what confused me. I never cooked one that small before.

MAID: (*whispers*) How could you stand to touch it? And do the necessary.

MARY: (*firmly*) I'm the cook.

MAID: You think he'll like it?

MARY: What is not to like? When I sauce it and you serve it he'll love it.

MAID: How do you <u>know</u>?

MARY: I know <u>exactly</u>. I'm the cook.

MAID: He never asks what he's eating?

MARY: He takes my word for it. I'm the cook. (*dinner bell rings from* LAB) You'd better bring the fish course. You know how he is about his fish.

MAID: (*picks up dish*) He's a pig. <u>That's</u> how he is about his fish. He's a <u>big fat pig</u>.

Blackout. Lights up on LAB.

LABORATORY: KOCH *belches. Rubs stomach. Belches again. Dead pig on table.*

KOCH: It's not anthrax. Not this time. It's something in the sputum or the urine or the feces. I know it. I'm <u>sure</u> of it. (*knock on door*) Alright, alright.

ASST: (*enters*) Your tea, Mr. Doctor.

KOCH: Alright, alright, uh, just put it . . . (*he gestures*).

ASST: (*sees pig, gets excited*) Are we finishing the pig, now, Mr. Doctor? Are we going to finish the pig?

KOCH: Yes yes, I'm afraid we have to. I hate to open up so large an animal but . . . (*shrugs*). It was showing all the symptoms of the bacillus.

ASST: (*very excited*) High fever! Uncontrollable diarrhoea! Rose spots on the abdomen!

KOCH: (*very excited*) Yes, yes. That's right!

ASST: It was much sicker than the rabbit.

KOCH: Yes, yes. It was. (*turns to table*)

ASST: (*thrusts spout of teapot in* KOCH*'s back*) Bang! Bang bang!

KOCH: Good god!

ASST: (*cackles fiendishly*) I'm sorry, sir. Ha ha ha it's just a teapot. Ha ha ha I wanted to play with it . . . ha ha ha . . . ever since I saw it in the kitchen. Hee hee hee.

KOCH: Pull yourself together, my boy. We've got to open up that pig.

ASST: (*weak hiccups*) Hoo hoo hoo. Oh <u>Jesus</u>. That was so much fun. Hoo hoo hoo. Bang bang! Hee hee.

KOCH: (*textbook voice*) Hysteria is often observed in inexperienced members of the medical profession before a dissection. (*cracks* ASST. *across the cheek*)

ASST: (*subsides into giggles*)

KOCH: There we are. All in one piece. We cannot dissect on a case of hysteria.

ASST: No sir, Mr. Doctor. (*goes to look at pig*) Oooh yuch. What's that. I never saw anything like that before.

KOCH: That is an ulcerated intestine, my boy. A sure sign of typhoid fever.

ASST: Oooh god. And look at that. That looks just like a can of worms. Heh heh heh. Wanna go fishing, Mr. Doctor? Heh heh heh.

KOCH: (*sternly*) I don't like to fish, my boy. This is the ravages of typhoid fever, you know. This pig did die in a horrible agony, you know.

ASST: Aha ha ha ha. Sorry, sir, I just can't seem to . . . Hee hee hee. Come over to my side, Mr. Doctor. Look at it from over here. There's just something extremely funny about . . . ha ha ha. Please Mr. Doctor. Come over here.

KOCH: (*looks*) Heh heh heh heh. Oh my god. This is indecent . . . heh heh heh heh.

ASST: See what I mean, Mr. Doctor? I know it's typhoid. I know it's terrible. But that part there looks just like Joseph Lister's nose! (ASST. *and* KOCH *collapse into each other's arms, hysterical with laughter*)

ASST: (*waving teapot*) Aha ha ha ha hee hee. Bang! Bang! Ha ha stick 'em up! Hoo hoo hoo.

KOCH: Joseph Lister's nose! Hee hee hee. (*wiping his eyes*) Oh my my my my. I haven't had a laugh like that in years.

ASST: God no. Me neither. Well you know what they say, Mr. Doctor.

KOCH: I certainly do, my boy. Nothing is funnier than death. That's what they say.

ASST: What does it mean, Mr. Doctor?

KOCH: (*belches*)

ASST: We had too much for dinner, Mr. Doctor.

KOCH: (*maniacal*) Yes yes we certainly did! (*serious*) If I establish a link between the bacillus and the disease and then if I identify the carrier . . . (*pauses, grins broadly*) I will have proven my postulate.

ASST: That reminds me, Mr. Doctor. What is the postulate?

KOCH: (*keeps grinning, belches again*).

ASST: (*holds his head*) I feel . . . hot. I feel . . . wet.

KOCH: (*busy at the pig*) You ate too much, my boy. You <u>laughed</u> too much.

Blackout. Lights up on KITCHEN.

KITCHEN: MARY *cuts vegetables,* MAID *enters.* MARY *very cheerful.*

MAID: Miss Mary. Miss Mary. What are you making for dinner tonight?

MARY: Boiled rabbit. (*looks in pot*) Oops there goes the bladder. I'm watching my temperatures very closely here. You have to be scientific about the boil.

MAID: There's a <u>bunny</u> in that pot, Miss Mary?

MARY: Oh you have to start your rabbit in the afternoon. It takes a <u>long</u> <u>time</u> to boil a rabbit. <u>Some</u> cooks won't boil them alive but those cooks are not <u>professional</u> cooks. <u>Professional</u> cooks always start from the ground up.

MAID: Miss Mary. Miss Mary. What's wrong with your right hand.

MARY: (*rolls dough*) You mean <u>this</u>. You mean my right <u>thumb</u>. All cooks who strangle their own rabbits have this thumb. It's called . . . <u>gamekeeper's</u> thumb.

MAID: It looks like you boiled it.

MARY: (*smiles*) I agree it's very red.

MAID: It doesn't hurt you?

MARY: No no. Why should it hurt? It's a perfect thumb. It's a <u>professional</u> thumb. It can cut radish roses so delicate, you would think they came from a florist. (*holds up a radish rose*)

MAID: What else. What else are you making Miss Mary?

MARY: (*as she chops*) A vegetable soufflé of brussel sprouts, broccoli, baby carrots, new potatoes, kohlrabi, and . . .

MAID: You'd think he wouldn't want to touch the main course.

MARY: You mean the rabbit.

MAID: That's what I mean. He <u>works</u> with rabbits. He sticks <u>needles</u> in their bellies. He <u>infects</u> them with jesus knows <u>what</u>. You'd think he wouldn't want to <u>eat</u> them.

MARY: Well you know what they say.

MAID: Yes yes I do.

MARY: Nothing is funnier than death.

MAID: That's what they say. (*pause*) What does it mean?

MARY: (*truculent*) It's not <u>his</u> choice what he eats. It's <u>me</u> who decides. It's <u>me</u> who's the <u>cook</u>. If I decide he should have rabbit . . . <u>he</u> <u>eats</u> <u>that</u> <u>rabbit</u>.

MAID: And the pork roast? He ate the pork roast after what happened to that laboratory pig?

MARY: Why shouldn't he eat it? It was perfectly cooked. A perfect roast. I've cooked that roast in twenty households to nothing but high praise. And even <u>more</u> than that.

MAID: Twenty households?

MARY: Twenty, at <u>least</u> twenty.

MAID: You've cooked for that many families?

MARY: <u>More</u> than twenty families. I'm only counting the pork eaters now.

MAID: Twenty families! <u>More</u> than twenty! How could you leave so many families? Me, I've only worked here.

MARY: Oh, you know how it is. People die. (*pause*) And so forth.

MAID: Twenty families <u>die</u>! You work for twenty families and they all <u>die</u>?!

MARY: (*firmly*) And so forth. You'd better serve the soup. You know how he is about his soup.

MAID: Oh he's good about his soup. He's a little bunny about his soup.

Blackout. Lights up on LAB.

LABORATORY: KOCH *in chair.* ASST. *separating things on table.*

ASST: I'm still hot. (*separates more*) Perhaps hotter.

KOCH: (*busy*) Yes yes, heat is everything. Heat is <u>life</u>.

ASST: And the soup made it worse.

KOCH: (*still busy*) <u>Hot</u> soup, was it?

ASST: You don't know what you ate?

KOCH: I ate what she cooked.

ASST: What was in that soup? It made me <u>sick</u>.

KOCH: (*shrugs*) <u>She's</u> the <u>cook</u>.

ASST: What was in that <u>rabbit</u>? (KOCH *shakes his head*) What did she put in the <u>soufflé</u>? The <u>pig</u>?

KOCH: (*his attention caught at last*) The pig? It was not anthrax, I can tell you that. It was certainly not anthrax in that pig.

ASST: I don't mean <u>our</u> pig. I mean <u>her</u> pig.

KOCH: (*bewildered*) <u>She</u> has a pig?

ASST: (*gives up*) I'll ask the maid.

KOCH: (*back to his notes*) Good idea. (*writes for a little*) You know something.

ASST: What is it, Mr. Doctor.

KOCH: (*sighs, stares into space*)

ASST: That's right, Mr. Doctor. Too many fevers. Not enough cures.

KOCH: Twenty pigs, twenty rats, twenty rabbits . . . (*sighs again*).

ASST: What's for dinner, Mr. Doctor.

KOCH: What? Dinner? I'm not the cook. Ask the cook.

   Blackout. Lights up on KITCHEN.

   KITCHEN: MARY *alone.*

MARY: I don't think he cared for the soup. I can <u>feel</u> he didn't care for the soup. (*uses egg beater moodily*) But he never says. Not a word. Not a word of praise, not a word of blame. Not a word about money. Nothing. And I'm here all day. Tasting, chewing, eating, testing, COOKING. (*she's happy as she says this; she smiles broadly*) COOKING.

MAID: (*enters speaking*) Miss Mary Miss Mary. He says you have to start washing.

MARY: Washing? I'm the cook.

MAID: Not laundry washing. <u>Hand</u> washing. <u>Pot</u> washing. The assistant told me you have to start washing the pots, the pans, and the vegetables.

MARY: (*slowly, with authority*) He's crazy.

MAID: The assistant says <u>he</u> says he wants the same . . . <u>something</u>, I can't remember the word, in the kitchen as there is in the laboratory.

MARY: Hygiene.

MAID: <u>That's</u> the word.

MARY: He's <u>completely</u> <u>crazy</u>.

MAID: The assistant says <u>he</u> says he's worried about . . . <u>something</u>, I can't remember the word, infecting the food.

MARY: Microorganisms.

MAID: That's not the word.

MARY: Bacilli.

MAID: That's not the word.

MARY: Germs.

MAID: <u>That's</u> the word. The assistant says <u>he</u> says the heat of the kitchen allows germs to breed.

MARY: <u>Heat</u>. <u>What</u> heat. It's always cool in here. Feel my hands.

MAID: Very cool.

MARY: Like ice. Like snowballs. I can't even hold a rolling pin properly, my hands are so cold.

MAID: Nevertheless, <u>he</u> says, <u>they</u> say, <u>someone</u> says he wants you to wash before and after you touch the food. <u>And</u> to wash everything in the kitchen that touches the food. (*great effort*) <u>And</u> to wash it all with soap and water that is very hot.

MARY: (*draws a deep breath, wipes hands on her apron in a final way*) It always comes to this. You know. It <u>always</u> comes to this.

MAID: It does?

MARY: That's right. Sooner or later, in every household I've ever worked in comes the same question: Who is to be cook in the kitchen? Is the master of the house to be cook in the kitchen? Or is the <u>cook</u> to be cook in the kitchen? That is always the question.

MAID: Is there an answer, Miss Mary?

MARY: To <u>that</u> question? There <u>is</u> an answer. (*pause*) <u>I am the cook</u>. That is the answer I always give.

MAID: It's true the dust protects the windows.

MARY: And the grease coats the pans.

MAID: And the dirt . . . (*searches unsuccessfully for the virtue in dirt*) . . . uh, the dirt . . .

MARY: If I washed my hands every time I touched something, I'd have no skin on them at all. Soap burns skin.

MAID: Perhaps he thinks it burns germs as well. Miss Mary . . . what <u>is</u> germs?

MARY: Something you cannot see. From which grows something you cannot cure.

MAID: He cuts open animals for something he cannot see?

MARY: Everyone says so.

MAID: How can he find what he's looking for if he can't see it or cure it?

MARY: I agree. I am the cook. (*proudly*) I see <u>everything</u> I do.

MAID: (*triumphant*) You don't see <u>taste</u>, Miss Mary. You don't see <u>smell</u>. And if there are germs in your cooking, you don't see them either.

MARY: (*picks up knife deliberately, with great calm*) Get out of my kitchen.

Blackout. Lights up on LAB.

LABORATORY: KOCH *and* ASSISTANT.

KOCH: She carried out my order?

ASST: Oh perfectly, Mr. Doctor.

KOCH: The kitchen is completely clean?

ASST: Yes yes, Mr. Doctor.

KOCH: You know this from your own eyes?

ASST: Uh . . . hearsay, Mr. Doctor.

KOCH: Hearsay is not verifiable, my boy. The kitchen is insanitary. Hearsay won't do.

ASST: I heard water running in the kitchen this morning, Mr. Doctor.

KOCH: The wrong pipe. I was taking my bath this morning.

ASST: I heard water running in the kitchen this afternoon, Mr. Doctor.

KOCH: Again a false conclusion. The rain barrels were being emptied this afternoon.

ASST: I heard water running in the kitchen just now, Mr. Doctor.

KOCH: Was it a <u>washing</u> sound, my boy?

ASST: (*thinks strenuously*) Uhhhhh . . .

KOCH: I thought not.

ASST: She's a stubborn woman, Mr. Doctor.

KOCH: Nevertheless, the kitchen must be disinfected. (*as though quoting*) Kitchens are the cradles of germs . . .

ASST: Germs are the mother of disease . . .

KOCH: Disease is the . . . <u>something</u>, I can't remember the word, of death . . .

ASST: And nothing is funnier than death, Mr. Doctor.

KOCH: As a general principle, yes, my boy. Nothing <u>is</u> funnier than death. But not in my kitchen. Death in my kitchen is <u>not</u> <u>funny</u>.

MAID: (*enters cheerfully with covered tray*) Here's dinner.

KOCH: So soon?

ASST: He didn't ring.

MAID: So what.

KOCH: Rude, but accurate. If dinner is ready no reason not to serve it.

ASST: I agree.

KOCH: What did she make.

MAID: Meat, vegetables, a sweet.

KOCH: I was hoping for a more specific answer.

ASST: You'll never get it from her, Mr. Doctor.

MAID: That's true. I operate on general principles.

KOCH: (*looks at her*) You're very flushed, my girl.

MAID: It's hot in here.

ASST: I agree. I'm hot all the time.

KOCH: That's funny. I couldn't be cooler.

ASST: You're always cool, Mr. Doctor. Your hands are like snowballs.

MAID: I've got to go. She needs me.

KOCH: (*hopefully*) You're cleaning the kitchen?

MAID: Oh no. She wouldn't consent to that.

ASST: Threatened you when you spoke of it, didn't she?

MAID: How do you know?

ASST: Hearsay. The kitchen walls are very thin.

MAID: She's a stubborn woman.

KOCH: Nevertheless, you must see that everything in the kitchen is perfectly clean.

MAID: Oh I couldn't do that, Mr. Doctor. <u>She's</u> the cook. (*leaves*)

KOCH: (*excited*) This is very suspicious.

ASST: I agree.

KOCH: <u>Very</u> suspicious.

ASST: (*emphatically*) I <u>agree</u>, Mr. Doctor.

KOCH: You think so?

ASST: Theories are made from less, Mr. Doctor.

KOCH: I think you're right, my boy. It <u>is</u> suspicious. Congratulations.

ASST: (*modestly*) I have a great example always before me, Mr. Doctor.

KOCH: Thank you, my boy.

ASST: What's for dinner?

KOCH: I forgot to look.

ASST: (*takes cover off food*) The usual.

KOCH: Oh yes?

ASST: Meat, vegetables, a sweet.

KOCH: But is it good?

ASST: (*excited*) It looks good. (*enthusiastic*) It smells good.

KOCH: Don't theorize ahead of your facts.

ASST: (*judicious*) But, of course, I haven't tasted it.

KOCH: It's hot?

ASST: The steam is rising off the platter. There is moisture on the cover of the bowl.

ASST: (*pleased*) Hot food. Still, I wish I knew what it was.

ASST: Um <u>um</u>.

KOCH: (*busy at test tubes*) What are you doing.

ASST: I'm tasting. Um <u>um</u>.

KOCH: What are you doing now.

ASST: (*mouth full*) I'm chewing.

KOCH: And now.

ASST: Eating. I'm <u>eating</u>. (*he swallows, grabs his belly, falls writhing to the floor*) Aaaoow! Aaow! It's the <u>cook</u>! It's the <u>cook</u>!

KOCH: (*impassive*) Too much salt.

Blackout. Lights up on KITCHEN.

KITCHEN: MARY *alone, in flowered apron. She hums "Four and Twenty Blackbirds" as she rolls out dough and reflours her board. Her first line is sung.*

MARY: Spring is in the air. (*considers a moment*) Spring is in the air. Spring is in the <u>air</u>? I wonder what that means. Doesn't spring start in the earth? In the <u>ground</u>? Doesn't everything grow from the ground <u>up</u>? And not from the air <u>down</u>? (*shrugs*) I'm the <u>cook</u>. I don't have to understand spring. (*Rolls pie dough*) I know they've been together. Several times at least. It takes a trained nose to sniff these things out. (*head left*) Snif snif. (*head right*) Snif snif. It takes a <u>cook's</u> nose.

MAID: (*enters disheveled*) You rang for me Miss Mary?

MARY: (*smiling*) It was my thoughts you heard.

MAID: (*surprised*) The walls are that thin?

MARY: (*a stern stare at* MAID's *stomach*) What have you got in the oven.

MAID: (*scandalized*) Miss <u>Mary</u>. <u>You're</u> the <u>cook</u>.

MARY: (*sternly*) I always know when something's in the oven.

MAID: (*a glance at her own stomach*) Oh you mean . . .

MARY: That's what I mean.

MAID: Nothing (*whispers*) I hope. <u>Nothing's</u> in the oven, Miss Mary.

MARY: Well, see that you keep it that way. There is only one cook in <u>this</u> kitchen.

MAID: Yes, Miss Mary.

Pause. MARY *returns to her pie.*

MAID: Miss Mary, Miss Mary. What are you making tonight?

MARY: It's game pie and vegetables.

MAID: What kind of game, Miss Mary?

MARY: (*significantly*) <u>Small</u> game. <u>Scientific</u> game.

MAID: And what sort of vegetables?

MARY: <u>Large</u> vegetables. <u>Root</u> vegetables. All in an oil pastry crust. (*she trims the pie*)

MAID: It sounds very good, Miss Mary.

MARY: Yes yes. I've served this dish in many households to nothing but high praise. Unfortunately, tonight, I put too much lard in the pie dough. ˉ

MAID: Is it possible.

MARY: I hadn't planned on it. The measuring cup made up its own mind. (*shrugs*)

MAID: That's terrible, Miss Mary. You know how he loves his game pie.

MARY: Baking a pie you didn't plan on is like being pregnant without knowing it. (*a look at* MAID's *stomach*)

MAID: I'd better get back to my dusting.

Blackout. Lights up on LAB.

LABORATORY: *Silent scene.* KOCH *is dozing over his notes.* MAID *and* ASST. *locked in sweaty embrace in corner of* LAB, *breathing very heavily.* MARY *is illuminated in* KITCHEN, *head raised suspiciously. She sniffs loudly and definitively.* SNIF. SNIF. SNIF. SNIF. SNIF.

Blackout. Lights up on KITCHEN.

KITCHEN: MARY *and* MAID.

MARY: Well? Well?

MAID: (*blank look*)

MARY: How did he like the pie?

MAID: He was very busy.

MARY: He said nothing? He made no remarks?

MAID: He asked if you had . . . <u>some</u>thing, I forget the word, the kitchen yet.

MARY: Disinfected.

MAID: That's the word.

MARY: What does he think? I conduct experiments here? I put bugs in the strudel?

MAID: He thinks you're responsible.

MARY: Responsible. He's right. I <u>am</u> responsible. I am the cook.

MAID: No no. Responsible for <u>some</u>thing.

MARY: For <u>cooking</u>.

MAID: For something <u>else</u>.

MARY: What is it?!!

MAID: I forget the word!!

MARY: (*shouts*) WHAT ARE YOU TALKING ABOUT!!?

MAID: (*shouts*) I DON'T <u>KNOW</u>!!

Blackout. Lights up on partial KITCHEN, *partial* LAB.

KITCHEN/LAB: MAID *is up to her elbows in seashells.* ASST. *is in front of his door.*

ASST: (*a loud whisper*) How about it?

MAID: I can't now.

ASST: I want you.

MAID: I have to beard the mussels.

ASST: I need you.

MAID: I have to scrub the scallops.

ASST: I want you.

MAID: I have to open the oysters.

ASST: You mean <u>kill</u> the oysters.

MAID: I'm not killing anything.

ASST: When you open the oyster shell you kill the oyster.

MAID: I didn't know that.

ASST: Marine biology. It's a new field.

MAID: I never thought of oysters as alive <u>or</u> dead.

ASST: They're bivalves. Bivalves are alive until you open their shells. And then they're dead.

MAID: You're smart.

ASST: You're smarter.

MAID: I agree.

> *Pause.*

ASST: (*irritated*) Why is she suddenly cooking seafood? She never cooked seafood before.

MAID: (*busy*) Really? <u>Never</u> before? My, but these are slippery.

ASST: Sexual. They're sexual.

MAID: That's stupid. They're not sexual, they're <u>oysters</u>.

ASST: But they <u>feel</u> sexual. They <u>look</u> sexual. Everyone <u>says</u> so.

> *Pause.* MAID *reflects.*

MAID: Then go fuck an oyster.

> *Blackout. Lights up on* LAB.

LABORATORY: KOCH *with test tube.* ASST. *in shadow.*

KOCH: I have the facts, now. I have the theory, now. Now the postulate appears. The next step is <u>action</u>.

ASST: (*suddenly appears behind* KOCH *with teapot*) <u>Bang bang</u>!

KOCH: Aieee! (*drops test tube*) Aieee!

ASST: Ha ha ha! Oh ha ha! Bang <u>bang</u>, Mr. Doctor. Bang bang bang!!!

Blackout. Lights up on KITCHEN.

KITCHEN: MARY *at table.* KOCH *stands in kitchen doorway.*

KOCH: Mary.

MARY: (*wheels around*) You're in my kitchen!

KOCH: I have a question for you.

MARY: Don't come too close, Mr. Doctor.

KOCH: It's a methodological question, Mary.

MARY: You think I don't know the word. <u>Hah</u>! I <u>know</u> the word. What do <u>you</u> know.

KOCH: I know something is wrong in this kitchen.

MARY: You have a formal complaint Mr. Doctor? Put it in writing.

KOCH: You know what I'm going to say.

MARY: (*terrible warning*) This is a clean kitchen, Mr. Doctor.

Pause. They look at each other. KOCH's *eyes waver first.*

KOCH: I'll be back. (*he leaves*)

MARY: (*triumphant, arms raised to heaven*) <u>I</u> <u>AM</u> <u>THE</u> <u>COOK</u>!

Blackout. Lights up on LAB.

LABORATORY: KOCH *absent.* MAID *and* ASST. *locked in sweaty embrace. Both breathe very heavily and make love as they speak.*

MAID: Where is he?

ASST: Talking to <u>her</u>.

MAID: You're joking.

ASST: Not about that.

MAID: He's crazy.

ASST: <u>I</u> think so.

MAID: He'll get himself nowhere.

ASST: He got himself into the kitchen.

MAID: Death is better than that.

ASST: Death is <u>funnier</u> than that.

Slight pause.

MAID: Are you always this hot?

ASST: Yes yes. Mmmm.

MAID: I mean your <u>skin</u>. It's burning up.

ASST: So is yours.

MAID: Are you sweating?

ASST: Feel this.

MAID: I'm in a soupbowl myself.

ASST: I have other symptoms as well.

MAID: So do I.

ASST: I don't want to say what they are.

MAID: I don't blame you.

   Pause.

ASST: Is this what love is like?

MAID: How should I know? (*pulls away*) Don't theorize ahead of your facts.

   Blackout. Lights up on KITCHEN.

   KITCHEN: MARY *and* MAID. *Tray of uneaten food.*

MAID: (*enters*) I think he's stopped eating.

MARY: That's bad.

MAID: Here. He's stopped eating here. He buys things other places.

MARY: That's <u>very</u> bad.

MAID: The assistant too.

MARY: You know this from your own eyes?

MAID: (*indicates tray*) The facts are before you.

MARY: This is a <u>serious</u> situation.

MAID: You're right, Miss Mary.

MARY: If no one eats, I'm out of work.

MAID: (*nods judiciously*) I agree.

MARY: I can't stay in a household where there's no work. I am . . . (*note of doubt*) the cook.

   Blackout. Spot on MARY's *hands rolling dough, lights up on* LAB.

LABORATORY: KOCH *and* ASST.

ASST: I'm <u>so</u> hungry.

KOCH: Have another sandwich, my boy.

ASST: (*bitterly*) You're the doctor.

KOCH: And <u>she's</u> the cook.

ASST: She's the cook alright. She cooks and cooks and we can't eat what she cooks.

KOCH: (*an order*) We <u>don't</u> eat what she cooks.

ASST: Yesterday she made Sacher torte.

KOCH: And the day before it was strudel.

ASST: I would give a lot, Mr. Doctor, for three pieces of Sacher torte and a strudel.

MAID: (*enters with pie plate, maniacally cheerful*) Here's a Sacher torte and three pieces of strudel. (*stops*) No. Wait. That's wrong.

KOCH: The walls are that thin?

MAID: They certainly are, Mr. Doctor.

KOCH: (*to* ASST.) Don't touch that plate.

Blackout. Lights up on LAB *again, spot still on* MARY *cutting dough.*

LABORATORY: KOCH *and* ASST.

KOCH: (*paper in hand*) She sent me a letter. A <u>letter</u>!

ASST: Ho ho ho. A <u>letter</u>. That's a hot one, Mr. Doctor. A letter. Ha ha ha. That's funnier than bang bang!

KOCH: You think it's funny for people to write?

ASST: I think it's <u>crazy</u>.

KOCH: For people to write to each other?

ASST: There's no each <u>other</u>, Mr. Doctor. There's only <u>her</u> in the next room writing to <u>you</u> in this one. Ha ha ha. A letter.

KOCH: I think it's . . . rather . . . touching.

ASST: Ooo hoo hoo hoo! Touching! Her! <u>Touching</u>! She probably spit in the ink!

Blackout. Lights up on KITCHEN.

KITCHEN: MARY *making dumplings.*

MARY: Germans are a very sentimental people. I know this from their style of cooking. (*holds up a dumpling*) The German style of cooking is so . . . crude. So . . . sloppy. That's it. German cooking is very sloppy. (holds up her dough-covered hands)

Blackout. Lights up on LAB.

LABORATORY: KOCH *in corner.* MAID *and* ASST. *on floor making love. Heavy breathing, kissing throughout. But it's Katzenjammer kissing.*

MAID: Why a letter? Why a letter? She's the cook. Cooks don't write. Cooks cook.

ASST: She cooks alright. But you're the hot one. Hee hee hee.

MAID: (*guilty*) I've got nothing in the oven. Believe me.

ASST: I mean your skin. You have very hot skin. And beautiful rose spots on your stomach.

MAID: (*stops panting*) I can't do this if you talk about it. Talk about something else.

ASST: Excuse me. Uh . . . He found the cause of typhoid today.

MAID: You mean the germ. (*proud of the word*)

ASST: No no. He isolated the germ long ago. He found the carrier.

MAID: It doesn't matter. The kitchen is still dirty.

ASST: It's not the kitchen. It's not the dirt in the kitchen. It's her. She's got it.

MAID: (*giggles*) That's funny.

ASST: I agree. Every time she licks a finger, or cracks an egg, or sneezes into a soufflé, another spoonful of death goes down someone's throat. (*they finish making love*) Ahhh.

MAID: Ohhh.

Pause. Rest of conversation continued in exhaustion.

MAID: You mean it's in her body? What he was looking for is in her body?

ASST: Everywhere in her body. In her blood, in her urine, in her sputum. Everything she touches turns to death.

MAID: That's funny. (*giggles*)

ASST: I agree.

MAID: (*recovers*) I mean it's something, I don't remember the word.

ASST: Me neither.

MAID: I never eat what she cooks.

ASST: No one does. Anymore.

Blackout.

End of Part I

Part II

KITCHEN: MARY *surrounded by pies, cakes, and broken cookies.* MAID *at oven.*

MARY: The thing is just to keep cooking. Cooking is its own reward. Everyone says so. I say so. Tasting, testing, chewing, eating . . . these are the small things. The big thing is cooking. The important thing is just to keep cooking.

MAID: (*clutches stomach, rocks back and forth*) Miss Mary, Miss Mary! My cake is fallen! My cake is burned!

MARY: Is it possible.

MAID: Miss Mary, Miss Mary! My cake is ruined! My cake is dead!

MARY: (*to the* MAID) Too much yeast. (*to the Audience*) I knew she had something in the oven.

Blackout. Lights up on LAB.

LABORATORY: KOCH *and* ASST. *trading pieces of paper back and forth very rapidly. What they do should look like double juggling.*

KOCH: (*breathing hard*) You see. (*puff puff*) My boy. (*puff puff*) This is (*puff puff*) how epidemics (*puff*) spread (*puff puff puff*).

ASST: (*passing paper bewilderedly*) From paper, Mr. Doctor? From touching paper?

KOCH: No no. Surely you don't think that. This is (*puff puff*) just an illustration of the rapid (*puff puff*) passage (*puff puff puff*) of (*puff puff*) epidemial (*puff*) infection. (*drops all the papers at once,* ASST. *stoops to pick them up*)

ASST: These are letters, Mr. Doctor! These are all letters.

KOCH: That's right, my boy. (*puff puff*) She wrote them to me. (*fondly*) Every one.

ASST: (*looks at a letter, shakes head*) Jesus.

KOCH: Alright, alright. Give them to me.

ASST: (*mutters*) Make me.

KOCH: (*cups his ear*) What did you say?

ASST: I said take them. (*holds letters out of reach*) But don't put them to your mouth, sir. On no condition, Mr. Doctor, should you put these letters in your mouth.

KOCH: Oh, I <u>agree</u>, my boy.

ASST: (*holds letters above* KOCH's *head.* KOCH *jumps for them*) You can't be too careful with laboratory material, Mr. Doctor. Remember the pig.

KOCH: I agree <u>absolutely</u>, my boy. (*intensely*) Give them here. <u>Give</u> <u>them</u> <u>here</u>.

ASST: So Mr. Doctor. You promise not to . . .

KOCH: Give them <u>here</u>! They're part of my postulate! (*finally jumps high enough to snatch them violently away, begins to kiss and lick them frantically*)

ASST: (*very casual*) Germans are such a sentimental people. I know this from their laboratory procedure. Their laboratory procedure (*a glance at* KOCH, *who is eating one of the letters*) is <u>very</u> <u>sloppy</u>.

Blackout. Lights up on KITCHEN.

KITCHEN: *Piles of food gone.* MAID *trimming green beans,* MARY *dozing in corner. Sound of beans hitting pan, plink plink plink.* MAID *cuts beans faster and faster. Soon she's just throwing them in the pan without cutting the ends, darting serious glances at* MARY *to see if she sees. When* MAID *finishes she pauses, grins broadly, then, slowly, moderately, distinctly, as though testing the phrase, repeats in a whisper:*

MAID: I . . . am . . . the . . . cook.

Blackout. Lights up on partial KITCHEN, *partial* LAB.

LAB/KITCHEN: ASST. *conceals a test tube under his shirt,* MAID *hides book under her skirt.*

ASST: Look what <u>I</u> have.

MAID: No <u>no</u>. <u>You</u> look what <u>I</u> have.

ASST: I asked first.

MAID: I <u>thought</u> first.

ASST: Awwww alright. What do you have?

MAID: (*pulls up skirt suggestively*) A <u>recipe</u> book.

ASST: What's a recipe.

MAID: How you cook a thing.

ASST: So it's a book of cooking. A . . . cook book.

MAID: It's a <u>cook's</u> book.

ASST: So what.

MAID: So nothing. I have a cook's book. That's it.

ASST: Pooh pooh. That's no fun.

MAID: I agree. What have <u>you</u> got?

ASST: (*coy*) Ohhhh. It's just a little something I play with.

MAID: Well. What <u>is</u> it?

ASST: Just a little something I keep in my pants to play with. (*suggestively*) <u>You've</u> seen it before.

MAID: I'd rather play house.

ASST: (*outraged*) This <u>is</u> house!

MAID: I mean house in the <u>kitchen</u>. Not house in the <u>bedroom</u>. I'd rather be the cook. (*she reads the cook book*)

ASST: (*disgusted*) You'd rather be the cook than see what I've got? (*he pulls out test tube and waves it*) You'd rather be the cook than play with <u>this</u>?!!

MAID: (*absorbed in book, but firm*) Oh yes yes. I'd <u>much</u> rather be the cook.

ASST: <u>Jesus</u>.

Blackout. Lights up on KITCHEN.

KITCHEN: MARY *alone, polishing knives.*

MARY: Why is it so warm. So <u>suddenly</u> warm. This was always a <u>cold</u> kitchen. (*she mops her brow*) I feel like I'm standing in a soupbowl.

MAID: (*enters with empty dishes*) Here's the dishes.

MARY: (*absorbed in polishing*) Dishes?

MAID: From the laboratory. And everywhere else.

MARY: The dishes are <u>empty</u>. They're <u>eating</u> again. (*big grin*)

MAID: I wouldn't say that.

MARY: You wouldn't?

MARY: Then where is the food? Where is the food that was on the dishes?

MAID: It's in test tubes. Or in the stomachs of rats. (*low voice*) Or in the garbage.

MARY: (*shaken*) The <u>garbage</u>!

MAID: He's proven his . . . <u>something</u>, I forget the word. And now he's acting on it.

MARY: (*automatic*) Postulate. He's proven his postulate. (*outraged*) Test tubes is proof? Garbage is action? Hah! I know what is proof (*brandishes a knife*). I know what is action (*polishes knife vigorously*)

Pause.

MAID: (*very innocent*) Miss Mary. Miss Mary. How would you cook a spring lamb? I mean if there was anyone to eat it. How long would you leave a spring lamb in the oven?

MARY: (*stops polishing immediately, whirls around, knife in hand, with a horrified intake of breath*)

Blackout. Lights up on LAB.

LABORATORY: KOCH *in foreground,* ASST. *lurks upstage.*

KOCH: It is exactly like peeling an onion. (*pause*) Did you hear what I said? Exactly like an onion. You cut and cut and peel and peel and what you have when you finish is something that will make you cry. (*sobs as he speaks*) Did you hear what I said? (ASST. *doesn't move*)

Blackout. Lights up on partial KITCHEN, *partial* LAB.

KITCHEN/LAB: MAID *in* KITCHEN, KOCH *in* LAB.

MAID: (*looks at* KOCH)

KOCH: (*looks at* MAID)

MAID: (*very agitated*) No. Wait. This is wrong.

Blackout. Instant illumination same scene.

LABORATORY: *Instant illumination on same scene, same position. But now the* ASST. *is in* KOCH's *place.* MAID *is exactly as she was.*

MAID: (*very cheerful*) It won't be long now.

ASST: Mmmm.

MAID: I know a hundred recipes now.

ASST: Mmmm.

MAID: I can light the stove now.

ASST: Mmmm.

MAID: Set a service for six now.

ASST: Mmmm.

MAID: Serve in the French style now.

ASST: Ummm . . . I think he'd prefer the <u>German</u> style.

MAID: The book didn't say anything about a German <u>style</u>.

ASST: Well, but the <u>question</u> is can you <u>cook</u>? The real question is can you <u>really</u> <u>cook</u>?

MARY *is illuminated over a mixing bowl, exalted, a martyr.*

MAID: Not yet.

Blackout. Lights up on partial KITCHEN, *partial* LAB.

KITCHEN/LAB: KOCH *and* MARY. MARY *furiously rolling dough.*

KOCH: I can't go on.

MARY: Keep your distance, Mr. Doctor.

KOCH: (*waving a letter*) You're writing me recipes! You're sending me oven temperatures!

MARY: Tell it to the maid, Mr. Doctor.

KOCH: You're not happy.

MARY: (*shrugs and grins*) Oh. Well. Happiness.

KOCH: You were born to cook.

MARY: I'm cooking.

KOCH: No one will eat.

MARY: I'm <u>still</u> <u>cooking</u>.

KOCH: No one will <u>ever</u> eat!

MARY: I'LL KEEP ON COOKING!

KOCH: YOU'RE COOKING POISON! YOU'RE COOKING DEATH!

MARY: The important thing is <u>just to</u> <u>keep</u> <u>cooking</u>.

Blackout. Lights up on LAB.

LABORATORY: KOCH *and* ASST. ASST. *is weak and flushed.*

KOCH: You don't look well.

ASST. No kidding.

KOCH: I don't like it.

ASST: I'm dizzy, I see spots, my bowels are running like a rat's, I feel I'm standing in a soupbowl. (*pause, a low tone*) I can't get the <u>maid</u> in bed anymore.

KOCH: I don't like it. Have you been in the kitchen?

ASST: I told you I'm <u>sick</u>, I'm not <u>crazy</u>. (*he peers*) You don't look so well yourself.

Blackout. Lights up on KITCHEN.

KITCHEN: MAID *counting silverware.* MARY *brooding in corner.*

MAID: Miss Mary, Miss Mary. The carving knife is missing.

MARY: (*raises head, smiling*) Look again.

MAID: (*looks*) It's still missing.

MARY: (*big grin*) Look again.

Blackout. Lights up on KITCHEN *again.*

KITCHEN: MARY *and* MAID *nose to nose.*

MARY: You've been reading my recipes.

MAID: (*frightened*) Miss Mary, Miss Mary.

MARY: And you've been testing my oven temperatures.

MAID: (*terrified*) Miss Mary, Miss Mary.

MARY: (*the ultimate*) Yesterday you boiled water!

MAID: (*a wail*) Miss Mary, Miss Marrry!

MARY: (*starts to strangle* MAID, *shrieks*) I AM THE COOK!

MAID: (*giggles*) That's funny, Miss Mary.

MARY: (*still screaming*) <u>What's</u> <u>funny</u>!

MAID: What you said about boiling water.

MARY: (*grins, takes hands from* MAID's *throat*) I agree. (MARY *starts to giggle, and in complete companionship* MARY *and the* MAID *put their arms around each other and laugh heartily into the blackout*).

Blackout. Lights up on partial KITCHEN, *partial* LAB.

KITCHEN/LAB: ASST. *standing,* MAID *reading. Each in their own doorways.*

ASST: This is your last chance.

MAID: Don't be silly.

ASST: Anything could happen.

MAID: Don't be silly.

ASST: You could die. I could leave. He could shut this place down. Anything could happen.

MAID: I'm not dying.

ASST: You know what I mean.

MAID: I'm not dying and you're not leaving. And we're <u>not</u> having anything to do with each other.

ASST: (*anguished*) <u>Never</u>? Never anymore?

MAID: (*back to her cookbook; definitively*) I <u>have</u> to learn cooking. I want to be a <u>cook</u>.

Blackout. Lights up on KITCHEN.

KITCHEN: MARY *alone, scalloping potatoes.*

MARY: It's not in my hands anymore. It's not in my spit or my blood anymore. It's not in the food. (*pause, a fiendish tone as she holds up a potato*) It's in the <u>ground</u>. It's growing from the ground up! And who is responsible? Who takes the blame? Why, it's the cook. It is the cook. That is the answer I <u>always</u> give. The cook did it. (*fiendish grin to Audience*) And I am the c . . .

Blackout. Lights up on LAB.

LABORATORY: KOCH *alone,* ASST. *behind door.*

KOCH: Cook. Cook. Perhaps it <u>is</u> a <u>cook's</u> postulate. Surely a rat dead for no reason is not a <u>scientific</u> proof. No no. Not at all scientific. (*pause, sigh, a low voice*) It seems to be everywhere now. Even in the ground.

ASST: (*from behind the door*) Mr. Doctor, Mr. Doctor. Something is wrong with the rats.

KOCH: (*to himself*) Yes yes.

ASST: Something is wrong with the rats, Mr. Doctor. They're all dying.

KOCH: (*louder, some inner recognition*) Yes <u>yes</u>.

ASST: (*appears in doorway*) They're dead. All the rats are dead and they died eating. (*pause*) I think I'm jealous of the rats.

KOCH: (*recognition is complete*) That's <u>it</u>. (*to* ASST.) You're theorizing ahead of your facts, my boy.

ASST: You think so?

KOCH: (*dismissively, he's thinking of something else*) Yes yes.

ASST: You think I shouldn't reason from rats to humans?

KOCH: That's right, my boy.

ASST: You think it <u>matters</u> if I reason from rats to humans?

KOCH: What? Oh no. Not at all. Not <u>now</u>. (*big smile*)

Pause.

ASST: (*violent*) Where are the letters! I want to see her letters!

Blackout. Lights up on KITCHEN.

KITCHEN: MARY *and* MAID. MAID *sits on stool, breathing loudly and moaning as though very sick.* MARY *is maniacally cheerful.*

MARY: (*clasps hands in pleasure*) Oh my. I am cooking something <u>wonderful</u> tonight. Something I have cooked in <u>many</u> households before. Something I <u>love</u> to cook. (*to* MAID) Have you checked the oven?

MAID: Uhnnmn. (*painful moan*)

MARY: That's <u>good</u>. Everything must be right tonight. Everything must go well. (*to* MAID) Did you shell the peas?

MAID: Uhnnmn. (*moans hideously*)

MARY: Scallop the potatoes?

MAID: Ahhhhh.

MARY: Julienne the carrots?

MAID: Ohhhhh.

MARY: Sauté the onions?

MAID: Uhnnnn.

MARY: (*expansive, gracious*) Oh that's <u>very</u> good. <u>Very</u> good. I have cooked this dish in many households. To the highest possible praise. And even more than that. But tonight I will cook it better than ever before. I can <u>feel</u> it. (*big grin*)

MAID: Ohhhhh. (*she slips off her stool to the floor and lies motionless*)

MARY: (*to the Audience, pure happiness*) No stuffing. She'll <u>never</u> be a cook.

Blackout. Lights up on LAB.

LABORATORY: KOCH *and* ASST. *quite weak.* KOCH *sets test tube down.*

KOCH: That's that.

ASST: What's what. (*points at* KOCH *weakly with tea cup*) Bang bang. Bang bang.

KOCH: (*kindly*) It doesn't really work without the tea pot, my boy.

ASST: (*sullen*) Bang. Bang. Bang. What's what, Mr. Doctor.

KOCH: (*very kindly, a little louder*) That is really <u>not</u> the teapot, my boy.

ASST: I <u>know</u>, Mr. Doctor. Bang. Bang. I'm <u>sick</u>, I'm not crazy. Bang. Bang. You said that's that. Now what's what.

KOCH: (*brightly*) The <u>postulate</u> is what, my boy. The postulate is <u>proven</u>. (ASST. *looks blank*) <u>Fully</u> proven. (ASST. *looks blanker*) I'll be publishing our results. (ASST. *looks away*) I thought you'd want to know.

ASST: (*touch of the old maniacism*) Oh yes <u>yes</u>, Mr. Doctor. I <u>do</u> want to know. (*pause*) I <u>did</u> want to know. (*pause, more energy*) There's something I want <u>you</u> to know.

KOCH: What is that, my boy.

ASST: I agree with you, Mr. Doctor.

KOCH: Well well, my boy. You agree with the postulate.

ASST: I agree with everything, Mr. Doctor.

KOCH: (*starts to giggle*) That's funny, my boy.

ASST: (*quickly*) I agree.

Blackout. Lights up on LAB.

LABORATORY: KOCH *and* ASST. *Same situation.*

ASST: (*points teacup randomly*) Ack ack ack.

KOCH: (*waves piece of paper*) Here's her latest.

ASST: (*halfheartedly points teacup*) Bang Bang bang. Pocketa pocketa pocketa.

KOCH: I think I will publish it along with the postulate.

ASST: Kabam. Pow. Ack ack.

KOCH: It's an invitation to dinner.

ASST: (*stops cold*) Is it possible.

KOCH: For this evening. At seven o'clock sharp.

ASST: (*very excited, dances around*) Let me see it! Let me see it!

KOCH: (*holds it out of reach*) Alright, my boy. Alright. You can certainly see it. But you must not touch it . . . (ASST. *grabs letter and begins to chew it*) . . . to your mouth. (*automatically*) Nothing from the kitchen should ever go into your mouth.

ASST: (*chewing frantically and pointing his teacup*) Bang Bang! Bang Bang! I'm eating! I'm eating! Hee hee hee. Bang Bang! (*teacup falls to floor*)

KOCH: (*straight to Audience*) It <u>never</u> works without the teapot.

Blackout: Lights up on KITCHEN.

KITCHEN: MARY *humming blackbird song again,* MAID *still on floor.*

MARY: Tum te tum. I wonder if he will dress for dinner, Tum te tum. I have never seen him dress for anything. Dum dum. Always with the laboratory coat on. (*stops*) Oh my. If he dresses for dinner does that mean that I must <u>also</u> dress for dinner? (*giggles*) That's funny. Keep your feet on the ground my girl. After all. Who is the cook in this kitchen?

MAID: (*weakly, from the floor*) <u>You</u> are, Miss Mary, <u>You're</u> the cook.

Blackout: Lights up on LAB *and* KITCHEN.

KITCHEN/LAB: *Both doors open at once.* MAID *enters* LAB, ASST. *enters* KITCHEN. *They stop and stare into the Audience.*

ASST: (*deadpan*) Wrong door.

MAID: (*exasperated*) His theory is <u>always</u> ahead of his facts.

Blackout. Lights up on LAB *and* KITCHEN.

LAB/KITCHEN: *Lights out on* KITCHEN. LAB *door opens,* MAID *and* ASST. *enter carrying plates and arguing.*

ASST: <u>He</u> said to put the dishes in the <u>laboratory</u>.

MAID: <u>She</u> said to put them in the <u>kitchen</u>.

ASST: <u>He</u> said to put the dishes in water.

MAID: <u>She</u> said to keep them dry.

ASST: Do you think it matters?

MAID: Oh no. Certainly not. Not <u>now</u>.

MAID *and* ASST. *set the table.*

ASST: I could eat the soup bowl. I could eat the table.

MAID: I couldn't eat anything.

ASST: (*lascivious*) Could you do something else? What about doing something else? (*nudges her*) Something <u>like</u> eating?

MAID: (*giggles*) That's funny.

ASST: (*sighs*) In a way.

MAID: Just let's set the table. It's almost seven o'clock. You <u>know</u> how she is about her timing.

ASST: Oh she's a killer about her timing. She's a <u>real</u> <u>killer</u>.

Blackout. Lights up on KITCHEN.

KITCHEN: *Silent scene.* MARY *opens oven, takes out pot, regards it intently as she sets it on work table, stands behind it, looks up. Enormous smile of satisfaction straight into the Audience.*

Blackout. Lights up on LAB.

LABORATORY: KOCH *in black tie and lab coat,* ASST. *with stiff collar. They stand behind lab table set for dinner.* MAID *enters, slowly, ritualistically, carrying covered kitchen pot. She sets it on table, moves to side.* KOCH *lifts the top.*

KOCH: Ahhhhh. At last a real meal.

ASST: Ummmmm. Food for a king.

MAID: Hmmmmm. It's like <u>something</u>, I don't remember the word.

MARY: (*in lab doorway, holding carving knife*) Postulate. It's like a postulate.

MAID: That's the word.

KOCH: (*cups his ear*) Cook's what? Cook's <u>what</u>?

ASST: Postulate. It's the <u>cook's</u> <u>postulate</u>. (*sticks his finger in the pot, licks it, falls laughing to the floor*) Hee hee hee. It's the COOK'S POSTULATE. Ha ha ha ha HA. (*he lies still;* MAID *and* KOCH *watch the pot in horror*)

MARY: (*shakes her head at* ASST.) Too much pepper. (*looks up with conviction*) But still a <u>real</u> <u>meal</u>. (*she advances on the Audience and speaks with utter sincerity*) I have cooked this dish in twenty households at least. To the highest <u>possible</u> praise. And every time I cook it I know that cooking is its own reward. The big thing is cooking. The best thing is cooking. The important thing is just to keep on cooking. But I have <u>never</u> . . . <u>enjoyed</u> . . . <u>cooking</u> . . . so . . . <u>much</u> . . . <u>as</u> . . . <u>I</u> . . . <u>enjoyed</u> . . . <u>cooking</u> . . . <u>tonight</u>. (*and she thrusts her arms high in a gesture of victory, and laughs violently into the blackout*).

Freeze. Tableau. Blackout.

Finis

THE LAST OF
HITLER

THE LAST OF HITLER was first shown at The Changing Scene, Denver, 1982, directed by Michelle O. Serries. It was subsequently produced in experimental venues in the United States. The photographs are from the 1984 production at Theater for the New City, New York, directed by the author.

Characters

Heard and Seen

THE RADIO
REICH BROADCASTER
HITLER BROADCASTER
DR. REICH
EDMUND THE SKELETON
ADOLF HITLER
EVA BRAUN
SONYA FYEDOROVNA
NADYA LEOPOVNA

Heard

JOHN COLE
MARY LEE TAYLOR

Seen

THE HASSID
Assorted Nazis

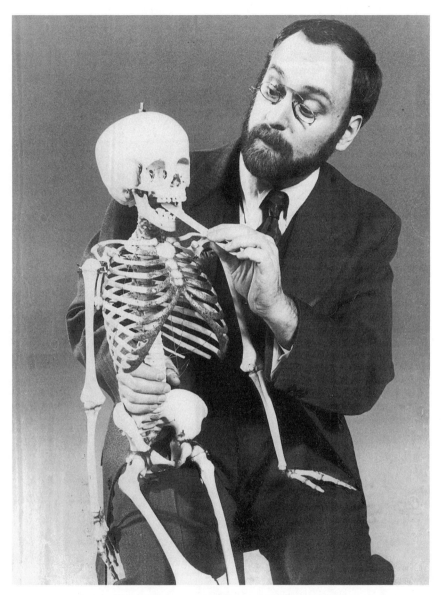

Left to right: EDMUND THE SKELETON, DR. REICH. (*Photo by Carol Rosegg*)

EDMUND: Reich, oh Reich, say Reich, look at that big audience out there. Isn't it nice to
˙ know so many people don't have television sets?

DR. REICH: Dignity, Edmund, dignity. We want to make a good impression.

Left to right: ADOLF HITLER, EVA BRAUN.

ADOLF: Palm trees. Coconuts. When I have held the Black Forest of Bavaria between my
thumb and little finger and roamed Western Europe like a wolf. Ach. I cannot <u>tolerate</u>
the colour green.

EVA: Oh, <u>green</u>. I thought you said dreams. I thought you said you could not tolerate your
<u>dreams</u>.

Left to right: ADOLF HITLER, THE HASSID. (*Photo by Barbara Ulrich*)

With an enormous jerk, the HASSID *disconnects the* RADIO *in mid-sentence and freezes against the red sky in silhouette, holding the huge, forked plug above his head. He looks like Lucifer and his black body and the black body of the* RADIO *stand together for an awful moment.*

Left to right: EDMUND, THE HASSID, ADOLF, EVA. (*Photo by Barbara Urich*)

The HASSID *looks on while* EVA BRAUN *follows* MARY LEE TAYLOR'S *radio instructions for How to Cook a Kosher Chicken.*

MARY LEE: (*overvoice*) How to Cook a Kosher Chicken. Grasp chicken firmly by the neck. Grasp chicken by the neck. Sever head and neck from body. Sever chicken head and neck from body. Grasp severed head firmly and remove gold fillings. Remove gold fillings and reserve for future use.

Left to right: DR. REICH, THE BROADCASTERS, ADOLF, EVA. (*Photo by Barbara Ulrich*)

DR. REICH: Excuse me, Herr Hitler. You're referring to Richard Wagner the German-Jewish composer?

ADOLF: ("*Jewish voice*") Yes, yes that's right! Mein old friend, mein hero, Richard Wagner used to say . . . "Adolf, Adolf, relax a little. Enjoy. <u>You</u> have a little dirty blood, <u>I</u> have a little dirty blood. So what. Drink your seltzer. Eat your nice vegetables, Adolf. Be proud. Yes. We should be proud that in der ganse meshugeneh velt, we don't have <u>more</u> dirt in our blood."

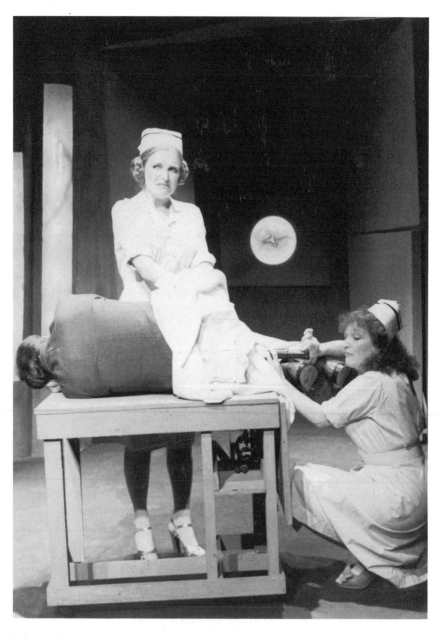

Left to right: DR. REICH, SONYA FYEDOROVNA, NADYA LEOPOVNA. (*Photo by Barbara Ulrich*)

SONYA: Nadya Leopovna. Nadya Leopovna. Hold the chicks. Hold the chicks or I will nefer be capable to insert this pipe further in poor old man's rrrectum.

NADYA: Hold chicks yourselve, Sonya Fyedorovna. Iss dizgusting vork for voman. Iss vork forrr manooal laborrrorrrr.

THE LAST OF HITLER

Part I

Mise en Scene:

The Proscenium is outlined as the upper face of a console Radio of the 1940's. (Its design will be repeated by the UPSTAGE CENTER *Radio described below). Perhaps the top third of what would be the Radio's illuminated dial strip stretches across the lip of the stage and forms the bottom of the Proscenium square. As the dial of the* UPSTAGE CENTER *Radio is manipulated, the needle of the Proscenium strip moves back and forth.*

UPSTAGE CENTER, STAGE RIGHT, *and* STAGE LEFT *must be illuminated as three separate territories, each with its accompanying times, lights and temperatures. All stage directions are given from the point of view of the Audience.*

UPSTAGE CENTER *is dominated by a huge console Radio of the 1940's. It is perhaps eight or ten feet high—the largest Radio in the world. It is oak-veneered and magnificent; its electric cord trails away to an end we cannot see. Its cabinet details are exaggerated: elaborate, illumined green dials focus like eyes in the dark; a long line of broadcasting frequency numerals rests on a glass pocket through which an enormous moving mouth can be seen when the Radio says words or delivers speeches. The Radio is a theatrical expression which, nevertheless, must appear perfectly capable of transmitting sound waves. Its unseen interior proliferates wires or antennae or headsets whenever necessary, and all broadcast must seem to come from its cloth-covered speakers. Behind and above the Radio, two* BROADCASTERS— *the* REICH BROACASTER *and the* HITLER BROADCASTER—*sit in a rectangle of illumination at a low table holding 1940's table mikes. Above and behind them is a screen rolled up like a window shade. The* REICH BROADCASTER *resembles* DR.

REICH *and has a faint Yiddish accent. The* HITLER BROADCASTER *reminds us of* ADOLF HITLER *and continually does dreadful things with a piece of string. Both* BROADCASTERS *sit at ends of their table which correspond to the stage territories of their prototypes: i.e., the* REICH BROADCASTER *is on the* STAGE LEFT *end, which is* DR. REICH's *territory, the* HITLER BROADCASTER *is on the* STAGE RIGHT *end, which is* ADOLF HITLER's *territory.*

STAGE RIGHT *is always some version of* ADOLF HITLER's *and* EVA BRAUN's *home in a Southern state. In the first scene, it represents Berchtesgaden in the Southern state of Bavaria. In all successive scenes it becomes the interior of a Kozy Kabin in a Florida swamp, fifteen miles from a resort city frequented by American Jews. In order that the Hitlers might always appear to be "playing house," all furnishings and objects* STAGE RIGHT *are child-sized.*

STAGE LEFT *represents* DR. REICH's *laboratory/office in the North Woods of New Hampshire. The light is crepuscular, the windows upstage back are long and narrow and half-covered by cheap shades with crocheted pulls—like the blackout shades used in North American homes during the Second War. The furniture* STAGE LEFT *is also pediatric, scaled to children, and the walls and galleries are hung with medical charts. Everywhere opulent instances of Hoch Deutsch Kultur are imprisoned in collecting cases. A bust of Wagner stares out from a side stand; to the left of it is a desk; cater-corner to the desk is an examining table. Near the table, on a handsome rack, hangs the perfectly polished skeleton of a child. Perhaps one of its fibulae is crooked.*

As the Audience drifts in, UPSTAGE CENTER *is eerily illuminated (a light cast by Radio dials, vacuum tubes, something of that sort), and the faint outlines of the Radio are perceptible.* STAGE RIGHT *is dark and* STAGE LEFT *is as dimly lit as a dream. The* BROADCASTERS *are in high relief in their rectangle, waiting for their show to begin.*

Stage Left:

Through the half-covered windows, light begins to redden in long lines, like a sunset on a sea beach. We see, or think we see, DR. REICH, *limping and wearing white gloves and eyeglasses, raising then rapidly lowering a nutrition chart (behind which is momentarily spotted Hermann Goering in drag), rolling and unrolling one window shade (an arm stiffened in the Fuehrer salute is visible out the window), opening a medical cabinet (Joseph Goebbels in full dress uniform is crouched inside), adjusting the skeleton of the child, and, finally, removing piles of papers from file cabinets, going to his desk with them and sitting down. He can continue to repeat his exposure of Nazis in various places and positions in his laboratory until most of the Audience is seated.*

Upstage Center:

When the house has more or less filled, Goering will flounce out from behind an eye chart and begin the play by twisting a dial on the Radio. Immediately, UPSTAGE CENTER *is fully illuminated and a medley of popular German songs of the*

1940's issues from the Radio—Dietrich singing Lili Marlene, Lotte Lenya doing Kurt Weill, etc. The music becomes louder, more persuasive, more insistently classical. It spreads to stain the entire house with its enthusiasm and, yes, it sounds like Wagner, some huge choral piece which drowns the Audience and their talk. As the music crescendos, the houselights go down and other characters from the play move by the Radio, intercutting the Wagnerian piece by changing the stations. One of the Nazis chooses "Deutschland uber alles," SONYA FYEDOROVNA gives us "Ochichonia," etc. We hear, in short, the Second War fought in the clichés of popular song.

The last character to approach the Radio is a male HASSID in traditional black hat and suit. He comes from nowhere. He has payess, pale skin, a bad beard. There is something repulsive about him which the Audience must immediately repress. The Radio resists him absolutely (its first act of this kind) and the moment he touches the dial, the overture stops. He turns the dial, finds ten seconds of shtetl wedding music, then static. As he tries to tune in, there is a clarifying silence. Finally, the HASSID raises his shoulders in the ancient gesture of resignation and moves out of the light.

The moment the HASSID disappears, the HITLER BROADCASTER unrolls the screen behind him, twists his fingers around his string, and the REICH BROADCASTER begins their show by speaking into his microphone. Projections of a can of Pet Milk and a box of Rinso Blue fill the BROADCASTERS' screen. The BROADCASTERS' speaking should be heightened, manipulative, very much "on microphone." As they introduce each character, he or she should be momentarily illuminated.

REICH B.: Good <u>evening</u>, ladies and gentlemen. This evening we are pleased to bring our American Radio Audience a premiere of the airwaves. Direct from postwar . . . (City and state in which play is being performed) . . . a narrated and dramatized version of THE LAST OF HITLER.

HITLER B.: (Hand over mike) Great <u>guy</u>, that Hitler. (Into mike) Presented to you without commercial interruption by our generous sponsors <u>Pet</u> <u>Milk</u> and <u>Rinso</u> <u>Blue</u>. (Hand over mike) What in hell is <u>Rinso</u> <u>Blue</u>?

REICH B.: (Hand over mike) A cleaning solution? <u>I</u> don't know. (Into mike) My colleague and I would like to take this opportunity to thank both our sponsors—<u>Pet</u> <u>Milk</u> and <u>Rinso</u> <u>Blue</u>—<u>and</u> the American government for allowing us to include <u>highly</u> <u>sensitive</u> <u>biographical</u> <u>material</u> in this family broadcast.

HITLER B.: In order of appearance, the characters in tonight's radio drama are . . .

REICH B.: Dr. Reich and Edmund the skeleton . . .

HITLER B.: Eva Braun and the Fuehr . . . (REICH B. jabs him in the side) . . . and Adolf Hitler.

REICH B.: The famous Dionne quintuplets . . .

HITLER B.: Who are never seen or heard from.

REICH B.: Two Russian nurses and assorted silent figures from Germany's Third Reich.

HITLER B.: (*Cynically*) Which the United States of America, Radio Audience, has just gloriously defeated.

REICH B.: (*Hand over mike*) I thought <u>Russia</u> defeated Germany.

HITLER B.: (*Hand over mike, good-natured*) You shithead! Josef Stalin isn't paying for this broadcast. Pet <u>Milk</u> is paying.

REICH B.: (*Eyes to heaven, then speaks into mike*) The drama takes place in the mysterious Dr. Reich's laboratory in New England . . .

HITLER B.: And in Berchtesgaden and the Kozy Kabin of Herr and Frau Hitler, fifteen miles from a large (*Contemptuous*) <u>Jewish</u> resort community in the United State of Florida . . .

REICH B.: And so, Radio Audience of America, we are proud to present to you . . .

HITLER B.: THE LAST OF HITLER. (*His right arm twitches automatically upward in the Fuehrer salute, but the* REICH B. *brings it down sharply*)

The Radio music rises and the Radio itself appears to swell in size and illumination. DR. REICH *limps to the Radio.*

REICH B.: (*Portentously*) In the New England laboratory of the mysterious emigré Dr. Reich, guardian of the most famous quintuplets in North America, the Radio is turned on.

DR. REICH *clicks the Radio dial nearest him, consults his watch, shakes his head, and clicks the dial off.*

REICH B.: (*On top of the situation*) The Radio is turned on . . . too soon.

Stage Left:

DR. REICH *returns to his desk, picks up his microscope, and focuses it intently.*

DR. REICH: (*An oddly displaced accent*) Here it is again, once again. I focus my microscope on a silver slide and I see . . . an ocean beach. (*A Coney Island beach covered with Jewish immigrants appears on a shade behind* DR. REICH) In this landscape, there is no difference between the sea and the sky. In the center of the beach is the largest Radio in the world. It is . . . how do you say . . . oak-veneered, its thick electric cord trails away to an end I cannot see. To the left of the Radio, I can make out the slowly drying body of a young mermaid. The sea has cleaned the mermaid of everything but her character—even her scales are gone—but I can see what a <u>beautiful</u> woman she must have been. Beside her body are a few . . . gold . . . teeth. (*Straight into the Audience*)

DR. REICH: I have suffered this vision repeatedly since the summer of 1942. They say I work magic with the quintuplets—people always think of magic when they are shown the final solution and not the process by which the solution appears—but here, I see no solution. Here I see only the problem, only the problem.

Once again, DR. REICH checks his watch, limps to the Radio, clicks it on, returns to his increasingly illuminated desk, removes his gloves, and begins to shift uncomfortably. He half-raises from his chair, thinks better or different of it, and sits firmly down again. During the following Radio broadcast, he checks, from time to time, the Nazis in his closets and responds appropriately to what he hears on the Radio.

Upstage Center:

Just before DR. REICH clicks the Radio dial, the REICH B. makes his announcement, then the MARY LEE TAYLOR SHOW comes on. All sound effects of the show must be extremely exaggerated.

REICH B.: And once again, in Dr. Reich's New England laboratory, the Radio dial is turned to a <u>very</u> <u>important</u> <u>program</u>.

JOHN COLE: Good morning, ladies and gentlemen. It's 10:00 A.M. B-U-L-O-V-A Bulova Watch Time and John Cole has the pleasure of announcing that another Mary Lee Taylor Radio Demonstration is in progress in the Pet Milk Kitchen. <u>This</u> morning we bring you Mary Lee Taylor's Stuffed Kosher Chicken as a perfect example of the creative genius which reigns over this kitchen. Now you may be saying to yourself that the word "kosher" is unfamiliar to you—but you needn't worry about that. Mary Lee Taylor always explains unfamiliar culinary terms in the second or "cooking" program of our two-part series. Or you may be saying to yourself that this dish isn't news to you at all. In fact, you may have already passed through a Jewish neighborhood in your city and smelled, from every kitchen, the rising aroma of Stuffed Kosher Chicken. <u>Or</u> you may have second-guessed us and found the recipe in the newest Pet Milk Cook Book called *Delicious Wholesome Meals For Two or Four or Six*.

MARY LEE: And now good morning to everyone in my nice audience from Mary Lee Taylor. If you could look into this Pet Milk Kitchen through your loudspeaker, I know you'd think that this Kosher Chicken I've been preparing all morning is the most beautiful bird you ever saw. The gorgeous bread stuffing drizzling with golden yellow chicken fat or schmalz (*She gives it a broad "a"*) as the Jewish people call it, has John Cole's mouth watering.

JOHN COLE *chews very audibly.*

JOHN COLE: And the third and fourth leg will hit the spot too, Mary Lee.

MARY LEE: Now, John. Everyone knows a Jewish chicken only has two legs.

JOHN COLE: Why you're right, Mary Lee. But remember. Even though a Jewish chicken only has two legs, it certainly does have a lot of money.

JOHN COLE *and* MARY LEE TAYLOR *laugh hysterically until they cry. Sounds of* MARY LEE TAYLOR *dabbing at her eyes.*

MARY LEE: Well, well, Radio Audience. We hope you enjoy John Cole's little jokes as much as he does.

JOHN COLE: (*Self-deprecatingly*) Now, Mary Lee . . .

MARY LEE: (*Clears her throat and resumes her recipe voice*) Like all our Pet Milk Recipes, Mary Lee Taylor's Stuffed Kosher Chicken will have the amounts of the ingredients announced in the order in which they should be used in the second or "cooking" part of our two-part series. But I see that our B-U-L-O-V-A Bulova Watch Time has almost run out and I must leave you until next Tuesday morning when Part Two of my Stuffed Kosher Chicken Program will be broadcast. Let me remind you that Daylight Saving Time will be over on next Sunday night and the return to Standard Time may make a difference in the hour when you'll be hearing me next Tuesday. In the meantime, you may want to consult the Pet Milk Recipe Book *Delicious Wholesome Meals for Two or Four or Six* for a preview of my Stuffed Kosher Chicken.

JOHN COLE: (*Sounds of* JOHN COLE *licking his fingers and sucking on chicken bones throughout this announcement*) To obtain this book, just write your address (*Crunch, slurp, etc.*) on the back of a Pet Milk label. If you have a baby or small child and <u>don't</u> have a copy of our new booklet "Better Babies," just add the words Baby Book to the back of the Pet Milk label. We'll mail it right out and you'll learn why children thrive so well on irradiated Pet Milk, Nature's most nearly perfect food. Doctors all over this country have followed the lead of the famous Dionne Quintuplets' famous physician and put their little patients on irradiated Pet Milk. And the results they've obtained have made a sensation in the medical world. Ask <u>your</u> doctor about feeding <u>your</u> children irradiated Pet Milk. Without hesitation he'll say Pet Milk is good enough for the Dionne Quintuplets—perfectly pure and absolutely safe. As safe as if there were no disease germs in the world.

A final slurp from JOHN COLE *and* DR. REICH *clicks off the Radio in disgust.*

Stage Left:

Offstage we hear:

NADYA: Doktor! Doktor!

SONYA: Doktor! Doktor!

DR. REICH looks up from the Radio dial.

REICH B.: Nadya and Sonya, nurses of North America's most famous little quintuplets, burst into the mysterious Dr. Reich's mysterious laboratory.

NADYA *and* SONYA *stick their heads around* STAGE LEFT *side of the Radio, then strike a pose.*

NADYA: Doktor! Doktor! Quintooplets crrrying forr theirrr milllk!

SONYA: Da, da, doktor. Annette, Yvonne, Marrrie, Emilie and Cecile shrrrieking forrr theirrr calllcioom.

DR. REICH: (*Very annoyed*) How many times must I tell you Nadya? How often must I reiterate, Sonya? Milk clogs the eliminative systems of young bodies. Milk is the <u>worst</u> thing you can give growing children. <u>Germs</u> breed in milk. (*The clincher*) <u>Milk</u> <u>makes</u> <u>mucous</u>.

NADYA: Gerrrms!

SONYA: Muuuucous!

NADYA: (*Crosses herself*) God forrrbid!

DR. REICH: (*Points to the skeleton*) Look at Edmund there. <u>Look</u> at him. (*They look*) <u>That</u> is an example of a milk-fed child. (REICH BROADCASTER *and the* HITLER BROADCASTER *wince*) Give the quintuplets <u>tea</u>, Nadya. Always <u>tea</u>, Sonya. <u>Only</u> <u>tea</u>.

Perhaps a slide of China appears on one of DR. REICH'*s shades.*

SONYA: Rrright away, doktorr.

NADYA: Samovarrr prrractically in hand <u>now</u>, doktorr.

NADYA *and* SONYA *withdraw their heads,* DR. REICH *goes back to his studies. He begins to look at photographs of* HITLER *and* EVA BRAUN. STAGE LEFT *lights down a bit and up on the* BROADCASTERS.

Upstage Center:

REICH B.: Adolf Hitler was one of us, ladies and gentlemen. We knew that all along. We should not forget it now.

HITLER B.: (*Touching his moustache*) He <u>looked</u> like us. He <u>thought</u> like us. He spoke <u>for</u> us—<u>better</u> than we did, more . . . theatrically—but the words he used were <u>our</u> words and we wanted to hear every one of them.

REICH B.: We were <u>obsessed</u> with him. He <u>was</u> like us and, at the same time, he was so far above us . . . (*Uncertain, as though losing his place in the script*) And <u>she</u>. Eva Braun . . .

Stage Left:

DR. REICH *holds what appears to be a photograph of* EVA BRAUN *and speaks to it. During the* BROADCASTERS' *narrative, photos of Francis Bacon self-portraits are projected on their screen; during* DR. REICH's *monologue, Bacon's first portrait of Isabel Rawsthorne appears on a shade behind him.*

DR. REICH: She was a Rhine Maiden, a mermaid, our National Socialist Naiad. In the long desert of our lives, she was the cool oasis, the fruited palm, the illusory pool of water towards which we crawled . . . (*He sighs*) gasping with relief.

Upstage Center:

HITLER B.: (*Malevolently*) Let me tell you Radio Audience, Adolf Hitler's greatness was undermined by his own policies. That Marxist doctor Reich spied upon . . . (*He shakes off the urgent hand of the* REICH BROADCASTER) . . . the Fuehrer's government, corrupted its eugenics program with (*Contemptuous*) Jewish psychology, and applied it to the five most famous children in the world. And what did he gain by this? International acclaim and fascinating results. And what did the Fuehrer get?

Stage Right:

Spot up immediately on ADOLF HITLER's *face in profile. He holds a tiny telescope, which is focused upon* DR. REICH's *laboratory. The telescope is dropped,* ADOLF's *head turns and delivers straight into the Audience:*

ADOLF: You know what I got. You all know what I got.

ADOLF *picks up the tiny telescope and, once again, trains it on* DR. REICH's *laboratory. Blackout.*

Upstage Center:

ADOLF *and* EVA *are in front of the Berghof's famous window, their bodies outlined against all the mountains of Bavaria.* ADOLF *looks and moves as we have always imagined him. He is facing the enormous upstage window and wearing a headset whose wires are plugged into the Radio.* EVA *is in young and determined profile with something of the ocean about her. She appears to be organized (in the manner of certain convalescents) around a central, physical "misery." Static from the Radio.*

EVA: Adolf. Adolf. The Radio.

ADOLF: (*Absorbed*) Pardon?

EVA: The Radio. The noise.

ADOLF: It's static.

EVA: The static. It's bad for my head. You know what the doctor said.

ADOLF: I'll turn it off in a minute.

Crackling from Radio stops.

EVA: It's off.

ADOLF: (*Turns around at last*) Very obedient. It must be Japanese. (*Laughs a little*)

EVA: It's a <u>German</u> Radio, Adolf. It's from Munich.

ADOLF: (*Turns again to the window*) Ahh München. Well, if it's German, it's <u>correct</u>, then, not obedient. <u>Correct</u>, Eva, ha ha ha, do you understand? Germans are <u>correct</u>.

EVA: (*Sighing*) I understand, Adolf. I <u>always</u> understand. (*Slight pause*) What are you listening to, Adolph?

ADOLF: I'm listening to a broadcast from Canada.

EVA: Oh Adolf, what do you want with Canada?

ADOLF: Nothing Eva. There's nothing in Canada to <u>want</u>. They're all mongrels there.

EVA: Then why are you listening, Adolf.

ADOLF: The broadcast is American, liebchen. It's about the quintuplets. You know I like to listen to broadcasts about the quintuplets.

Pause

EVA: Sometimes I think the doctor's not telling me the truth.

ADOLF: (*Completely involved in the broadcast*) He's telling you the truth.

EVA: Sometimes I think he doesn't want me to know.

ADOLF: The quintuplets' doctor is also secretive. It's in the nature of doctors, liebchen.

EVA: But to keep cancer a secret.

ADOLF: You have migraines, Eva, Dr. Morell diagnosed them.

EVA: They're not migraines.

ADOLF: Recurrent attacks of migraine headache. Every three to five days since you shot yourself. (*Pause*) The quintuplets are never ill.

EVA: Propaganda, Adolf.

ADOLF: No, Eva. They're kept in a germ-free environment. My spies confirm it.

EVA: Little experimental rats. That's what they look like.

ADOLF: Not at all, Eva. The American government is imitating my eugenics program. Quite intelligently too.

EVA: Poor motherless rats . . .

ADOLF: Think of the <u>father</u>, Eva, not the <u>mother</u>. Think of the <u>father</u> who could produce five children like <u>that</u>. (*Snaps his fingers*) In a single stroke.

EVA: (*Suggestively*) Let us hope, Adolf, that for such a production, the mother and father enjoyed more than a single stroke.

ADOLF: (*Prissily*) I was referring, Eva, to the father's <u>artistic</u> nature. Five at one . . . blow is very . . . <u>artistic</u>. I am often surprised at how the mongrel races overreach themselves.

EVA: (*Shaking her head in admiration*) He must be hung like a horse.

ADOLF: Eva!

EVA: I meant, of course, Adolf, that in the matter of inferior races, there is a simple explanation for everything. I read it in that pamphlet of Herman's—how is it called? The one with the funny name.

ADOLF: "Listen, Little Man" is the name. It is true I have heard that people in that barbarous country follow the quintuplets' father into bathrooms . . .

EVA: (*Interested*) Just to get a look at his . . .

ADOLF: (*Embarrassed*) Yes, yes, that's it.

EVA: How quickly the world forgets biology, Adolf. (*Sagely*) You need eggs to make babies—yes, even for <u>those</u> poor little rats. You need eggs.

ADOLF: (*Importantly*) Well, I'm going to change all <u>that</u>, Eva. At this very moment, Joseph is in Poland, supervising certain experiments . . .

EVA: Adolf, Adolf, my headache is bad enough without hearing the details of Joseph's experiments . . . You know, Adolf, I think Dr. Morell doesn't want me to know what I really have.

ADOLF: (*Patient, barely listening*) What do you really have, liebchen.

EVA: A tumour on the brain. Yes, Adolf. A cancer sitting on top of the brain like a bonnet. I can feel it growing.

ADOLF: Drink your tea, liebchen.

The Radio seems to stop.

ADOLF: You know the quintuplets have tea three times a day. I heard it on the Radio. Their doctor says it calms the digestion.

EVA: Children hate tea, Adolf.

ADOLF: (*Grandly*) And every afternoon, their doctor has them held up to the hospital window and displayed to the primitive multitudes who gather to pay their respects . . .

EVA: Little rodents, poor little rodents.

ADOLF: (*Begins to speak, then*) Shh: Shh! The quintuplets are singing, I want to hear them.

EVA: They train them in that laboratory, Adolf. I read in the newspapers they make them perform twice a day.

ADOLF: Shhh. Shhh. They're on the last verse. (*He hums with them, "There'll Always Be An England"*)

EVA: Do you know what you're humming, Adolf?

ADOLF: I can't understand the words. Their little mongrel accents are too thick. Tum <u>tum</u> tum <u>tum</u> tum <u>tum</u> <u>tum</u>.

EVA: (*With utter satisfaction*) The name of the song, Adolf, is "There'll Always Be An England."

ADOLF: (*Removes headphones immediately*) The tune is dreadful.

EVA: (*Back to her subject*) My throat is cracking, Adolf. I think the cancer is in my throat.

ADOLF: (*Back to <u>his</u> subject*) Yes! Yes! That's how it should be done. Miracle children raised by a miraculous government. My idea. Perfection, Eva, perfection!

EVA: (*Satirically*) Perhaps you should write their doctor a letter of congratulations.

ADOLF: (*Pauses profoundly, then as though he didn't hear her*) Perhaps I will write their doctor a letter of congratulations.

EVA: (*Deadpan*) An excellent idea, Adolf.

ADOLF: (*Moves to serve himself some tea*) He keeps himself very much in the background, that doctor.

EVA: Not like Dr. Morell or our dear Joseph.

ADOLF: (*Pours half the sugar bowl in his tea*) He keeps himself in the background and he controls everything. (*Drinks*) That doctor has been totally infected by my policies, Eva. Totally. How I would like to meet him. (*Drinks*)

EVA: He might help you with your digestion, Adolf.

ADOLF: (*Bridling*) Dr. Morell has conquered my digestion.

EVA: Adolf. You've been breaking wind ever since the Radio was turned on.

ADOLF: (*A hard look, then decides to ignore it*) When I <u>think</u> of what that doctor must have to undergo . . .

EVA: (*Bored*) Enormous trials, I'm sure.

ADOLF: (*Pours more sugar*) In the North Woods of that degenerate mongrel nation without flush toilets or national principles . . .

EVA: (*Genuine curiousity*) What does he look like, Adolf? Is he a . . . handsome man?

ADOLF: When I think of his noble attempt to keep the world's most famous children under the iron hand of National Socialism . . . What do you mean is he a handsome man?

EVA: I was merely interested to know if he had the Nordic look. (*Slyly*) Anyone you admire would surely have the Nordic look, Adolf.

ADOLF: Yes, yes, of course. He . . . <u>must</u>.

EVA: And what is his <u>name</u>, Adolf?

ADOLF: (*Blustering*) His name. It's . . . ahem . . . I have it written down. (*Fumbles in his breast pocket*) The man is so secretive, his name disappears from . . . But I have it written . . . Ah, here it is. Right here. Dr. Krebs. Dr. Krebs of North America. (*Hugely pleased*) Well. I should have remembered <u>that</u> name. I should <u>certainly</u> have remembered <u>that</u> name.

EVA: (*Sighs*) Krebs is a German name, alright.

ADOLF: (*Exuberant*) A Teuton, a real Teuton! I knew it, of course, by his work! He is one of us, Eva. He is <u>absolutely</u> one of us!

ADOLF *picks up the tiny telescope and, once again, trains it on* DR. REICH's *laboratory. Blackout* STAGE RIGHT.

Upstage Center:

The HASSID *appears* UPSTAGE CENTER, *looking worriedly over his shoulder. He turns the Radio dial to the only station he can get, the Radio glows weirdly, and a consultation between* ADOLF HITLER *and* DR. REICH *comes on over the Radio.*

DR. REICH: You've got the name wrong, mein Fuehrer. My name is Reich, the <u>third</u> Reich, actually, (*They both chuckle*) my grandfather was the first to assume the name. But, of course, I only use it professionally. In my private correspondence, I've gone back to our family name, the name my grandfather abandoned. He went to Oxford, you know, and I suppose the English denotation of the name drove him mad.

ADOLF: And what denotation is that, Herr Doktor?

DR. REICH: It's death, mein Fuehrer. My secret name is Dr. Death.

ADOLF: (*Gasps in horror*) Ahhhhhhh.

DR. REICH: And now, Herr Hitler, as long as your mouth is open I can take your temperature and we will begin to discuss these alarming gastric symptoms of yours . . .

Static from the Radio, then an hysterical melange of air-raid sirens, snippets of news predicting the fall of various countries, Tokyo Rose seducing G.I.s to desertion—and out of what is clearly the Fall of Berlin, the lights come up slightly on DR. REICH *and* EDMUND *the skeleton.* DR. REICH *holds a piece of paper.*

REICH B: And back in the laboratory, Dr. Reich receives a letter.

Stage Left:

DR. REICH: (*Reads aloud in a steady, contemptuous voice*) Herr Doktor: The Fuehrer of the Thousand Year Reich salutes you and your experimental work, carried out, we are certain, in an atmosphere of extreme hostility against the grain of the Jewish-Democratic State in which you live. (DR. REICHS's *eyes slide to heaven as he mouths:* "Could he mean New Hampshire?" *in disbelief. He puts the letter down*) I wonder if <u>she</u> knows of this letter? I have heard that she is interested in the rearing of children. <u>Blond</u> children, of course.

Upstage Center:

Radio sounds intersect DR. REICH's *voice, the Radio's station indicator moves wildly up and down the dial, and the* REICH BROADCASTER *and the* HITLER BROADCASTER *read, very fast, the supposititious statistics of Jewish annihilation during the Second War. The* REICH BROADCASTER *might doven a little as he reads; the* HITLER BROADCASTER *produces a little dreidl around which he has wound his string, and maliciously spins it on the broadcasting table during the recitation. After the first two or three statistics, they shorten the lines to the name of the country and the number of deaths. As they read, the statistics flash on the screen behind them, piling up like bodies.*

POLAND:	3,000,000 Jews killed, 90% of the Jewish population.
BALTIC COUNTRIES:	228,000 Jews killed, 90% of the Jewish population.
PROTECTORATES:	80,000 Jews killed, 89% of the Jewish population.
SLOVAKIA:	75,000 Jews killed, 83% of the Jewish population.
GREECE:	54,000 Jews killed, 77% of the Jewish population.
NETHERLANDS:	105,000 Jews killed
HUNGARY:	450,000 Jews killed
WHITE RUSSIA:	245,000 Jews killed
UKRAINE:	900,000 Jews killed
BELGIUM:	40,000 Jews killed

REICH B.: Total Jewish population of Europe before Hitler: 8,861,800.

HITLER B.: Total Jewish population annihilated by the Fuehrer: almost six million.

REICH B.: (*Funereal tone*) That's what it amounts to, ladies and gentlemen, six million Jews.

HITLER B.: (*Sprightly tone*) That's right. The war is over and so is European Jewry.

REICH B.: And in the laboratory, Dr. Reich's favorite . . . uh (*Doubtfully*) <u>former</u> patient is being examined . . .

Lights up on EDMUND *the skeleton and* DR. REICH STAGE LEFT, *who is testing* EDMUND's *reflexes. The conversation <u>we</u> hear comes from the* BROADCASTERS *as they turn off their mikes.*

HITLER B.: Kee-rist! What a lot of dead Jews.

REICH B.: (*Slowly, stunned*) Six . . . million. I didn't realize . . . <u>six</u> <u>million</u>.

HITLER B.: (*Reminiscing*) We had a Jew in my neighborhood. Once.

REICH B.: (*Controlled trepidation*) What happened to him.

HITLER B.: (*Remembering with some pleasure*) Oh, they burnt his house, they killed his dog, and they, yes, they crippled his child. The four year old, I think. I never understood why.

REICH B.: (*Hopefully*) Why they hurt the child?

HITLER B.: (*Exasperated*) Why they killed the <u>dog</u>, shithead. There was nothing wrong with the <u>dog</u>. The <u>dog</u> wasn't Jewish.

Stage Left:

DR. REICH *gets a particularly bouncy reaction from* EDMUND's *bad leg which flies up and hits him in the nose.* DR. REICH: "Wonderful, wonderful." *Then* ED-MUND's *jaws snap loudly.* DR. REICH: "Good, Edmund."

Upstage Center:

REICH B.: (*Tentatively, very "Jewish"*) You know what I heard? I heard the quintuplets' mother was a Jew.

HITLER B.: And <u>I</u> heard the father was.

REICH B.: That's funny. The quintuplets don't <u>look</u> Jewish.

HITLER B.: They're <u>girls</u>, dummy. It doesn't show so much on the <u>girls</u>.

Slight pause

REICH B.: (*Indicates the doctor*) I wonder where Dr. Reich is from? He looks . . . familiar.

HITLER B.: <u>Germany</u>, where else. <u>All</u> doctors come from Germany.

REICH B.: And I wonder what his first name is.

HITLER B.: It's not in the script.

REICH B.: Well, it's probably Bill. Every American's first name is Bill. (*A mild joke*)

HITLER B.: (*Malicious*) Matter of fact, I think it's Julius. Dr. Julius Reich. Hell of a name for a pediatrician.

REICH B.: Pediatrician? He never touches children.

HITLER B.: That's OK with me. I don't touch children myself. I don't even touch my own child and he's right here in the studio. Children are full of infection. (*Looks appraisingly at* REICH B.) Do you have any children?

REICH B.: (*Looks down*)

HITLER B.: (*Menacingly*) I wonder where you're from?

REICH B.: (*Stiffly*) What do you mean by that?

HITLER B.: Well, there's just something . . . funny! about you. Something that makes me wonder if you're a real American.

REICH B.: (*Slightly "Jewish"*) And why should you wonder that?

HITLER B.: Ohhh, you could call it a nose for news. My mother used to say you could always tell a (*Contemptuous*) foreigner by the smell.

REICH B.: Keep your nose to yourself you swine! It's not me who's hiding a picture of Adolf Hitler in his desk drawer! (*Indicates* HITLER B.'*s side of the table*)

HITLER B.: (*Again holds up the dreidl which he pulls from the* REICH B.'*s side of the table*) No, my friend. You prefer to hide toys. (REICH B. *winces*) And, by the way, where were you during the war?

REICH B.: (*Freezes*)

Stage Left:

DR. REICH'*s voice is immediately audible, as though it is he who is answering the* HITLER BROADCASTER'*s question. He has left* EDMUND *and speaks, once again, to himself.*

DR. REICH: There was never any water during the war, never. People went unwashed for years. And the children. (*Utter disgust*) Children, who are naturally unclean, became filthy during the war. (*Reflecting and holding up his once-again white-gloved hands*) I no longer touch children with my hands. (*Points to Edmund*) There is a perfect example of a child who went unwashed during a war. A mild rash, a headache, a spreading infection, no water applied, and that is the result. (*Pause*) You can never expose yourself to too much water. No no never too much. (*Slight pause*) I believe New Hampshire has more flowing water than any other New England state.

Blackout STAGE LEFT

Upstage Center:

Florida scenes flash on the BROADCASTERS' *screen.*

HITLER B.: And, in a swamp somewhere in southern Florida late in 1948, Adolf and Eva Hitler are living in a Kozy Kabin . . .

REICH B.: (*Interrupting, hand over mike*) What's a Kozy Kabin?

HITLER B.: (*Shrugs, covers mike*) Search me. (*Into mike*) . . . a Kozy Kabin, fifteen miles from a resort city frequented by American (*Contemptuous*) <u>Jews</u>.

Stage Right:

Lights up on the HITLERS' *Kozy Kabin in southern Florida. Instead of the enormous Bavarian window, there's a raised shade at the top of a long window with a Florida view: jungle, perhaps a snapping alligator or two, green, tangled abundance. There is a signed photograph of Henry Ford on the wall. Two older, sick people,* EVA *and* ADOLF, *are in the Kabin.* EVA *is propped up in a bed,* ADOLF *is in a wheelchair with his back to us. We do not recognize him immediately.*

ADOLF *wheels himself to the window, still with his back to us. He pulls on the window shade—and an exact, painted duplication of the Berchtesgaden view of the Bavarian Alps unrolls to cover the jungle. He stares at it a moment with his telescope, then wheels, muttering, to the Radio.*

ADOLF: (*Back to us*) Palm trees. Coconuts. When I have held the Black Forest of Bavaria between my thumb and little finger and roamed Western Europe like a wolf. Ach. I cannot <u>tolerate</u> the colour green.

EVA: What is it, liebchen?

ADOLF: (*A little louder*) I said I cannot <u>bear</u> the colour green.

EVA: Oh, <u>green</u>. I thought you said dreams. I thought you said you could not tolerate your <u>dreams</u>.

ADOLF: I have no <u>dreams</u>, Eva.

EVA: No dreams? Well, well, perhaps it's the climate.

ADOLF: The heat is <u>awful</u>. I'm perpetually running in sweat.

EVA: Or the language. Perhaps you don't know what <u>language</u> to dream in.

ADOLF: My tongue twists on their consonants.

EVA: Could it be the strange vegetables.

ADOLF: (*A lament*) No purple cabbage, no cauliflower, no real potatoes.

EVA: It's the lack of medical care. How can you dream properly when your digestion is unattended.

ADOLF: This flatulence gets worse and worse.

Pause. They both sigh.

EVA: We shouldn't have left home.

ADOLF: Even the <u>Radio</u> reception is terrible here.

EVA: (*Nods sagely*) Humidity. Radio waves cannot travel comfortably through air which is perpetually soaked in water. I read it in the newspaper.

Pause

ADOLF: We shouldn't have left home.

EVA: We left in order to grow old.

ADOLF: It was a bad choice.

Pause. Radio crackles, ADOLF *continues to adjust it.*

EVA: (*Childlike*) Bring me my tea, Adolph.

ADOLF: In a minute, liebchen.

EVA: (*Again childlike*) Now. I need it now.

ADOLF: The static. I'm adjusting for the static.

EVA: My throat is cracking. I'm sure the cancer is in my throat.

ADOLF *continues to twist the dials, his wheelchair looking very small against the gigantic Radio.*

EVA: It's cracking <u>now</u>. Not at the end of the static.

ADOLF *suddenly turns and wheels towards her and we see one whole side of his face is a mass of burn scars.*

ADOLF: (*Carefully, paternally*) I'm coming with the tea, tösserl. Be calm.

EVA: (*Drinks greedily*) Ah, Adolf. The tea is wonderful. So heartening.

ADOLF: (*Spooning and spooning sugar into his cup*) Tea gives courage, Eva. Tea <u>sustains</u>. During the worst of their troubles in the colonies, English governors always drank tea. I heard it on the Radio.

EVA: Not when the tea was half <u>sugar</u>, Adolf. Not when it was half sugar syrup. (*With authority*) Sugar eats up the brain cells, Adolf.

ADOLF: A few teaspoons. That's all I use, liebchen. Three or four teaspoons to adjust the taste.

EVA: Seven, Adolf. It's always been seven. Before you needed the energy, I would watch you empty the whole sugar bowl into your cup.

ADOLF: It's because I don't eat meat. I don't dine on corpses like most humans. I need the strength of sugar—and my chocolates.

EVA: (*Shuddering*) Bring me my shawl, Adolf.

ADOLF: (*Looks at his wheelchair*) In a minute, tösserl, the wheel is stuck.

EVA: Frau Wagner always called for her shawl when she was frightened. (*Slight pause*) You were much too attentive to Frau Wagner.

ADOLF: (*Tenderly*) Are you frightened, my darling.

EVA: Well, certainly I'm not cold, Adolf. I certainly don't shudder from the cold.

Pause while ADOLF *uses his telescope on* DR. REICH's *laboratory.*

ADOLF: You know, Eva. Sometimes I think I can almost see Germany again. (*Holds up telescope*) This is an appropriate instrument, Eva. A very appropriate instrument for a man of vision.

EVA: (*Is silent*)

ADOLF: (*Needs the confirmation*) What did you say, liebchen?

EVA: (*Very suggestively*) I said, Adolf, that there are instruments which interest me more than the telescope.

ADOLF: (*Looks woundedly at her*)

EVA: (*Hurriedly, to cover*) Microscopes, for instance. Yes. Laboratory equipment. I am fascinated by laboratory equipment.

ADOLF: Ach! The toys of academicians, Eva. To take scrapings from little silver slides when you could be scanning the greater galaxies . . . (*Pause*) I would give my chair here for one winter's day at Obersalzburg.

EVA: Only your chair?

Slight pause

ADOLF: (*A sudden change in tone*) They think we're Jews, do you know that? The . . . natives here think we're Jews. I heard them talking on the verandah yesterday. They think we're Jews and from this they deduce that I have a Jewish nose.

EVA: You shouldn't have shaved your moustache, Adolf.

ADOLF: My moustache has nothing to do with it! This nose is not semitic! This is an Aryan nose! In an Aryan face! Temporarily trapped in a Jewish state!

EVA: (*Sighs*) I'm so hot.

ADOLF: Here, tösserl. Have a nice piece of fruit.

EVA: Fruit is full of sugar, Adolf. I don't care for sugar. Cancer cells feed on sugar. (*Sighs, closes eyes*) It's hot as an oven. I feel as though I'm being <u>baked</u>.

Pause

ADOLF: (*Confidentially*) They say the governor of this state is a Jew.

EVA: Why, that's impossible, Adolf. Even in <u>this</u> . . . (*Contemptuous*) country, Jews don't get elected to office.

ADOLF: Perhaps it's the lieutenant-governor then. <u>One</u> of them is Jewish.

EVA: (*Punctilious*) Lieutenant-governor is not an elective position, Adolf. I read it in the newspaper. The lieutenant-governor is appointed by the <u>governor</u>.

ADOLF: One of the <u>chosen</u> people, eh? Ha ha ha. Then it <u>must</u> be the lieutenant-governor who's Jewish. Ha ha ha. One of the chosen people. Did you understand, Eva? <u>Chosen</u> <u>People</u>.

EVA: (*Patient*) Yes, Adolf. I <u>always</u> understand. Chosen people are the people who have no choice.

ADOLF *sighs, then starts and stops to clear the tea things.*

ADOLF: How is Herman.

EVA: Katha says not well.

ADOLF: How long can they hold him?

EVA: As long as they like. It's considered quite serious here.

ADOLF: What he did. Gott. These Americans! Serious!

EVA: It was in a schoolyard, Adolf.

ADOLF: A schoolyard! Katha didn't tell me that.

EVA: He exposed himself in a schoolyard. What they call here a grade school.

ADOLF: (*Head drops*)

EVA: (*Experimentally*) During the recess. Katha told me three little boys were affected.

ADOLF: He <u>touched</u> them?!!

EVA: No, no! he <u>never</u> touches them.

ADOLF: Poor little rats. (*Slight pause*) Herman should have been eliminated in '42. With the other misfits.

EVA: Adolf! Herman is loyal to you.

ADOLF: Thank gott for plastic surgery that covers such loyalty.

EVA: They'll never find out who he is.

ADOLF: Joseph was thorough. A good doctor.

EVA: Joseph was a <u>great</u> doctor, Adolf. A brilliant scientist!

ADOLF: He had enough practice, gott knows. All of Poland to experiment upon!

EVA: If Joseph were here right now I would not have this cancer sitting on my brain, Adolf! I can tell you that!

ADOLF: They say he's still alive.

EVA: Yes.

ADOLF: Alive and in Uraguay.

EVA: Paraguay. It was in the newspapers.

ADOLF: (*Definitively*) Argentina. I heard it on the Radio.

EVA: It doesn't matter.

ADOLF: Of course it doesn't.

EVA: (*Sighs heavily*) Not any more.

    Radio crackles. ADOLF *wheels his chair around and heads for the Radio.*

Upstage Center:

REICH B.: (*Jiggling his mike*) The microphone is dead.

HITLER B.: That's impossible. These are <u>German</u> instruments!

Stage Right:

ADOLF: Gott! It's almost time for the broadcast!

EVA: (*Indicates the tea tray*) Adolf! The tea things!

ADOLF: (*Fiddling madly with the dials*) Later, Eva, later! I don't want to miss the quintuplets! They're making their first Communion tonight on the Radio.

EVA: Will Dr. Reich be on the broadcast, Adolf? I would love to hear his voice.

ADOLF: (*Ecstatic*) I've got it, Eva! I've got it! To the devil with the humidity! I found the station! And the reception is <u>perfect</u>!

    Lights half-down on ADOLF *and* EVA. ADOLF *remains in ecstatic listening position, while* EVA *does a few suggestive things with his telescope.*

Upstage Center:

BROADCASTERS *take off their headhones.*

HITLER B.: (*Rattles his script in disgust*) Florida! My god what a script!

REICH B.: (*"Jewish" intonation*) What's wrong with Florida? I've got relatives in Florida.

HITLER B.: Florida stinks that's what's wrong with it. It's full of old Jews in new vacation homes just flushing their toilets into the swamps. Why, the whole state is running in piss.

REICH B.: (*Aghast*) You think the <u>Jews</u> are responsible for <u>drainage</u> problems?

HITLER B.: Well, it's not the Germans peeing into those swamps. You can bet it's not the Germans.

REICH B.: (*Picks up headphones grimly*) The quintuplets are almost finished with their broadcast.

HITLER B.: (*Listens*) By god, you're right. The sound man should have cued us. It's a shame to miss the religious music. I think the sound man is a <u>Jew</u>. (*He taps the* REICH B.'s *mike*) Well here's <u>one</u> place you won't find any Jews.

REICH B.: (*Profoundly uncomfortable*) What do you mean?

HITLER B.: The <u>Radio</u>, shithead. They haven't let the Jews take over the airwaves yet.

The HASSID *appears again, standing quietly by the Radio, waiting to tune in to another consultation between* DR. REICH *and* ADOLF HITLER. *Meanwhile, the* BROADCASTERS *begin the following narration, during which biological slides of infected tissue and cancerous cells appear on the screen behind them.*

REICH B.: Adolf Hitler could do anything. He dictated statutes which determined the religion of household servants, the colours artists could use in paintings, the way lobsters were cooked in restaurants, and how physics should be taught in universities. He decided whom his subjects might marry, what they could name their children, and where they could be buried. (*Pause*) He designed their cars, he built their roads, he engineered their buildings. How could we . . . uh, how could <u>they</u> live without him? (*Pause, a lower, more ominous tone*) And during all this time, the whole of Germany was a vast circulatory system transmitting poisons to infected cells.

HITLER B.: (*Brightly*) Yes, they say that infection spread from human tissue to human tissue like a terrible stain . . .

Voices from the radio interrupt the HITLER BROADCASTER.

RADIO: You've got it!

She's got it!

No, no these are not the spots!

This is not the rash! I'm <u>blushing</u>, that's all.

<u>Blushing</u>?!

She must have caught it from a <u>Jew</u>!

HITLER B.: The Fuehrer, of course, saw a different pathology. Something . . . outside himself. The Fuehrer thought of it as a kind of cancer that must be cleansed from the body politic. Everywhere he looked he saw an infected Jew ready to prey upon the tissue of healthy German cells. What he did not understand was . . .

REICH B.: (*Interrupting harshly*) There was nothing Hitler understood. He understood <u>nothing</u>.

HITLER B.: All the while, Dr. Reich was investigating the causes of the Fuehrer's rise . . .

REICH B.: (*Interrupting*) <u>Disease</u>. Not Hitler's rise. Dr. Reich was investigating <u>Hitler's</u> <u>disease</u>.

HITLER B.: (*Starts again*) . . . the Fuehrer's <u>disease</u> from the very beginning. Reich's reasons were better than most. He was fascinated by the Fuehrer and thought he saw his own future in a lampshade. (*Nasty smile*)

Stage Left:

DR. REICH: (*In a small pool of light with his microscope*) Really, the symptoms were so obvious, I didn't need my microscope. I didn't need my microscope at <u>all</u>. (*Tosses it over his shoulder*)

Upstage Center:

REICH B.: (*An approving nod toward* DR. REICH) Hitler himself . . . (*His voice sinks, he shakes his head*)

HITLER B.: (*Brightly, picking up the narrative*) Why, they say that even the rain was a different colour in Hitler's Germany. It came down like a golden shower. (*Another nasty laugh*)

The HASSID *switches the Radio to his favorite station, then moves out of the light. Fragments of the consultation between* DR. REICH *and* ADOLF HITLER *come on again.*

ADOLF: You know, doktor, I always imagined Eva as a mermaid.

DR. REICH: (*An unguential tone*) Is that so, Herr Hitler? Perhaps you would feel more comfortable lying down.

ADOLF: Thank you doktor. Yes, that's quite nice. (*Sounds of* ADOLF *reclining*)

DR. REICH: (*Gently prompting*) You say you thought of her as a sea creature . . . ?

ADOLF: Yes, yes, a mermaid, a Rhine Maiden. When we met that day in Hoff-man's studio, I swear to you that the hours began to run in rivers and I could hear the sea rising in my ears.

The HASSID *turns off the Radio disgustedly and moves out of the light again.*

REICH B.: And, once again, in Dr. Reich's laboratory in New England, his re-searches are interrupted by the excited entrance of Nadya Leopovna and Sonya Fyedorovna.

Stage Left:

Lights up on STAGE LEFT. DR. REICH *is rolling up his charts. We are surprised to find no one behind them. Small crinkling and bubbling sounds are coming from the Radio—it's warming up for the Quintuplets' Broadcast—but the sounds are not distracting. The moment before the* REICH BROADCASTER *stops speaking,* NADYA *and* SONYA *burst into the laboratory, gesticulating wildly. They are dressed, very sloppily, in white laboratory coats and are clearly beside themselves.*

SONYA: Doktor! Doktor!

NADYA: Doktor! Doktor!

DR. REICH: (*Turns wearily to them*)

SONYA: Be qviet, Nadya Leopovna.

NADYA: Qviet yourselve, Sonya Fyedorovna. Doktor can hear nossing ven you scrich like ow-val.

DR. REICH: (*Low and tense*) What is it? Something is wrong with the children?

SONYA: Chillldren fine, Doktor Reich.

NADYA: Chillldren vunderful. Iting, slipping, going to bassroom—just perrrfect!

SONYA: Da, da, iss true.

NADYA: (*Ticking off*) Leetle Marie behaves brrrilliant . . .

SONYA: Yvette rrrecites poitry like genyuss . . .

NADYA: Cecile its like horrrse . . .

SONYA: Annette slips like dog . . .

NADYA: Emillie prrrays like hangel.

SONYA: (*Grasping the subject*) Ve come hyere so you not be late for brrroadcast.

NADYA: Da, Doktor. Een ten minoots de girrrls go on airrr and make comm-mooonyon and direktor vants you make beeeg spyich.

SONYA: Nyet, nyet, Nadya Leopovna. Not spyich, Doktor. Meerrly introdoooc-
tory rrremarks to rrreligious event. You know, the mirrracle off mooltipool
births, etc., etc., etc. (*She gestures suggestively*)

NADYA: (*Disappointed*) No beeeg spyich?

SONYA: Oh Doktor, I tell you, iss useless knocking on doorrr off deaf voman.

NADYA: Vat doorrr you rrreferr to, Sonya Fyedorovna?

SONYA: Doorrr of your brrrain, Nadya Leopovna. Vich iss perrrmanently closed.

DR. REICH: Ladies. Please. You know I cannot take the time for public relations.
(NADYA *and* SONYA *droop*) Let the girls go on as usual. They have learned their
songs?

NADYA: Voice of hangels, doktor.

DR. REICH: And they've had their tea.

SONYA: Like fife little vite mice drrrinking from kops.

DR. REICH: (*Nods head approvingly*) Correct behavior is what we want. Children
are confused by too many choices, you know. My latest studies show . . .
(*Looks at* NADYA'S *and* SONYA'S *eager faces and gives up all hope of explanation*)
Never mind what they show. Do the Radio technicians have their surgical
masks?

NADYA: Whole ssstudio loooks like Leningrrrad after poison gasss is drrropped.

DR. REICH: Good. Good. I won't have anyone breathing on them. We cannot
risk the infection.

SONYA: God forrrbid.

NADYA: Infection.

They both make the sign of the cross.

DR. REICH: And the parents. Where are the parents?

SONYA: Ass ussooal.

NADYA: Locked out.

SONYA: The Papa threatens. Ass usssooal.

NADYA: And the Mama blames the Jews. Also as ussooal. Iss sad.

DR. REICH: Terrible, terrible. They don't understand how <u>safe</u> the children are in
the laboratory. Now that I am approaching a cure.

SONYA: Oh Doktor! Iss vanderful news. You heeeeerr, Nadya Leopovna? Doktor
has almost found currre.

NADYA: Oh, hoppy, hoppy day! I alveys said it, Sonya Fyedorovna. You can't deny I always said Doktor vass <u>genyuss</u>.

SONYA: Ve both verrry, verrry hoppy.

NADYA: (*To* SONYA *sotto voce*) Sonya Fyedorovna, Excusse pliss my intorrruption, Doktor. Von't tek long. Sonya Fyedorovna. Currre for <u>vat</u>? Vat for Doktor find currre?

SONYA: Come to theeenk, I don't know, Nadya Leopovna. Vy don't you ask?

NADYA: OK, Sonya Fyedorovna, I ask. But if I ask, no more knocking on door off deaf voman. (*In a louder voice*) Doktor, excusss my ignorance but vat you are currring pliss?

DR. REICH: I thought you knew. It's the plague. I'm curing the emotional plague. I am seeking a cure for Hitler.

NADYA *and* SONYA *make crosses in the air, spit three times, and raise their right hands as though taking an oath.*

NADYA: <u>Hitler</u>.

SONYA: <u>Hitler</u>.

NADYA: May turrrnips grow in his belly.

SONYA: May he lie down in a grrraveyarrrd and have Mengele for a neighbor.

NADYA: May he haf house vit a tousand beds and be found dead in every vun of them.

NADYA *and* SONYA *spit and cross themselves.*

NADYA: Ve had no ideee, Doktor.

SONYA: Ve knew perhops you refugeee from Second Var just like us.

DR. REICH: (*Steely*) How did you know that.

NADYA: (*Vague*) Ohhh, ve listen to Rrradio Brrroadcast, here, there.

SONYA: (*Nudges* NADYA) Da, da. Isss nice to be heeere in vat dey call it cold climate Doktor, where Rrradio rrreception iss ssso goood.

NADYA: Da. Veather rrreminds me of gurrrlhood in Siberrria.

Radio crackles.

SONYA: Almost time for brrroadcast.

NADYA: If you not come Doktor, ve got to go.

SONYA: Da, da mek surre little gurrrls do nice on big Rrradio.

NADYA: Ve give your luf to qvintuplets, Doktor.

SONYA: Neverr mind pooting vords in mouth of Doktor, Nadya Leopovna, ve be late forr Brrroadcast. Move the feet!

NADYA: Move the feet, yourselve, Sonya Fyedorovna . . .

They exit flailing and recriminating. DR. REICH *turns his back immediately and moves to his microscope. He is quiet for awhile as though thinking, holds a microscope slide up to the window light, inspects his charts again (as he raises and lowers the nutrition charts we see Goering's feet), opens a medical cabinet (only Goebbels's uniform is there), and goes to stand before* EDMUND *the skeleton. We see that there is a tag encircling* EDMUND's *left wrist bones.* DR. REICH *raises it and reads.*

DR. REICH: "Edmund from Germany. Age six. Death resulting from complications of an attack of measles." (*He looks up*) I remember his eyes—so remarkably blue—and his habit of eating cake with his dirty hands. I could do nothing for him. (*Reads again from the tag*) "Family medical history: Mother died of tumour of the breast, Father of apoplexy, elder sister suspected of idiocy, elder brother believed to be in hiding in America." (*Looks up in wonderment*) No one . . . gassed? No one . . . burned? No . . . experiments? (*Looks at tag, reads its last line*) "Body donated to science." They all died in their beds. How . . . unusual.

The Radio begins to glow suggestively. DR. REICH *looks at* EDMUND *for a moment, then takes him off his rack and sits with him like a ventriloquist—articulating his joints horribly to make images appropriate to the sentences he says. Like a ventriloquist, he must move his jaw whenever* EDMUND *speaks.* EDMUND, *naturally, uses the voice of* CHARLIE MCCARTHY, *and* DR. REICH *will have* EDGAR BERGEN's *upperclass articulation.*

EDMUND: Reich, oh Reich, say Reich, look at that big audience out there. Isn't it nice to know so many people don't have television sets?

DR. REICH: Dignity, Edmund, dignity. We want to make a good impression. You'd better watch your step.

EDMUND: I'll watch my step, Reich, if you watch your lips.

DR. REICH: Edmund. Tonight an investigation is being conducted into the lives of some of the most important figures in modern history.

EDMUND: Well thank you Reich. You didn't have to go to all this trouble just for little old me.

DR. REICH: Alright, Edmund, never mind, never mind. You know, Edmund. I have studied children for a very long time.

EDMUND: It shows, Reich, believe me it shows.

DR. REICH: I've put them through every laboratory test I could devise. Like little mice, just like little mice.

EDMUND: Maybe you should have been a veterinarian, Reich.

DR. REICH: I know the colour of their eyes and their urine, the texture of their skin and hair under a microscope. I know how they react to frustration — don't I, Edmund?

EDMUND: I'll say, you skinflint.

DR. REICH: . . . and how they should react. I have cultured their tissues, analyzed their feces . . .

EDMUND: Yuch.

DR. REICH: . . . raised bacteria from their baby bodies.

Impressive pause.

DR. REICH: And what, Edmund, has this long labour brought me to? To what secrets of the soul have I been directed?

EDMUND: Search me, Doc.

DR. REICH *considers* EDMUND *for an instant, then abruptly wrenches his left arm upwards in the Fuehrer salute.*

EDMUND: Aoowww!

DR. REICH: This is what I found. (*Lets the arm fall, then raises it emphatically and fixes it in position*) Here is what I came upon. It is Hitler, Edmund, Hitler!

EDMUND: Now don't be hasty Reich.

DR. REICH: Hitler is what I saw. Understand me? In the bodies of babies I have found . . . Hitler.

EDMUND: Down, boy, down.

DR. REICH: At the center of human cells, I have seen sitting a tiny Hitler, directing the ebb of acids, the flow of fluids.

EDMUND: You sure about that, Reich?

DR. REICH: I have seen him, one layer thick, spread out on a silver microscope slide.

EDMUND: Awww come on now.

DR. REICH: (*Breathing stertorously*) I swear to you Edmund, that in the very marrow of your bones I have identified a representation of the German government of 1942!

Upstage Center:

The Radio crackles and lights up fully for a moment. UPSTAGE CENTER *lights down except for the faintly glowing Radio.*

REICH B.: *(Shaking his headset)* I can't hear a <u>word</u> Charlie McCarthy's saying.

HITLER B.: *(Shaking his microphone)* I tell you this is German equipment and German equipment <u>never</u> <u>fails</u>.

REICH B.: *(Jewish and resigned)* Is that so? Why don't you tell that to the Italians? They'll believe anything.

Stage Left:

EDMUND: *(A hard, Nazi voice)* Alright Reich, cut the crap. That's enough. I <u>order</u> you to find the answer. Get down on your knees.

DR. REICH: Here Edmund? Here, sir? This is a latrine, sir.

EDMUND: Ah, you noticed. Get down on your knees in the slime. Rub your face in the filth. The answer, Herr Doktor, is in the mountain of shit you have hidden in this hole. But when you get up, you'd better be clean, you understand? <u>Clean</u>. We want no sheisskopfs in the Fatherland.

DR. REICH *begins to sink to his knees, holding* EDMUND *high above his head. A tableau of* EDMUND *triumphant in the Fuehrer and salute, then blackout* STAGE LEFT.

UPSTAGE CENTER, *the Radio lights up fully for a moment (the Quintuplets are broadcasting), then blackout.*

Upstage Center:

REICH B.: And once again, Radio Audience, we are inside the Hitlers' Kozy Kabin in Florida. Adolf and Eva have been listening to the Radio.

Stage Right:

Inside the Hitlers' Kozy Kabin. EVA *is sitting on the edge of the bed;* ADOLF *is slumped in his wheelchair, the picture of disappointment. His headset dangles from the chair arm. During this scene—and the process is barely perceptible—* ADOLF's *and* EVA's *mannerisms must become increasingly "Jewish."* EVA *begins cheerfully, the draining of* ADOLF's *energy has somehow pleased her.*

EVA: Never mind liebchen. I'm sure he'll speak again. I'm just as disappointed as you are. Why I was myself <u>dying</u> *(too much emphasis in the <u>dying</u>)* to hear him.

ADOLF: Weeks, Eva, I waited weeks for that broadcast. Weeks to hear Dr. Reich speak of his researches. And he doesn't even appear on the program. The man is hiding something, Eva. You can be <u>sure</u> of it.

EVA: Adolf. <u>Adolf</u>. An interesting man in that position. What could he be hiding?

ADOLF: What do you mean interesting? Whatever it is, it ruined my digestion. I'm blocked again, Eva. Blocked.

EVA: Impossible, Adolf you eat like a sparrow.

ADOLF: Nevertheless, Eva, an entire division of panzers has driven over my duodenum and wedged its way into my lower colon.

EVA: (*Eyes to heaven*) Always the war. Have some cake Adolf. A nice piece of cake.

ADOLF: (*Takes the cake, starts to eat it with his hands, then flings it down*) Ach! Who can eat on such an occasion? Even the quintuplets were a disappointment.

EVA: (*Terribly pleased*) You shouldn't say it, Adolf.

ADOLF: Yes, yes. Their singing was flat, their retorts were sharp, I could hear the starch crinkling in their communion dresses . . . I'm beginning to think they're not being raised correctly.

EVA: It's the confinement, Adolf. Children cannot stand to be confined. I read it in the newspaper.

ADOLF: All that training, all my policies—gone to waste. Oh I tell you Eva, I'd like to get my hands on that doktor. His behaviour has been totally incorrect. Totally . . .

Enormous static from the Radio.

Upstage Center:

REICH B.: (*Hand over mike*) We'd better take a station break, no? The transmission is completely fermisht . . . <u>confused</u>.

HITLER B.: (*Snaps his fingers*) It's little Wulf.

(REICH B.: (*Terrified*) An animal? There's an animal in the studio?

HITLER B.: It's my son, dummy. I told you he was here. We call him Wulf for short. Damn little bastarrd's probably up on that transmitter. (*Faintly proud*) He climbs everything in sight so he can look at the buildings. Says he wants to be as good an architect as Albert Speer. (*Matter-of-fact, an ordinary threat*) You get on down from there Wulf, or I'll break your leg!

Lights down UPSTAGE CENTER.

Stage Right:

EVA: (*Sighing*) It's the children again.

ADOLF: (*Furious*) They will not stop from shaking that antenna! Filthy little things! Children should never be touched, Eva. You can catch <u>terrible</u> <u>infections</u> from children!

EVA: They're only playing, Adolf.

ADOLF: You know what they call me, Eva?

EVA: (*Nods*) Never mind liebchen.

ADOLF: (*Between his teeth*) Mr. Monster.

EVA: Because of the burns, liebchen. Children don't like scars. I read it in the newspaper. Scars make them feel insecure.

ADOLF: (*Menacing*) Perhaps I should offer them some of my candy.

EVA: (*Alarmed*) Leave them alone, Adolf.

ADOLF: Little bags of candy . . .

EVA: (*Warning*) <u>Adolf</u> . . .

ADOLF: Tasty little pieces of chocolate . . . rolled in prussic acid.

Slight pause.

ADOLF: Even when <u>I</u> was a child, Eva, even <u>then</u> the little Bavarian bastards did not persecute me as these children do.

EVA: Americans are animals, Adolf. Everyone knows that.

ADOLF: The quintuplets are always <u>perfectly</u> behaved. The broadcast—bad as it was—<u>insisted</u> upon that.

Static from the Radio.

ADOLF: (*Points his telescope toward the imagined transmitter*) Those children are ruining my reception! (*Broods*) Mr. Monster! They scribble that name on walls, it appears on neighborhood mailboxes, sidewalks, even ceilings when they're low. (*The final horror*) One day I saw it nailed to a <u>tree</u>.

EVA: Finish what's on your plate, Adolf.

ADOLF: Maybe it was a bush.

EVA: The cake, Adolf.

ADOLF: No, not a bush. There are no bushes in this barbarous state.

EVA: (*Ironically, a quotation*) "No Jews," either. Remember what dear Joseph said?

ADOLF: Ach! <u>Why</u> do you remind me? "No vegetation," Mengele said. "The state to which you are fleeing has no vegetation that will interest you. And no noble wildlife. No wolves. Just snakes and insects. But, mein Fuehrer, you can console yourself with the complete absence of international Jewry." With five hundred thousand of the filth not fifteen miles from my front door, drinking, breathing, <u>vacationing</u> as though my plans to extinguish them never took form in this world. By god, I hope Mengele finds Argentina as uncomfortable as this scorched piece of earth.

EVA: <u>Paraguay</u>, Adolf, Joseph is in Paraguay. (*She moves to the sink with the cake plate*)

The Radio tries to communicate something.

ADOLF: (*Turns to wheel to the Radio*) If my Radio is ruined, there won't be a child left alive in this entire nation! <u>Not</u> <u>one</u> <u>single</u> <u>child</u>!

EVA: (*At the sink*) Adolf! Look look! At last! A little water pressure! You can have a shower, liebchen. Think how good that will make you feel.

ADOLF: <u>One</u> shower. One. When I have been accustomed to five showers a day and a washing of the hands every twenty minutes all my life! Well, alright, Eva, turn it on, turn it on quickly. God knows how long the water will last!

Lights down STAGE RIGHT.

Upstage Center:

The HASSID *drags himself into the dim light. His confidence is gone. He moves like a death-camp Musselman—without lifting his feet from the floor. His body appears vacated, without tendencies. He lifts his hand two or three times before touching the Radio dial. As he changes the stations a series of soap commercials come over the loudspeaker; sounds of the shower* ADOLF HITLER *is taking run under them.* ADOLF *is visible, scrubbing himself in his chair as though under a shower;* EVA *can be seen opening and closing her oven repeatedly, as though trying to identify a strange smell.* DR. REICH *remains* STAGE LEFT, *sterilizing some instruments, then peering into his microscope.*

The following soap commercials come on the Radio sequentially whenever the HASSID *clicks the dial.*

RADIO: L-A-V-A. Nothing cleans dirty hands faster, yet more gently, than lava soap.

Ivory snow, Ivory snow is what your dishes need.

For a wash that's white without bleaching use Oxydol with lively, active hustle-bubble suds. Recommended by Oxydol's own Ma Perkins.

HITLER B.: (*Hand over mike*) What's <u>happening</u>? Where did these commercials <u>come</u> from? The sponsors will <u>exterminate</u> us!

REICH B.: (*One hand over mike, the other on his forehead*) Oy vey! Competitors!

RADIO: Lever Bros. Co., the makers of new Rinso Blue with solium the sunlight ingredient brings you . . .

REICH B.: (*Hand over mike, yelling to imagined engineer*) That's good, that's good! Stay with <u>that</u> one!

The HASSID *switches to the continuing consultation between* DR. REICH *and* ADOLF HITLER, *during which* ADOLF *continues to shower,* EVA *continues to open her oven and,* STAGE LEFT, DR. REICH *continues to sterilize his instruments. The shower sounds run under the consultation, as do sounds of* DR. REICH's *note-taking.*

DR. REICH: Well, we're coming along quite nicely, Herr Hitler. Now that we've got you . . . <u>dreaming</u> again.

ADOLF: (*Decidedly "Jewish"*) Ach! Dr. Reich. Such dreams a <u>criminal</u> shouldn't have! They're terrible, terrible. And I had them again. (*Sighs and speaks as though seeing it*) The ghetto is in flames around me, the sky is as red as a throat that's been cut. The luftwaffe is bombing, panzers are shelling, the screams of the dying are worse than the howling of devils in hell. I run outside, and I trip and I fall into a filthy hole. Would you believe it, it's a sewer. I'm swimming in a sewer hole. And Eva is swimming just above me, out of reach, legs locked, covered with shiny scales, flicking her fin in my face.

DR. REICH: Tell me, mein Fuehrer, in what sort of water are you swimming?

ADOLF: Sea water, doktor. It is <u>always</u> sea water. And it is <u>always</u> filled with forbidden flesh. Crabs! Lobsters! Shrimp! Abalone! Trayfe! All trayfe! I'm sure if I looked around I could see communion wafers swimming by my side. Well, to continue, I swim straight ahead and . . . (*interrupts himself*) By the way, doktor. I have heard that sea water is made from the . . . uh . . . body fluids of mermaids. Do you think this is correct?

DR. REICH: (*An indulgent tone*) Why don't you just go on with the dream, Herr Hitler?

ADOLF: (*No response*)

DR. REICH: Well, how often do you have this dream?

ADOLF: Every night, doktor, every night. And when I wake up from the horror, the sea is in my mouth, I am bathed in sweat, and I have to shower five times a day to keep the salt from my imagination.

DR. REICH: Ahhh . . . the word <u>shower</u>, mein Fuehrer. I see by my notes that this is not the only time we have associated the word shower with you. In the matter of six million members of the Jewish faith . . .

STAGE RIGHT EVA *freezes with a hand on the oven door.*

ADOLF: (*Interrupts with his Nazi voice*) RACE, not <u>faith</u>! RACE! RACE! RACE!

A poison bacilli breeding into the bloodstream of the Fatherland! Filth! Filth! A mountain of dreck! They're dreck and all the showers of the world couldn't wash them away!

Pause. Sounds of note-taking stop.

DR. REICH: (*Perfectly neutral*) If I remember correctly you haven't yet finished your dream. Why don't you finish your dream, Herr Hitler?

ADOLF: (*Perfectly calm, "Jewish" again*) Ach! With a memory like that, doktor, who needs notes? (*Clears his throat*) I am in a room where nothing is dry . . .

Stage Right:

Voices of EVA *and* ADOLF *from* STAGE RIGHT *interrupt the Radio consultation.* EVA *has moved from the oven to the sink.*

EVA: <u>Ask</u> me, <u>ask</u> me, you swine! I'm ready!

ADOLF: I beg you liebchen. Please my darling. <u>Now</u> <u>now</u> NOW MEIN FUEHRER!

EVA turns the sink water up fully and the consultation is dissolved in sounds of flooding water from the Radio. EVA's back is to ADOLF; ADOLF *is in a kind of ecstasy as he is flooded with imaginary fluids. The* HASSID *abandons his Musselmanner movements and, in his eagerness to extinguish the Radio, stumbles and falls grotesquely.*

Out of the flooding water sounds, EVA, *washing dishes at the sink, mutters into an environment of light which constantly flickers and darkens and brightens as though filtered through sea water.*

EVA: I have been marooned in this desert too long. (*Holds up her hands*) My scales are drying out. (*Picks up fork*) My trident is dull (*Holds a cracked glass to the light*), the necklace of shells I wear to bed is broken. My mouth has lost the shape all mermaid mouths assume when they are near the ocean. (*Runs fingers over her mouth*) There are still bits of seaweed between my teeth, but I suffer a constant headache from the static. (*Gestures toward Radio, which crackles obligingly*) I, who was not made for a stinking swamp but for the bed of a conqueror, sometimes dream that Dr. Reich will carry me across this desert and into the water once again. (*Pause*) Perhaps . . . it was something I read in the newspapers.

ADOLF: (*He scrubs himself frantically in his wheelchair, breathes heavily as he speaks*) I know there are parts of my body that have never been clean. (*One hand scans his body, pauses at the genitals, then decides not to deal with them*) The bottoms of my . . . <u>feet</u>, for instance, have not been correctly attended to. Terrible infections can start with the <u>toes</u>. Yes, with the <u>toes</u>. I once heard Frau Goebbels, when she thought I was napping, say to <u>Joseph</u> something about the softness of his feet. I walked too much in the <u>war</u> for soft <u>feet</u>.

(*Hideous contempt*) <u>Goebbels</u> had the <u>feet</u> of an academician. (*Straight into the audience, without warning*) They've got me! They've trapped me in the showers! Zir habt mir in bud!

Upstage Center:

Cellular images of infection spread across a map of Germany on the BROADCASTER's *screen, in the manner of 1940's newsreels.*

REICH B: (*Ludicrously*) As with all great plagues, the infection that conquered Germany was both preceded and followed by the death of kings and presidents, profound political upheavals, magnetic phenomena of all kinds, and the destruction of Jews on a large scale.

Stage Right:

EVA *sniffs loudly at her oven door.*

EVA: Adolf. <u>Adolf</u>. Come out from the shower. I think the oven is leaking again.

Upstage Center:

HITLER B.: Before the onset of the disease, the outer body was covered with pale red spots which the victim only noticed if they darkened unexpectedly.

REICH B: These spots are merely the outer signs of an interior revolution. (*A dream tone*) Much the way waves reveal a disturbance of the ocean's floor or the drying of a mermaid's scales indicates something . . . <u>heavy</u> at her heart.

HITLER B.: (*Looks at* REICH B. *pityingly*) In any case, the sufferer's head soon become horribly painful and the primitive brain . . .

REICH B.: (*Interrupts slyly*) . . . the National <u>Socialist</u> brain . . .

HITLER B.: . . . begins to boil. (*Rapidly, a sort of laundry list*) The inner body's molecules separate from each other; the center of every cell is sucked away; small squads of self-destroying viruses implant themselves, producing cells that function without inhibition, cells that have shed the mechanism which restrains growth.

REICH B.: (*Hand over mike*) Moron! Dummy! That's the wrong <u>disease</u>! We're supposed to be describing the plague and you're talking about <u>cancer</u>.

On the BROADCASTERS' *screen, the slides should alternately show cancer tissue and infected plague cells. The images should shift as rapidly as the* BROADCASTERS' *argument does.*

HITLER B.: (*Hand over mike*) <u>Cancer</u> is what the Fuehrer <u>saw</u>. And <u>cancer</u> is what should have struck <u>Columbus</u> before he discovered <u>Pet</u> <u>Milk</u> and <u>Rinso</u> <u>Blue</u>!

REICH B.: (*Hand over mike*) Cancer is what the Fuehrer <u>had</u>! Cancer is what the

Fuehrer <u>was</u>! Everyone else got the <u>plague</u>! Do you understand? The <u>plague</u>! (*Broadcasting again*) This rash, ladies and gentlemen, is not the most terrible form the plague can take.

HITLER B.: The most terrible plague is the one that does not reveal its symptoms. (*Almost as an afterthought he takes off his mustache, then puts it back on*)

The HASSID, *prostrate throughout this narration, arises briskly and goes to stand by the Radio.*

REICH B.: And back in Dr. Reich's laboratory, strange sounds are heard in the middle of the night.

Stage Left:

Lights up on EDMUND *the Skeleton, who glows weirdly* (*Radioactively*) *from within.* EDMUND *is back on his rack, near the examining table. Upstage, slightly behind the table, stand* NADYA LEOPOVNA *and* SONYA FYEDOROVNA *in a pool of light. They are clearly up to no good. Soft sounds come from the Radio—operation music, perhaps. On the examining table, its head turned away from us, is a faintly familiar male body covered primly with a sheet. It is* DR. REICH *got up to resemble* ADOLF HITLER.

NADYA *and* SONYA *fuss and bumble about and, finally,* NADYA *plugs what appears to be a primitive electrocardiagram machine into an outlet on the Radio. The Radio "respires"—"uh"—as the plug is thrust into it. The ladies begin to assess the body before them.*

SONYA: Ooooh, Nadya Leopovna. Isss so in-terrresting hafing body of rrreal grrrown perrrson to loook at.

NADYA: Da, da, Sonya Fyedorovna, I know vat hyou mean. Whole carrreeer spent vit infants.

SONYA: Isss nice change, though (*Looks hard at body*), come to theenk, thees body isss not so nice.

NADYA: Qvite, how you say, smelly.

SONYA: Nadya Leopovna! Smelly iss not prrrofessional descrription.

NADYA: Qvite rrrright, Sonya Fyedorovna. (*Tries again, sniffing*) Let me put it another vey. Old man <u>stinks</u>.

They look some more, poking and prodding and giggling like children playing doctor.

SONYA: Hyou know, Nadya Leopovna.

NADYA: Vat iss it, Sonya Fyedorovna.

SONYA: De tyeeth on dis old mon are very fonny.

NADYA: Vell, de dyental vork is German, nachurlik . . .

SONYA: Bot de qvality is hyighly expansif.

NADYA: Da, da I see vat you myean. Loook at de gorgyous golden cccrowns. Vort mony, mony hrubles. (*She looks longingly*)

SONYA: And someting else, Nadya Leopovna.

NADYA: Vat more else, Sonya Fyedorovna.

SONYA: Dis old mon hass too many hhholes in de skyinn.

NADYA: Vat myean you, hhholes in de skyinn. Everrrybody hass hhholes in de skyinn, Sonya Fyedorovna. Iss called hyere <u>pores</u>.

SONYA: (*Exasperated*) Nyet, nyet no <u>pores</u>. Hhholes like from needles. Tousand hhholes from needles. See hyere. Hyere. Hyere and hyere.

NADYA: Ooooh hyou so hhhright, Sonya Fyedorovna. Hyou haf eyes like Comrrrad Joseph Stalin. Hhhe could pick poisoner out of feefty pyeeple at dinerrr tyable and haf him executed by desert. You t'ink dis old mon is how hyou call it hyere junkie?

SONYA: Nyet, nyet, come to look closer, these <u>not</u> nyeedle hhholes. Morrre like pustuuuules, you know, peemples dat haf opened.

NADYA: Ooooh! Rrright again, Sonya Fyedorovna. Vat diagnostic brrrilliance. If ve vere back in Rrrussia vhere vomen allowed to be doktors, you vould cerrrtainly be imporrrtant physician.

SONYA: Verrry grrracious statement, Nadya Leopovna.

NADYA: Isss merrrely acknowledgement of talent. You perrrfectly correct. Rrrotten old mon isss coverrred vit pale rrred spots.

SONYA: Ay yi yi! Rrred spots firrrst sign of drrread infection! Qvickly, Nadya Leopovna, let us finish test and rrremove ourselfs.

NADYA *begins to affix one of the electrocardiogram's many wires to the chest of the body of the examining table. When the printout comes, it will appear on the* BROADCASTERS' *screen* UPSTAGE CENTER.

SONYA: <u>Nyet</u>, Nadya. <u>Dat</u> vun, <u>dat</u> vun. Hyou vant to keel de old monster?

NADYA: Qviet, Sonya Fyedorovna. Pyatient rrresting.

SONYA: Qviet yourrrself, Nadya Leopovna. Pyatient hupset. Be calm meester vat's-your-name. (*To* NADYA) Vat de nyame of dis old mon?

NADYA: (*Looks at tag on body's left wrist*) Gerrrman nyame. Too harrrd for Rrrussian to prrronounce.

SONYA: Vell, nefer mind yourrr nyame. Ve do dis test anyvay.

Body flinches as SONYA *applies paste to chest before affixing suction cup attached to electrocardiogram wire.*

SONYA: Oooo iss cold, dis leetle pyaste, bot nyecessary to poot on brrreast.

NADYA: Brrreeeze diply, brrreeeze diply meester vot's-yourrr-nyame, so it vill rrregister nice on machine.

RADIO *makes protesting noises. Electrocardiogram printout begins to appear on the* BROADCASTERS' *screen.* SONYA *and* NADYA *turn to look at it.*

SONYA: See? Hyou see, Nadya Leopovna? Just look at dat. Deed I not tell hyou?

NADYA: You deed not, Sonya Fyedorovna. You deed not say vun vord.

SONYA: Never-de-less he hass it. De pyatient hass de vurst form of de disease and hyere is de prrroof.

NADYA: (*Looking in disbelief*) Nyet, nyet, Hwho vould beleef such a t'ing . . . bot you rrright again. De leetle line neverrr lies.

SONYA: Dere it iss. Black and vite. De old mon hass not <u>vun symptom</u> in de <u>hear-rrt</u>. Not <u>vun</u>.

NADYA: (*Still marveling*) Verrry <u>serrrious</u>, Sonya Fyedorovna.

SONYA: <u>Verrry</u> serrrious, Nadya Leopovna. (*Shakes her head*) Dis rrrotten old mon has de healthiest hearrrt I everrr saw.

The body on the table turns its face toward us grinning luridly and we see that it is DR. REICH *got up to resemble* ADOLF HITLER. *Immediate blackout on everything but the body's face and* EDMUND *the skeleton, who lingers a bit, in a Radioactive way. Then both images gutter out.*

Upstage Center:

HITLER B.: (*Unctuously*) And now, ladies and gentlemen, we'll pause for a station break. Although this program is broadcast without commercial interruption, we'd like to suggest that during this time you might want to refresh yourselves with a glass of Pet Evaporated Milk or perhaps start that load of laundry you've been postponing all week with just a little of our sponsor's miraculously mild detergent, Rinso Blue.

REICH B.: (*Disdainful look at the* HITLER B.) We'll return to bring you the last of THE LAST OF HITLER in approximately five minutes.

End of Part I

The Entre-acte

As the Audience files out to drink, to relieve itself, or simply to quit the theatre, Wagnerian music swells once again from the Radio—which might appear to enlarge a little with every crescendo.

Stage Left:

Lights up a bit STAGE LEFT *where* NADYA, SONYA, *and the body have vanished without a trace. We see* DR. REICH *leafing through his library.* EDMUND *the Skeleton hangs in a very lively position on his handsome rack. The bust of Wagner appears unusually prominent—perhaps it glows suggestively from within.*

DR. REICH *chooses a volume of Nietzsche, goes to stand by the bust of Wagner, changes his mind or merely his direction, unhooks* EDMUND (*who might seem to struggle a bit*) *and sits down, facing front, with skeletal* EDMUND *on one knee and the volume of Nietzsche on the other. Throughout their conversation,* DR. REICH *continues to manipulate* EDMUND *and to mime the ventriloquism.*

DR. REICH: Edmund old boy.

EDMUND: What is it now, Reich.

DR. REICH: I want you to hear what Friedrich Nietzsche has to say about Richard Wagner.

EDMUND: Oh oh. I think I'd rather listen to the Radio.

DR. REICH: (*Leafing through the book*) Where is it, now? Ah, <u>here</u> we are.

EDMUND: I think I'm missing an important appointment, Reich.

DR. REICH: Quiet, Edmund. Listen to what the great Nietzsche said. (*Clears his throat*) "I dislike all music that has no higher ambition than to persuade the nerves. Wagner's music is simply bad music, perhaps the worst that has ever been made. He wants effect, he wants nothing but effect. He has, in this respect, the unscrupulousness which everyone possesses who is connected with the stage." (*Slight pause while* DR. REICH *turns slightly to glance at the* HITLERS STAGE RIGHT) Well what do you think of <u>that</u>, Edmund?

EDMUND: I think I'd rather snack on your communion wafers, Reich.

He tries to extract something from DR. REICH's *breast pocket.*

DR. REICH: <u>Edmund</u>. Stop that. The wafers are for the quintuplets.

EDMUND: (*Provocatively*) I just wonder where you got all that Jewish blood from.

DR. REICH: What are you talking about, Edmund.

EDMUND: Oh come off it, Reich. <u>Every</u>one knows communion wafers are made from the blood of Jewish children.

DR. REICH: (*Warning*) That's quite enough of that kind of talk.

EDMUND: OK, OK. Listen doc, I got some great jokes for you.

DR. REICH: (*Stiffly*) What do you mean jokes Edmund.

EDMUND: Listen to <u>him</u>. I mean <u>jokes</u>, Reich. Snappy little stories to make you smile.

DR. REICH: Oh yes, yes, <u>those</u>. Of course.

EDMUND: Well here we go with the first joke. I need some light on the carpals for this one, please.

Lights spot EDMUND's *fingerbones so that their shadow seems to be cast on the* BROADCASTERS' *screen.* DR. REICH *turns* EDMUND *sideways so that the right hand bones appear to be the top shadows, the left hand bones the bottom ones. In fact, the image should be created with a short film. The five spread fingers of the left hand point upward, the five fingers of the right hand point downward and are wiggled as in the illustration. During this little shadow play, the* BROADCASTERS *are earnestly engaging in a round of cat's cradle with the* HITLER BROADCASTER's *string. Lights spot their hands as well. Here is the image* EDMUND's *carpals should make:*

EDMUND: OK Reich. What's this? (DR. REICH *is silent*) Give up? (DR. REICH *nods re-luctantly*) It's the five quintuplets under the showers. (EDMUND *turns his left*

thumb downward) OK now. What's <u>this</u>? (DR. REICH *is again dumb*) One of them just bent over to pick up the soap. Ha ha ha. Did you get it, Reich? Did you understand? She's in the showers and she just bent over to pick up a bar of <u>soap</u>.

DR. REICH: (*Sighing*) I understand it, Edmund. I <u>always</u> understand <u>that</u> joke.

The moment DR. REICH's *last line is delivered, the* HITLER BROADCASTER *brings his hands together in a sharp sound. The game of cat's cradle is over. As soon as the hand sound is heard, dim figures of supposititious Jews of every identifiable class appear in little pools of light behind the suddenly immobile* EDMUND *and* DR. REICH. *They all concentrate on the same action—which is to raise every shade in the laboratory.* NADYA LEOPOVNA *appears as a shtetl grandmother who spits three times before raising a window shade (The Fuehrer salute is still behind it); the* REICH BROADCASTER *appears as a pushcart vendor whose cart is heaped with old eyeglasses, watches, gold fillings, etc. He goes straight to a collecting cabinet and begins to fill it with what he has in his cart; then he wheels over to the* HITLER BROADCASTER, *puts on a veil, and the two* BROADCASTERS *appear as a rich wedding couple whose groom (the* HITLER B.) *continually mimes the breaking of wineglasses under his foot, and whose bride (the* REICH B.) *continually rolls up one of* DR. REICH's *body charts, which continually forms a chupa over the heads of the couple.* SONYA FYEDOROVNA *plays a current inmate of Dachau (still in stripes) whose numbered arm is horribly illuminated as she reaches for a pair of eyeglasses from the pushcart in order to see* DR. REICH's *eye chart before she rolls it up.*

The activity by the supposititious Jews should be extremely brief, extremely intense, extremely illuminating. It might be intercalated with little flashes of EVA STAGE RIGHT *at the oven or* ADOLF *in the shower, but, in any case, it must give the effect of two minutes in the dream life of a whole culture. It ends abruptly with a blackout on everything but* EDMUND *who fades, as usual, more slowly than anyone else. Wagner doesn't fade at all. His bust is left glimmering, his music (or, preferably, music like his) comes up loudly on the Radio, which again appears to expand to accommodate it. The* HASSID, *more or less defeated, crawls offstage.*

End of Entre-acte

Part II

The House:

The House lights flicker uncertainly; there is confusion in the House.

Those members of the Audience who were trapped in their seats for the Entre-Acte will not know if the play is over. Those members of the Audience who left their seats before the Entre-Acte began and are now returning will wonder if they have re-entered the right play. This confusion is salubrious and should be encouraged in every way. The BROADCASTERS *will clarify the situation when they begin to speak.*

Upstage Center:

The Wagnerian music stops abruptly and the Radio, in the absense of the HAS-
SID, *begins to adjust itself. The dial selector moves up and down, scanning the
field, catching parts and particles of soap commercials as it goes. It seems about to
accede to some monologue from* DR. REICH, *who is adjusting his body behind the
desk* STAGE LEFT *with the apparent intention of reading from a sort of scroll.* DR.
REICH *will not be fully lit until the* REICH BROADCASTER *announces him.*

Stage Right:

EVA *is in the painful stages of preparing a meal.* ADOLF *is plugged into the
Radio, but dozing.* EVA *wears conspicuous makeup and toys, from time to time,
with a pair of rhinestone-studded sunglasses with which she conceals an apparent
headache. She continues to check the pans, rattle a few pots, and sniff suspiciously
at her oven.* EVA *and* ADOLF *will not be visible until the* HITLER BROADCASTER *announces them.*

Upstage Center:

HITLER B.: Welcome, ladies and gentlemen, to the second part of THE LAST OF
HITLER, brought to you directly from postwar (*city of performance*) without
commercial interruption by our sponsors Pet Milk and Rinso Blue.

REICH B.: (*Hand over mike*) What in god's name <u>is</u> Rinso Blue?

HITLER B.: (*Ignoring him*) We last left Nadya Leopovna and Sonya Fyedorovna,
nurses to the most famous quintuplets in North America, up to no good in Dr.
Reich's laboratory . . .

REICH B.: But they're gone now and the mysterious doctor has repossessed his research and sits quietly at his desk, reading from a sort of scroll.

HITLER B.: In the Hitlers' Kozy Kabin, a meal is being prepared . . .

REICH B.: (*Portentously*) When suddenly Dr. Reich gets up and turns the Radio
dial to a very familiar program . . .

Stage Left:

Carrying his scroll with him, DR. REICH (*very <u>un</u>-suddenly*) *goes to the Radio,
clicks the dial, then returns to his desk. He reacts with some annoyance to the
sound of* JOHN COLE's *voice.*

Upstage Center:

The MARY LEE TAYLOR SHOW *begins immediately.*

JOHN COLE: Good morning, ladies and gentlemen. It's 10:00 A.M. B-U-L-O-V-A
Bulova standard watch time and once again John Cole has the pleasure of announcing that another Mary Lee Taylor Radio Demonstration is in progress

in the Pet Milk Kitchen. <u>This</u> morning we bring you part two of Mary Lee Taylor's program, How To Cook A Kosher Chicken. And here to tell you about it is Pet Milk's Own Mary Lee Taylor.

MARY LEE: Thank you, John Cole. And good morning once again to my nice Radio Audience. As you know, this is our How To Cook A Kosher Chicken Show and I have been doing some <u>very</u> interesting research into the quaint customs of the quiet people for whom kosher (*she give it the "osh" of Oshkosh*) chicken is the staff of life.

JOHN COLE: <u>Quiet</u> people? Now Mary Lee Taylor. When have you last heard Jews being <u>quiet</u>.

MARY LEE: Well, John Cole. To be perfectly honest, I can't say that I've <u>ever</u> heard Jews.

JOHN COLE: What about Eleanor Roosevelt, Mary Lee? I guess you've heard <u>Eleanor</u> <u>Roosevelt</u>.

MARY LEE: Why, John Cole. I didn't know Eleanor <u>Roose</u>velt was Jewish.

JOHN COLE: That's what they say, Mary Lee. They all say Eleanor Roosevelt is a Jew.

MARY LEE: My, my, isn't that interesting. As you know, Radio Audience, John Cole often interjects his thoughts on current events into our broadcasts and I hope you enjoy his special knowledge as much as <u>I</u> do.

JOHN COLE: Let's get back to that chicken, Mary Lee. My mouth is still watering from last week. (*Drools audibly*)

MARY LEE: Well, John Cole, we <u>will</u> get back to that chicken, but what I want you <u>and</u> my nice Radio Audience to remember is that it's a <u>kosher</u> chicken— and that makes <u>all</u> the difference. You see, John Cole, <u>kosher</u> chickens are not like <u>other</u> chickens.

JOHN COLE: Of course not, Mary Lee. <u>Kosher</u> chickens are food for <u>Jews</u>.

MARY LEE: Well, John, (*A little laugh*) it's a little more complicated than that and I'd like to explain the term kosher to you <u>and</u> to my nice Radio Audience.

JOHN COLE: (*Testily*) Explain as much as you like Mary Lee Taylor, as long as you <u>cook</u> the darned thing. It's almost B-U-L-O-V-A Bulova <u>lunchtime</u>, you know.

MARY LEE: Now John Cole. You know my cooking is usually worth waiting for.

JOHN COLE: (*Slurps and drools*) You're absolutely right there, Mary Lee Taylor. Take your B-U-L-O-V-A time. Heh heh heh.

MARY LEE: Kosher, or koshér as the Jewish people sometimes call it, refers to a way of killing animals for human consumption.

JOHN COLE: (*Interjects*) Well, Mary Lee, I guess this part of the program should be called how to <u>kill</u> a kosher chicken, not how to <u>cook</u> a kosher chicken.

MARY LEE: (*Between her teeth*) That's very clever, John Cole. I hope my nice Radio Audience enjoys your sense of humour as much as I do. (*Resumes*) For koshering, the Jewish people say the slaughtering knife has to be so sharp that you can kill the animal with one quick cut.

The HITLER BROADCASTER *takes a real interest in this part of the* MARY LEE TAYLOR SHOW. *He reacts to her descriptions of koshering (i.e. Drawing a finger across his throat to illustrate her last line about the quick kill), strains to hear* MARY LEE's *exchanges with* JOHN COLE, *and does many illustrative bits of business with his string throughout.*

JOHN COLE: <u>I</u> never had a knife that sharp, did you, Mary Lee?

MARY LEE: (*Ignores him*) And the Jewish people say you can't shoot the animal. Shooting is <u>definitely</u> not allowed. You have to cut its throat in the presence of a . . . (*Hesitates, then mispronounces it*) . . . rābbi.

JOHN COLE: Ha ha ha. You just <u>try</u> sneaking up on a chicken with a rabbi and a knife and cutting its throat, Mary Lee. Be a darn sight easier to cut the <u>rabbi's</u> throat.

MARY LEE: And then the Jewish people say you have to put the animal in salt water to drain all the blood out of its body.

JOHN COLE: Jews <u>hate</u> blood, Mary Lee.

MARY LEE: Of course, not every animal can be used for koshering. Some animals are kosher, and some are not. Horses aren't kosher. Animals with split hooves are. Sea fish without scales or sea animals who . . . uh . . . evacuate in their shells aren't kosher.

JOHN COLE: (*Scornfully*) <u>Evacuate</u>? I'm going to evacuate to a French restaurant if we don't get to cooking this chicken <u>real</u> <u>soon</u>, Mary Lee.

MARY LEE: Why, John Cole. I do believe you're more impatient than ever. You're drooling right down on to your tie.

JOHN COLE: (*Plaintively*) All this talk about Jewish people is making me hungry, Mary Lee.

MARY LEE: Now, now, it won't be long, John Cole. You know how I like to keep my nice Radio Audience informed. Now where was I? Oh yes. Did you know, John Cole, that fertilized eggs aren't kosher? The ones with that little speck of blood in them?

JOHN COLE: (*Proof of the pudding*) I've said it a million times, Mary Lee. <u>Jews hate blood</u>. They won't eat blood with anything. And you know what <u>that</u> means, Mary Lee Taylor?

MARY LEE: Why, I don't know that I <u>do</u> know what that means, John Cole.

JOHN COLE: It <u>means</u>, Mary Lee, that Jewish people have to wait six hours after eating a lamb patty to drink a glass of buttermilk. And <u>then</u> they go and drink that milk in a different kitchen from the kitchen they ate the lamb patty in. I heard it on the Radio. All Jews have <u>two</u> <u>kitchens</u>. Can you beat it? That's why they have to make so much money.

MARY LEE: (*Regaining control of her program*) Well, now, let me tell <u>you</u> something, John Cole. If a butter knife from one Jewish kitchen happens to touch a piece of meat from the other Jewish kitchen, the Jewish people <u>in</u> that kitchen have to run outside and stick that knife in the ground to purify it, to keep it kosher. It's an awesome thought, isn't it, Radio Audience. All your Jewish neighbors with their backyards full of silverware.

JOHN COLE: <u>Filthy</u> I call it. No wonder everyone around here is sick. It's a known fact, Mary Lee. Jews spread infection. That's what my mother always said.

MARY LEE: I guess the Germans felt just like your mother did, John Cole.

JOHN COLE: Why I guess they did, Mary Lee. Of course the Germans went about it all wrong. You know what <u>I</u> always say, Mary Lee.

MARY LEE: No, John Cole. What <u>do</u> you always say.

JOHN COLE: Well, Mary Lee. <u>I</u> always say a <u>gun</u> is the only way to kill anything you hunt. (*Brightly*) Jewish people included.

Stage Left:

On MARY LEE TAYLOR's *line,* "Some animals are kosher and some are not," DR. REICH *begins to read very fast and low in a singsong voice from the scroll he's holding. (It is the Mishnah) He rocks as he reads. He should finish on John Cole's line,* "That's what my mother always said." *Intelligibility is secondary to effect here; the only word that needs to come through is* "blood." *With the first sentence of the Mishnah, the* HASSID *appears and stands quietly by the Radio.*

DR. REICH: The law of the covering up of the blood is binding both in the Land of Israel and outside the Land, both during the time of the Temple and after the time of the Temple, for unconsecrated beasts but not for animal offerings.

　　If the blood was mixed with water but still has the appearance of blood, it must be covered up; if the blood was mixed with wine, this is looked upon as though it was water.

　　If the blood was mixed with the blood of cattle or of an animal that is still living, this is looked upon as though it was water. Rabbi Judah says: Blood cannot make other blood of no effect.

　　Splashings of blood and blood that remains on the knife must be covered up.

　　With what may they cover and with what may they not cover up the blood? They may cover the blood up with fine dung or with fine sand, with lime or with pieces of potsherd. Rabbi Simeon ben Gamaliel laid down a general rule: They may cover up the blood with aught in which they can grow plants; they may not cover up the blood with aught in which they cannot grow plants.

Upstage Center:

REICH B.: (*Covers mike with his hand*) For godssake what's going on with these meshugeneh . . . uh, these crazy Americans?

HITLER B.: (*Covers mike with his hand*) If that old hag doesn't cook the chicken soon, we'll have to scramble her signal.

MARY LEE: And now, Radio Audience, the recipe you and John Cole have been waiting for: How To Cook A Kosher Chicken. And remember, as you follow my instructions, Mary Lee Taylor will be cooking right along with you.

Stage Right:

Lights up fully on EVA, *who has a chicken and who begins, automatically, to follow* MARY LEE TAYLOR's *instructions.*

Upstage Center:

MARY LEE: (*The voice is consciously slowed so that hundreds of homemakers can imitate her instructions*) HOW TO COOK A KOSHER CHICKEN. Grasp chicken firmly by the neck. Grasp chicken by the neck. Swing it, <u>swing</u> it three times around your head. Swing chicken three times around your head. Pluck all feathers. Pluck all feathers and reserve for future use. Sever head and neck from body. Sever head and neck from body. Remove inner organs with particular attention to bladder. Reserve bladder for future use. Grasp the severed head firmly and remove gold fillings. Remove gold fillings and reserve for future use.

Stage Right:

EVA *follows the cooking instructions automatically until she realizes she is searching the head and neck of a chicken for gold fillings and eyeglasses and, shrieking: "*<u>Eye</u>glasses! <u>Gold</u> <u>fill</u>ings!,*" she flings the chicken in the direction of the Radio. It hits the* HASSID, *who scuttles behind the Radio in terror.*

Upstage Center:

HITLER B.: (*Pulls his string tightly around the neck of a toy chicken*) I <u>got</u> her! I <u>got</u> her, by god! The <u>last</u> thing the Fuehrer needs is another <u>cooking</u> lesson.

Heavy static from the MARY LEE TAYLOR SHOW.

REICH B.: I'm sorry, ladies and gentlemen, but we're having some transmission problems. We ask you to be patient while they're being corrected.

HITLER B.: Let us return to supper time at the Hitler's Kozy Kabin.

Stage Right:

ADOLF *sleeps with his telescope in his lap.*

EVA: Adolf. Adolf. Wake up. The soup is ready.

ADOLF: (*In a stupor*) Soup?

EVA: <u>Vegetable</u> soup, Adolf. Just as you like it.

ADOLF: (*Removes headset greedily*) With cabbage, liebchen. Does it have <u>cab-bage</u>.

EVA: There is no cabbage in this part of the country Adolf.

ADOLF: (*Hopefully*) Potatoes, then. A few potatoes?

EVA: Potatoes don't grow in warm climates Adolf. The newspapers all say that.

ADOLF: (*Discouraged but pursuant*) Lima beans, liebchen. Surely you made it with lima beans.

EVA: It's a beet soup Adolf. Remember how you used to like beets.

ADOLF: (*Slower, less certain*) No . . . no . . . (*Hopeful again*) . . . uh . . . Beets have sugar in them, don't they liebchen? A great deal of sugar?

EVA: A dangerous amount, Adolf. I read it in the newspaper.

ADOLF: (*Satisfied*) Ahhh. Wonderful. Wonderful. (*He wheels up to the small dining table and shudders*) You know, liebchen, it's in the stars. It's really all in the stars.

EVA: (*Wrapping her fringed shawl around him*) Here Adolf. Take my shawl. You're shivering with fever.

ADOLF: And my cap, Eva. Bring the cap. My head is very bad. Covering up the head relieves headache. I heard it on the Radio.

EVA *hands* ADOLF *a brimless cap, which he settles on the back of his head. He looks now very like a Jew about to pronounce the Sabbath blessing and, in fact, he bows his head momentarily—but it is only to smell the soup before him.*

ADOLF: Ummm. What a smell that is Eva. It's the <u>salt</u>. You use more salt in your soup than my mother did. Ahhhh.

Upstage Center:

The HASSID *appears from wherever he has crawled to, eyes fixed in horrified attention at the spectacle of* ADOLF HITLER *in a talis and yarmulke.*

The BROADCASTERS' *screen begins, once again, to show slides or films of invasive forces; bacteria, armies of ants, etc. If the lips in the Radio's glass pocket are operative, they should be slightly out of synchronization with the following narration by the* BROADCASTERS. *The effect should be that of an inexpertly dubbed foreign language film. Lights down* STAGE RIGHT.

REICH B.: Despite certain clandestine attempts to contain it, the plague spread throughout all of Western Europe. We watched it march into Czechoslovakia, into Poland, it conquered France, Bulgaria, Rumania, but seemed always to stop at the edge of the sea.

HITLER B.: Some people said that salt water washed away the infection.

REICH B.: Even before the war, it was rumoured that Eva Braun, (*Corrects himself*), that Hitler's secret lover had contracted the disease. Given her constant exposure to the source of the infection, this was not surprising to any of us.

Stage Left:

DR. REICH: (*Looks suddenly from his scroll, a dreamy tone*) I see her lying on a bed of seaweed, those opalescent scales spotted and drying in the sun, the silvery slits behind her ears opening convulsively in the rhythm of her headache, trying to suck oxygen from water that is no longer there. (*Goes back to his scroll*)

Upstage Center:

HITLER B.: Hitler's mother had the infection in its most extreme manifestation. It found its painful way into her breast. (*Slight pause*) I often imagine him as an infant suckling that cankered dug. And I have wondered <u>many</u> <u>times</u> if the growing of him in her womb for those nine months was not the first symptom of her (*Corrects himself*) . . . of <u>our</u> fatality.

Pause.

REICH B.: Did you ask the name of the infection? Did someone inquire for the source of the disease? The answer is always the same, my friends.

Slight pause.

HITLER B.: It is Hitler, of course.

Full pause. Radio lips are synchronized with the next line—and the HITLER BROADCASTER *grins broadly for it.*

HITLER B.: The answer is <u>always</u> Hitler.

REICH B.: (*Ludicrous tone*) And, once again, in Dr. Reich's laboratory, Nadya and Sonya are conducting a private investigation . . .

Stage Left:

Lights down on DR. REICH, *who is asleep at his desk, forehead on hand, downstage. Lights up (follow spots) on* NADYA *and* SONYA, *who have turned from playing doctor to playing detective. They giggle fiendishly as they ransack the doctor's pa-*

pers, nod excitedly as they find his Mishnah, and whoop joyfully as they come upon a pair of striped pyjamas (Auschwitz issue) at the bottom of a file case. Breaking and entry is obviously their regular entertainment.

Upstage Center:

As NADYA *and* SONYA *cull the laboratory, the* BROADCASTERS *have the following conversation, hands covering their mikes.*

HITLER B.: You know, I never get tired of listening to those quintuplets.

REICH B.: If your little Wulf would climb down from the transmitter, we might hear <u>more</u> of them.

HITLER B.: (*Ignores him*) They <u>did</u> sound a little off tonight, though. And someone must have put cement in their underskirts. I could hear the damn things crackling all through the show.

REICH B.: Perhaps they heard the news.

HITLER B.: <u>What</u> news.

REICH B.: (*Happy to be the bearer of bad tidings*) The six o'clock news, Mr. Broadcaster. We have an infection here. Children are dropping like flies.

HITLER B.: (*Interested*) Is that so?

REICH B.: There's a little girl in (*Local name*) hospital right now who's twisted up like a . . . how do you say . . . pretzel. The infection went straight to her brain.

HITLER B.: (*Impressed*) Is <u>that</u> <u>so</u>?

REICH B.: That's how it starts. First, a few red spots . . .

HITLER B.: (*Joins in joyfully*) Then the head begins to ache . . .

REICH B.: The body stiffens . . .

HITLER B.: (*Happy as a clam*) The temperature rises . . .

REICH B.: After that, you might as well say kaddish . . . uh, deliver the eulogy.

HITLER B.: (*Suddenly irritable*) Why don't you button your lip. You're giving me a headache . . . (*Stops short*)

REICH B.: (*With malicious interest*) What did you say?

HITLER B.: Nothing. I didn't say a thing.

REICH B.: (*Again, with malice*) Is that a . . . <u>rash</u> there on your hand?

HITLER B.: (*Pulls his hand away*) It's a <u>heat</u> rash. The microphone's too hot. (*To distract*) Ten to one that infection started with the Jews.

REICH B.: (*Ironically*) Naturally. <u>Every</u>thing starts with the Jews.

The Radio crackles.

HITLER B.: (*Thrilled with the diversion*) Kee-rist. It's Wulf on the transmitter again. I'm going to <u>murder</u> that boy.

REICH B.: I can't remember the reception <u>ever</u> being this bad. I'm afraid the wires are damp.

HITLER B.: Well, it's a damn shame about that infection.

REICH B.: (*Rattles his script*) Dr. Reich says here that it's an imported disease. He says he saw it start up in Europe twenty years ago.

HITLER B.: (*Sagely*) Plenty of Jews in Europe <u>then</u>. (*Looks up at slight noise*) What the . . . (*A report*) Look at that. The sound man just unhooked little Wulf from the transmitter and he's dragging him down the ladder. Look at Wulf <u>kick</u>. What a boy. Now he's sinking his teeth into the sound man's arm. <u>Look</u> at him. What a <u>boy</u>. By god, he's going straight for the sound man's throat. Here they come clawing and scratching. Look at . . . My god. Look at <u>Wulf</u>. He's covered with . . . spots. He's got <u>big</u>, <u>red</u>, <u>spots</u> <u>all</u> <u>over</u>!

Stage left:

Lights up fully on STAGE LEFT *as* NADYA *backs into* EDMUND (*glowing softly as usual*) *and gives a shriek that awakens* DR. REICH.

SONYA: A heeedeeous death awaits yourrr stooopidity, Nadya Leopovna! (*Faces* DR. REICH *dripping with sweetness*) Oooo doktor. Excussse pliss my clumsy friend hyere. Ve haf no intyention of waking you.

NADYA: Da, da doktor. Isss imporrrtant for famoooss currre dat hyou get beeyooty slip. (*She pushes his head back down on the desk*) Put head back on flat surrr-face and ve vill go.

DR. REICH: (*Extricates himself*) Ladies, <u>ladies</u>! What are you doing in my labora-tory at this advanced hour?

SONYA: (*Always a quick thinker*) We herrre to leave you note on condition of qvin-tuplets, of courrrse doktor.

NADYA: Eggsactly rrright, doktor. Verrry suspicious symptoms appearring in darrr-ling little girrrls.

SONYA: Eeets the pirogis, doktor. I tell Nadya Leopovna rrrepeatedly, you cannot stoff leetle childrren with rrraw dough and expect them to haf beeyutiful skyin.

DR. REICH: (*Fully awake*) The skin. Their skin is affected?

NADYA: Dats rrright, doktor. Dots. They haf dots. Five leetle girrrls coverrred with—how you say hyere—(*Triumphant*) peenk polka dots.

SONYA: Da, doktor. Strrrange bot trrrue. (*Double-edged*) Nadya Leopovna slaves overrr hot oven for darrrling leetle childrrren and rresult is serrious allerrr-genic rrrreaction!

DR. REICH *stands up in horror.*

NADYA: And dots arre not all, doktor.

SONYA: (*Maliciously*) You so rrright, Nadya Leopovna. Besides loooking like chip pyiece of materrial, doktor, leetle girrrls developing <u>otherrr</u> strange rreactions to Nadya Leopovna's cooking.

NADYA: Not my cooking vun leetle bit, Sonya Fyedorovna! Hyou know perrr-fectly well iss not my coooking making dots on leetle darrlings.

SONYA: (*Overrides*) Otherr symptoms developed by qvintuplets, doktor, iss beeg pain in leetle heads.

DR. REICH: They have <u>head</u>aches? They have <u>spots</u> and <u>headaches</u>?

NADYA: Isss trrue doktor. Marie and Emilie both complain of bad headache. They say sounds of Rrradio go right through theirr brrains.

SONYA: But you shouldn'y worry doktor. We fix everything. Problem is solved.

NADYA: Da, doktor. You alvays say water iss curre for every thing . . .

SONYA: So naturlich ve poot qvintuplets in bathtub.

NADYA: Da, da. Cheeldrren splashing hoppily avay rright now doktor.

DR. REICH: (*In horror*) You left the quintuplets alone in the <u>water</u>? The five most famous children in the world are now unattended in a <u>bathtub</u>?

SONYA: Come to theenk, Nadya Leopovna, qvintuplets <u>are</u> alone.

NADYA: Perhops not such grrreat idea to abandon childrren in water, Sonya Fye-dorovna.

SONYA: Goood thinking, Nadya Leopovna. (*To* DR. REICH) Don't vorry doktor. We haf made prrrofessional decision to go rrright now and drrrain tub before disaster strikes. Come, Nadya Leopovna.

NADYA: (*As they exit quarreling*) I alvays said, Sonya Fyedorovna. I alvays said wa-terr is hyighly unnatural element for small chilldrren.

DR. REICH *collapses at his desk, then wheels around as the Radio crackles again. He picks up his microscope and as he looks into it, a slide of one of Francis Bacon's self-portraits appears on a shade in his office.*

DR. REICH: (*Low and obloquial*) There is no progress, of course. Simply an ex-change of conditions. (*Lights up* STAGE RIGHT *on* ADOLF HITLER *who rallies, waving his telescope for this next line, which he says in unison with* DR. REICH)

DR. REICH: (*Disillusioned*) The idea of an advance in a <u>forward</u> direction is <u>absurd</u>.	ADOLF: (*frantic*) The idea of an advance in a <u>forward</u> direction is <u>inspiring</u>.

On the last word, they turn slightly towards each other, then ADOLF *lets the telescope sink to his lap.*

DR. REICH: (*Repeats*) . . . <u>absurd</u>—and far more suitable to the linear conceptions of plane geometry than to the web of confusions against which life beats its hopeless wings.

Radio crackles once again and DR. REICH *turns to face it.*

Upstage Center:

Some illumination on the Radio before which the HASSID *is standing impassively. He does not attempt to touch the dial. Another crackle from the Radio and the* MARY LEE TAYLOR SHOW *concludes itself.* STAGE RIGHT, ADOLF *and* EVA *eat their meal throughout the broadcast, occasionally responding with their bodies or attitudes to a word or a phrase.*

JOHN COLE: (*Expansive and affable as after a good meal, he chomps and slurps audibly as he speaks*) Well, (*Slurp*) Radio Audience, this is John Cole for the Pet Milk Kitchen Hour once again. I understand that, due to transmission difficulties, etc., you missed the best part of our (*Chomp, grind*) broadcast this morning. Radio transmission is a real problem when the wires get wet. Must be showering over the whole Western world this morning. I know if Mary Lee Taylor were still with the show she'd be just as disappointed as I am that you missed her moving description of the best way to render chicken fat or schmalz as the Jewish people say. And I know <u>I'm</u> disappointed that you missed our lively discussion over the correct oven temperature for cooking kosher chickens. I <u>do</u> want to say that my mother's point of view prevailed as it usually does—600 degrees for the first fifteen minutes and lots of salt. And I also want to say one more thing which I know will go a long way towards easing the shock of this morning's tragedy. My generous sponsors, the Pet Milk People, have promised me that the unfortunate accident occurring in the struggle over oven temperatures that resulted in the death of Mary Lee Taylor, America's most beloved homemaker, will not affect future broadcasting of the Mary Lee Taylor Show. (*The clipped suggestion of an SS accent in the next sentence*) My own mother, Klara Pölzl, was a renowned cook in the little Bavarian hamlet where she grew up and I am looking forward to demonstrating many of her favorite ethnic recipes to you in the weeks to come. As for now (*Slurp, lick, slurp, chomp*), I can only say that (*Drool, slurp*) this particular program has been a fitting memorial to America's favorite homemaker and the tastiest darn little chicken I ever had. I hope all of you in my Radio Audience followed the kosher chicken recipe a little closer than I did though. <u>I</u> forgot to take off Mary Lee's eyeglasses before I carved her up, and (*Belch, slurp*) they've sure given me one heck of a case of indigestion.

And now it's that B-U-L-O-V-A Bulova signoff time again and I'd like to leave my new Radio Audience with a final, inspirational thought. Mary Lee Taylor, wherever you are . . . we want you to know . . . that every week . . . at this time . . . we'll be lighting the ovens . . . just for you.

The HASSID *attacks the Radio dial, moving the selector frantically up and down. The half-phrases, the snatches of music, the static come this time not from the Radio but from the suddenly frozen characters present on stage—* DR. REICH, EDMUND, ADOLF, *and* EVA. ADOLF's *"Ahhhhh" of pleasure after finishing his meal might begin the mimesis by turning into what sounds like static from the Radio. The sounds should pass from one character to another like an electrical storm. The effect must be one of the Radio's pervasive voice having been finally and terribly internalized by the characters.*

REICH B.: (*Through the imitated Radio noises*) I'm sorry ladies and gentlemen, but we're having transmission problems once again. The dampness seems to have saturated the airwaves. We ask you to be patient. (*Covers the mike*) What in hell is <u>happening</u>?

The HASSID *finally tunes in to his favorite Radio station which brings us, once again, a fragment of the consultation between* ADOLF HITLER *and* DR. REICH. *During the consultation, the* HITLERS STAGE RIGHT *will be seen attempting some dessert;* ADOLF *occasionally straining to hear the Radio,* EVA *primping from time to time.* EDMUND STAGE LEFT *bounces expectantly on his rack and* DR. REICH STAGE LEFT *rolls another scroll (The Torah this time) and peruses his papers. Perhaps an occasional uniformed member of the Third Reich appears in a compromised position in* DR. REICH's *laboratory.*

ADOLF: Did you know, doktor, that the biblical story of Adam and Eve is a complete falsification.

DR. REICH: (*Soothingly*) Is that so Herr Hitler. Why don't you relax the neck a little more. I'm trying to <u>relieve</u> your headache, not encourage it.

ADOLF: Yes, yes doktor, the story of Adam and Eve was one of the many lies spread by the Elders of Zion.

DR. REICH: (*Sounds of note-taking continue*) You would perhaps be interested to tell me <u>your</u> version of the Creation Myth, Herr Hitler? And as you speak, I'm going to press very hard on your solar plexus. For the solar plexus is the seat of your sorrow, Herr Hitler.

ADOLF: Uh! Uh! I hope you are correct, doktor.

DR. REICH: (*Unctuous*) I <u>am</u> correct, Herr Hitler. All my researches have led me to this moment. And that is why my art takes precedence over your policy, Mein Fuehrer.

ADOLF: Uh! Uh! Why is that, Herr Doktor?

DR. REICH: Because sadness is a larger thing than social misery, Herr Hitler. So—much—larger. (*Punctuated by sounds of pressings on the abdomen*)

ADOLF: (*Quickly, terrified and gasping*) I will now tell you the true story of how god created the ur-parents in the Garden. Uh! Uh! Contrary to common belief, the first organ god made was the male bladder . . .

DR. REICH: (*Very excited*) I see it, I see it, I see the accursed head of the Dybbuk coming from your mouth! Indigestion be damned! You've got a devil inside you, Mein Fueher! A little more pressure and we'll have him out!

ADOLF: (*A long scream*)

The HASSID, *with a careless flick of the wrist, turns the Radio off.*

Stage Left:

EVA *appears briefly in a mermaid's tail to* DR. REICH, *who moistens his lips with water, then embraces her sexually, slowly, as his scrolls fall to the floor. The whole appearance must absolutely be in slow motion; the kind of terrified, unwilling slow motion that is experienced in a dream of hideous pursuit.*

Upstage Center:

As DR. REICH *and* EVA *embrace, the* BROADCASTERS *have the following exchange, hands covering their microphones.*

REICH B.: You know, she really is a beautiful woman. And everyone agrees. Even here in America. Look. Here's her picture on a seltzer bottle. (*Holds up bottle of White Rock*)

HITLER B.: Kee-rist. That's not <u>seltzer</u> you dummy. It's <u>soda</u>. It's <u>White Rock soda</u>. (*Viciously*) <u>Americans</u> call it <u>soda</u>.

And the White Rock Girl, looking remarkably like EVA BRAUN, *appears briefly on the* BROADCASTERS' *screen.*

Stage Right:

ADOLF *and* EVA, *finished with their meal, go to their respective mirrors and commence a kind of toilette.*

EVA: Adolf, Adolf, we forgot the candles.

ADOLF: Why candles on a Friday night, liebchen. It's not even dark yet.

EVA: To keep off the insects, Adolf. The mosquitoes are holding conventions here on the weekends. I'm sure these spots on my skin are mosquito bites. (*Then, coquettishly*) Adolf, I have a surprise for you. Close your eyes.

ADOLF: (*Very excited*) It's chocolate, isn't it Eva? You found me some German chocolate in this underdeveloped country.

EVA: Not exactly, liebchen. But it <u>is</u> something sweet. Keep the eyes <u>closed</u>, Adolf. I'm getting ready. (*She does her makeup*) You know, Adolf, I had the strangest dream last night. I was in the laboratory of Dr. Reich . . . (*Trails off; she's finished her makeup and she puts on a sheidl*) I'm ready. It's from Warsaw, Adolf, do you like it? I carried it all the way from Berlin hidden in my trunk. (*She puts her rhinestone sunglasses on*) <u>I</u> think it's <u>perfect</u> with the sunglasses.

ADOLF: Gott. Gott. The color of blood! You <u>know</u> how I hate blood, Eva.

EVA: But I thought you'd love it, Adolf. We never dress up anymore. See, I've put a little color on the lips; a little scent behind the ears. You know how I adore to have well-groomed people around me. It keeps up the spirits in this terrible heat.

ADOLF: A million times I've told you, Eva. Lipstick comes from the filth of sewers and perfume is made of boiled cat.

EVA: What am I to do, Adolf? My head aches constantly, my limbs are stiffening, these red spots on my skin won't go away. And you. You have your Radio, Adolf. Your telescope. You no longer embrace <u>me</u>.

ADOLF: Eva, it is forbidden to be touched by a woman during her menstruation. You know how the sight of blood affects me.

EVA: (*Rising panic*) Blood? Don't worry about <u>blood</u>, Adolf. Ever since we came to this horrible country my menstrual fluid has been as clear as sea water. I don't understand it. I'm dry as a bone.

ADOLF: Then drink, Eva. For godssake drink a little seltzer for the dryness and have a little compassion for <u>my</u> condition. Do you think the quintuplets carry on like this?

EVA: Little laboratory animals don't need cosmetics, Adolf. (*Malevolently*) Especially sick little laboratory animals. I read it in the newspapers. The quintuplets have caught something serious.

ADOLF: That's impossible, Eva. That traitor Reich watches them far too closely for anything to hap . . . (*Remembers something*) Perhaps I heard something like that on the Radio . . . But, no. It was the static. All I <u>hear</u> is static. That Radio must have been made in Italy.

EVA: (*With satisfaction*) Tokyo, Adolf. We ordered it from Tokyo before the Axis broke. (*Continues to examine her makeup*) Mussolini would <u>never</u> have sent us something that didn't work well. (*Provocatively*) A handsome man like that.

ADOLF: <u>Handsome</u>?! Mussolini <u>handsome</u>! With a name like a sauce for spaghetti and a nose like an orthodox Jew. (EVA *goes back to her cosmetics*) Eva, Eva, if you could only see the bodies of the animals from which your cosmetics are made. Have I ever told you about the day I visited the slaughterhouse in Linz?

EVA: (*Controlling a yawn*) Many times, Adolf, many times.

Upstage Center:

The HASSID *cannot bear another minute of this talk and switches the Radio once again to the consultation between* DR. REICH *and* ADOLF HITLER, *during which he stands impassively in front of the Radio.*

ADOLF: Yes, doktor, it was the Elders of Zion who infected our kultur with this dreck, this poison, this racial cancer.

DR. REICH: (*Note-taking sounds*) You see it, then, as a disease, Herr Hitler. Some . . . contamination that can be socially transmitted? How can it be transmitted, Herr Hitler. What are the signs of the cancer.

ADOLF: I will tell you, doktor.

The HASSID *turns immediately to profile, casting a huge black shadow on the Radio. He models for* ADOLF's *speech, moving or touching parts of his body as they are referred to.*

ADOLF: (*Nazi voice*) I will gladly tell you the signs. Just before the body begins to express the worst of the infection, the nose hooks and points downward, the lips swell and turn outward, the skin darkens, the left side—where the acquisitive instincts are located—begins to ache, and the shoulders start to shrug involuntarily. (*An admiring pause*) Our dear Wagner said it took five thousand years to develop these characteristics in the genetic chain of a race.

DR. REICH: Excuse me, Herr Hitler. You're referring to Richard Wagner the German-Jewish composer?

ADOLF: (*"Jewish" voice*) Yes, yes that's right! Mein old friend, mein hero, Richard Wagner-the-greatest-German-composer-he-should-rest-in-peace, used to say "Adolf, Adolf, takes five thousand years develop traits like that in human people. Relax a little. Enjoy. You have a little dirty blood, I have a little dirty blood. So what. Drink your seltzer. Eat your nice vegetables, Adolf. Be proud. Yes. We should be proud that in der ganse meshugeneh velt, we don't have more dirt in our blood. Remember Adolf," he used to say, "things could always be worse."

DR. REICH: (*In a neutral tone*) You remember that Richard Wagner said these things to you?

ADOLF: Of course, he said them to me. And much more than that, Herr Doktor. But that doesn't mean Wagner was correct. Oh no. Even genius has its flaws. Wagner, may he rest in peace, was much too easy on the Jews.

The HASSID *turns and tugs frantically on the Radio's electric cord—trying, unsuccessfully, to pull it out of wherever its socket is. Enormous static.*

REICH B.: (*Covers mike, holds left side*) Uh! This is awful.

HITLER B.: It's not only awful. It's <u>embarrassing</u>. Hitler was a great guy. A <u>really</u> <u>great</u> <u>guy</u>.

REICH B.: Not the <u>show</u>, you donkey, the <u>pain</u>. I have terrible pain in my left side.

HITLER B.: The Fuehrer always said cancer started on the left side of the body.

REICH B.: (*Vicious*) The <u>Fuehrer</u> should not deliver diagnoses without a medical license. And if I remember correctly, the <u>Fuehrer</u> had problems with his <u>own</u> left side.

HITLER B.: The Fuehrer's only problems were untrustworthy associates.

REICH B.: Ach. It's not enough to sit here in agony, underpaid by American soap merchants. I have also to listen to commercials for the Third Reich.

HITLER B.: (*Suddenly*) Where were you during the war?

REICH B.: <u>What</u> war. <u>Which</u> war.

HITLER B.: The BIG ONE. Hitler's war.

REICH B.: Ah, <u>Hitler's</u> war. I was in Poland, Mr. Detective. I was in Poland. . . . in detention. (*Points quickly to* HITLER BROADCASTER's *microphone hand*) What <u>are</u> those spots on your hand? (*And before* HITLER B. *can respond,* REICH B. *speaks quickly into his mike*) And back in Dr. Reich's laboratory, Edmund and the doctor discuss a sad event . . .

Stage Left:

Lights up again on EDMUND *and* DR. REICH *who approaches* EDMUND, *chair in hand, for one of their conversations. He unhooks* EDMUND *from the rack and sits down with him. Their exchange this time does not depend so much on the structure of jokes. Once they are seated,* EDMUND *bounces up and down on* DR. REICH's *knee.*

DR. REICH: Calm down, Edmund. Calm down, now. Think of your audience.

EDMUND: (*Demonically excited*) Oh boy oh boy oh boy! They're dead, Reich? Huh? <u>Huh</u>? The girls are really <u>dead</u>?

DR. REICH: It's terrible. The quintuplets succumbed to the plague tonight while I was in the laboratory. Edmund, will you stop <u>bouncing</u>? I didn't see them before they passed away. I have such trouble entering the nursery. (*Sighs*) The smell of infant . . . waste matter is not something I enjoy. But I have kept every one of their files, Edmund. Every one.

EDMUND: Gee that's great, Reich. Who needs those rotten kids, anyway. It's the <u>records</u> we want.

DR. REICH: (*Warning*) Edmund. Control yourself. (*In a sudden reverie*) I delivered them, you know. Pulled them from the womb of that screaming woman, covered with blood and urine . . . It was a wonderful thing about the quintuplets, Edmund, that not <u>one</u> of them resembled Adolf Hitler. Not <u>one</u> of them.

EDMUND: Babies are supposed to look like Winston Churchill, Reich. Or Eisenhower. You sure you got your dictators straight? For <u>my</u> money, the little rats were dead ringers for Emperor Hirohito.

DR. REICH: Edmund. <u>Please</u>. My work with those children is crucial to curing the terrible plague that has taken this country.

EDMUND: Really, Reich? I thought the plague <u>started</u> with the quintuplets.

DR. REICH: What are you talking about Edmund?

EDMUND: I heard it on the Radio, Reich. The quintuplets are Jewish. Or they <u>were</u> Jewish. Maybe it was . . . <u>half</u> Jewish.

DR. REICH: What has <u>that</u> got to do with it, Edmund.

EDMUND: C'mon Reich. Everybody knows that the infection started with the Jews.

DR. REICH: Edmund! I forbid you to speak like that!

EDMUND: Whatsa matter, Reich? You Jewish too?

DR. REICH: (*Silence*)

EDMUND *makes a* "say, look at <u>him</u>" *gesture.*

EDMUND: Say, Reich.

DR. REICH: What is it now, Edmund.

EDMUND: Where did you spend the War?

DR. REICH: What War, Edmund. Which War.

EDMUND: The BIG ONE, Reich. Hitler's War.

DR. REICH: Ah, <u>Hitler's</u> War. (*Pause*) I was in . . . Poland, Edmund.

EDMUND: (*Nazi voice*) Is that so, Herr Doktor Reich.

DR. REICH: I was in Poland . . . in detention.

EDMUND: You were in detention? And for what crime were you being detained, Herr Doktor Reich?

DR. REICH: For . . . racial impurities.

EDMUND: Sir.

DR. REICH: For racial impurities, <u>sir</u>.

EDMUND: Describe your duties in detention, swine.

DR. REICH: I cleaned the latrines, sir. Every day I cleaned the latrines of urine and fecal matter. And every night I had to clean myself for inspection.

EDMUND: What a story, Herr Doktor Reich. What a story. There was, of course, never any water in detention. So tell me, doktor, how did you manage to keep yourself clean?

DR. REICH: I . . . licked myself all over, <u>sir</u>. Every part of me that my tongue could reach I made clean. And every part that my tongue couldn't reach I . . . wiped on another Jew.

Immediate blackout on DR. REICH *and* EDMUND. *The* HASSID *rapidly switches the Radio to loud sounds of running water. Lights up on* EVA STAGE RIGHT *running water into a sink full of dishes, then down again.*

Upstage Center:

REICH B.: And once again, Nadya and Sonya are up to no good in Dr. Reich's laboratory.

Stage Left:

Lights up on NADYA *and* SONYA, *who are once again playing doctor with the body of* DR. REICH *got up to resemble* ADOLF HITLER. *This time they're taking turns pretending to look up a proctoscope inserted in the anus of the body.*

NADYA: I nefer recofer from death of little girrrls. Nefer, nefer, Sonya Fyedorovna.

SONYA: Life goes on, Nadya Leopovna. In tyeeth of terrrible infection, life goes on.

NADYA: Horrrible agony to looose little girrrls like that. I tell you I nefer recofe . . . Ooooooo. Look Sonya Fyedorovna. Loook at that.

SONYA: Nadya Leopovna. Nadya Leopovna. Hold the chicks. Hold the chicks or I vill nefer be capable to insert this pipe further in pooor old mon's rrrectum.

NADYA: Hold chicks yourselve, Sonya Fyedorovna. Iss dizgusting vork for voman. Iss vork forrr manooal laborrrrorrrr.

SONYA: OK Rrroyal Prrrincess. <u>I</u> hold chicks and <u>you</u> loook up pipe, you so smarrrt.

NADYA: Oooooh, nyet, nyet. Not my line, Sonya Fyedorovna. Not my medical speshoolty vun leetle bit.

SONYA: Ay yi yi, mooof out of vay, then. I tek ofer frrrom heeerr. You poosh pipe vun inch more it come out poor mon's brrain.

NADYA: (*Still looking*) Sonya Fyedorovna. Doo you see vat I see?

SONYA: How iss posssible? Rrroom only forrr vun eye on pipe at time.

NADYA: Vell, heeerrr. Haf gooood looook. Neferr in whole medical carrreeer did I see vun like dat.

SONYA: Vun <u>vat</u>, Nadya. Vat you spiking off.

NADYA: Just loook.

SONYA: (*Awestruck*) May I sufferrr strrrange death if I efer see <u>any</u>thing like dat beforrre.

NADYA: May you grow hairrr like monkey if you efer see anything like dat <u>again</u>.

SONYA: The bladderrr . . . (*She can hardly say it*) . . . Bladderrr . . . bladderrr of filthy old mon iss biggerr than two hearrrts.

NADYA: <u>Three</u> hearrrts, Sonya Fyedorovna. Bladderrr is biggerrr than <u>three</u> human hearrrts.

SONYA: You t'ink old mon vill burst?

NADYA: How do I know Sonya Fyedorovna? I am only nurse, thanks to god, only simple nurse and <u>not</u> complicated doktorrr.

Blackout on SONYA, NADYA, *and the body.*

Upstage Center:

The Radio tunes itself to the consultation between DR. REICH *and* ADOLF HITLER. *The* HASSID *introduces it with an ironic flourish.*

ADOLF: And it was just after Richard Wagner spoke to me for the last time—ach, what a dryness in the throat he left me with—that I found my Rhine Maiden, my little mermaid. And since that day, let me tell you doktor, we have never been out of the water together.

DR. REICH: Oh, what a happy story, Herr Hitler. Heart-warming, positively heart-warming. (*Slight pause*) Now I want you to follow my finger with your eyes. Ummm. No lateral movement whatsoever.

ADOLF: My strong point, Herr Doktor. I never deviate once I have decided on a policy.

DR. REICH: And, mein Fuehrer, let us discuss this lovely little fairy tale about you and Eva Braun. Is it true?

ADOLF: Not . . . precisely true, Dr. Reich. You see, certain changes in our economic condition produced a few—how shall I say it—headaches? in our relationship.

With a broad smile, the HASSID *turns the Radio down so only mutterings are audible under the following exchanges.*

HITLER B.: And back in Florida, Herr Hitler and his Frau continue their toilettes at home.

REICH B.: (*Hand over mike*) How can you say his "Frau." She was a <u>beautiful</u> <u>woman</u>. A <u>very</u> <u>beautiful</u> <u>woman</u>.

Stage Right:

ADOLF, *in bright light, swings his chair around the stage while looking intently into a hand mirror.* EVA, *faintly illuminated, continues her toilette.* ADOLF *looks up and speaks into his mirror, facing front. The* HITLER B., EDMUND, *and* DR. REICH *might mouth* ADOLF's *second line with him.*

ADOLF: The thing that I will never understand is . . . Do I still look like the Fuehrer? Do I really still look like the Fuehrer? The truth is . . . the truth is I was not meant to lead. The truth is . . . I was meant to serve. The truth is . . . everyone tells me . . . I look rather like a waiter.

EVA: (*"Jewish" voice*) Adolf! Enough, enough. As my grandfather used to say, "Hold up your dignity on the one hand and your pants on the other." If you had my problems . . . Look how my skin is spotted! Look how it lumps up! Mountains! Valleys! It looks like a map of Germany!

ADOLF: (*Cuts her off*) That slaughterhouse in Lindz was running in blood, Eva. They were beating animals to death with clubs. There was blood on the floor, on the knees of the butchers—but I changed all that. After my inspection, the blood was covered with fine sand and the animals were killed quickly with a sharp knife. (*Demonstrates*) Like that. And after my inspection everyone said: "Do not seek Adolf Hitler with your brains, you will find him with your heart."

Muttering from Radio stops.

EVA: (*An ironic look*) You know, Adolf, your posture is very bad. Look how stiff your spine is. President <u>Roose</u>velt never allowed himself to be photographed in a wheelchair.

ADOLF: (*Sighs*) President Roosevelt! A cancer should have taken Columbus before he discovered this awful country! (*Pause*) And when I returned from the slaughterhouse, and spoke before the Reichstag, the entire audience made sounds like the sea from the beginning of my speech to the end of it. (*He begins to rock slightly in his chair*) Beginning to end, Eva.

EVA: (*Turns to him wearing her sheidl and rhinestone sunglasses*) You know, I'm liking this wig more and more.

ADOLF: (*Hysterical*) Gott forbid there was any blood in the camps, Eva! We never had blood in the camps! Never! No trayfe. The solution was very clean.

We covered everything with fine sand and quicklime. And the trenches! The urine was cleaned from the trenches every day!

EVA: (*Very gently*) Adolf, Adolf, don't shout my darling. Shouting makes cancer in the throat. I read it in the newspapers. Why don't you listen to the Radio.

ADOLF *and* EVA *turn slowly to stare at the Radio, which illuminates fully and continues its expansion from "hardware" to "software."*

Upstage Center:

REICH B.: Dr. Reich's researches into the symptoms of the terrible plague revealed many truths to him. He was able to treat the viral strain that we all saw growing in Western Europe so many years ago. But the new genus, the new specie that crossed the salt waters to America . . . (*Sighs*) All his work with the quintuplets, all his studies of Hitler, could not stop the disease. He could only imagine dissolving the plague in some sterile solution. But what that solution might be . . . ? He did not know.

HITLER B.: (*Slowly*) The thing that I will never understand is . . . It was in us all the time. It was among us at every moment. This infection, this terrible plague, was always . . . one of <u>us</u>.

The HASSID *determinedly switches the Radio to the final consultation between* ADOLF HITLER *and* DR. REICH. *During this consultation, the Radio must become larger and more plastic. Smokestacks sprout slowly from the top of its cabinet.*

DR. REICH: And now, Herr Hitler, you must finish the dream for me. If I remember correctly, you haven't yet finished your dream.

ADOLF: ("*Jewish*" *voice*) <u>Any</u>thing, doktor, <u>any</u>thing to get your hands off my body. (*Clears his throat, regular voice*) I am in a room where nothing is dry. I lie on the damp floor on my back. Eva squats above me and I see that her scales are gone and her legs are divided again. I look up directly into her lower lips. You know what I mean doktor . . . doktor? (*Slight pause*) They curve and curl like the inside of a seashell. I am . . . <u>very</u> <u>excited</u> as I await the gift of the one sterile solution the body possesses. Suddenly, she rains a steady, golden stream near my mouth. In such a moment, I always feel she gives birth to my intentions. When all is finished, and I have begged her forgiveness for my vileness, we wash each other, tenderly, seriously, then separate as quickly as we can. I go back to my Radio and she swims away to whatever lower depths she inhabits when she is not with me. (*Pause. Nazi voice*) Herr Doktor Reich. What is the matter? You have stopped taking notes.

DR. REICH: Forgive me, mein Fuehrer. A sudden headache . . .

Static from the Radio.

REICH B.: The morning after the demise of the quintuplets, Dr. Reich himself was found dead in his laboratory, kneeling near Edmund, his favorite skeleton . . .

HITLER B.: A photograph of Eva Hitler when she was Eva Braun, clutched in his hand.

Slide of EVA BRAUN *appears on* BROADCASTERS' *screen.*

REICH B.: Some say the plague got him, for his body was very stiff.

HITLER B.: Others say it was the cancer the Fuehrer . . . (*Corrects himself*) Herr Hitler described that ended the doctor's life. (*Suggestively*) A cancer the doctor contracted when he was camp physician at Auschwitz.

Stage Left:

Lights illuminate the interiors of both EDMUND *the Skeleton and the bust of* Wagner *during the* BROADCASTERS' *narrative.*

Stage Right:

ADOLF *and* EVA *in fluid pools of light.* ADOLF *still in yarmulke and talis, holding the telescope in his hand. The headset dangles from the wheelchair.*

ADOLF: (*Low and awful, looking into his telescope*) The glass is clouded. I see nothing but . . . sand. (*"Jewish" voice*) Cover the mirror! Eva! Cover the windows! Tear your garments and close your heart! The children are dead, the children are dead! I never wanted a child, Eva, but think, think what we might have produced!

EVA: (*"Jewish" voice*) Adolf, Adolf. For a child you need sperm, you need eggs. No child can come from what I showered you with.

Instant blackout STAGE RIGHT. *Only the bust of Wagner and* EDMUND *glow softly in the dark of* STAGE LEFT.

Upstage Center:

DR. REICH's windows glow a lurid red and red streaks begin to colour the BROADCASTER's screen. At the moment the streaks join in a solid colour, the Radio proportions shift so that the eye level of the Audience drops and the Radio seems to be seen as from below. It turns to black against the red sky; it towers and obtrudes above us and its smokestacks are now horribly apparent. The whole front section opens like a furnace door. Inside, all is fire, a crematoria. The HASSID makes an attempt to tune the Radio. Crackling static, like the sounds of fire raging out of control, is all he can get. The HASSID moves STAGE RIGHT of the Radio and begins to doven, lips moving at last.

Stage Right:

Utter darkness. A match strikes and we see EVA *and* ADOLF *at the little dining table.* EVA *is lighting a Yahrzeit candle.* ADOLF's *head is bowed; his back, as at first, is towards us. He rocks and seems, perhaps, to be muttering the Kaddish. Tableau.*

Stage Left:

Accidental limbs of incidental Nazis dangle from cabinets which hold reliquaries of the Holocaust. The Fuehrer salute is visible through the fiery red light of the laboratory window, but the arm performing it is shaking badly.

NADYA *and* SONYA *dance out from behind the Radio wearing chef's hats, brandishing barbeque equipment, and singing: "Hey good lookin', vat ya got cookin'?" They buck and wing it towards the body on the examining table—whose legs are drawn up to its chest so that it resembles a large roasting chicken. It is still the body of* DR. REICH *got up to look like* ADOLF HITLER. NADYA *and* SONYA *happily salt and pepper the body, remove its eyeglasses and a gold filling or two from its mouth, then wheel the body on the examining table to the front of the Radio, which continues to crackle with fire. The bust of Wagner illuminates fully now and, as the table wheels past his rack,* EDMUND *the skeleton might try for the Fuehrer salute, but fail. His arm will not stay in position without* DR. REICH.

Upstage Center:

NADYA *and* SONYA *open the door of the Radio as widely as possible and pause, jauntily*:

NADYA: Sonya Fyedorovna.

SONYA: Vat iss it, Nadya Leopovna?

NADYA: You poot stoffing in body cavity, yet?

SONYA: No time for stoffing, Nadya Leopovna. Oven eggsactly rright temperrature.

NADYA: Just like vat's herr name Mary Lee Taylorr Rrradio Brroadcast say?

SONYA: Eggsactly like Mary Lee Taylorr Rrroadcast say. Six hondrred degreeees forrr first fifteen minoots, then use own crrreatif genyuss forrr rrrest.

They push the body in the open door of the Radio. It slides gently into the flames and is immediately consumed. NADYA *spits after it three times, then* SONYA *closes the door. They exchange complicit and satisfied nods, then exit giggling behind the Radio, jockeying for steering position on the examining table. Smoke billows from the Radio's stacks as the* BROADCASTERS *begin to speak. As soon as we hear their voices, the* HASSID *begins to move unobtrusively along the Radio's cord, past the dim tableau of* ADOLF *and* EVA, *tracing the presumptive plug that connects the Radio to its current. The* BROADCASTERS' *narrative must come out of the Radio.*

REICH B.: He will always be one of us. We knew that all along. We can <u>never</u> forget it now.

HITLER B.: He will always . . . look like us. He will always . . . think like us. And he will always speak for us.

REICH B.: ("Jewish" voice) The thing that I will never understand is . . .

With an enormous jerk, the HASSID *disconnects the Radio in mid-sentence and freezes against the red sky in silhouette, holding the huge, forked plug above his head. He looks like Lucifer and his black body and the black body of the Radio stand together for an awful moment.*

Stage Left:

The bust of Wagner flickers out.

Total blackout.

Finis

THE UNIVERSAL
WOLF

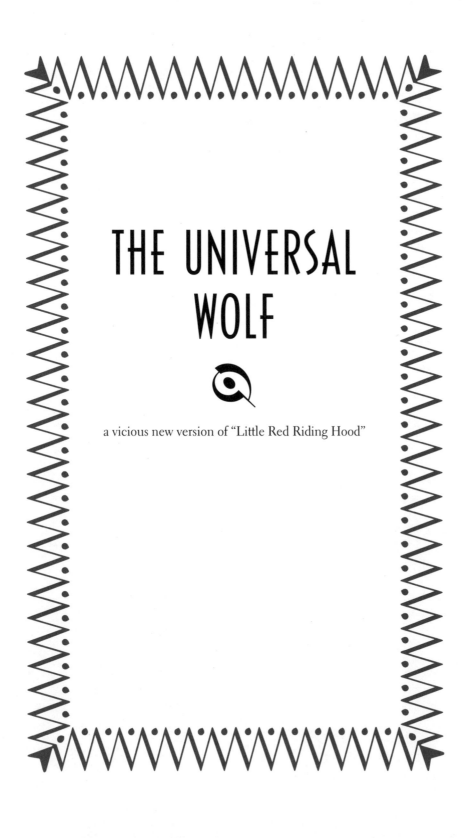

a vicious new version of "Little Red Riding Hood"

THE UNIVERSAL WOLF had its first showing at UBU Rep, New York City, 1991, directed by Virlana Tcasz. It has been subsequently produced in many experimental venues from Los Angeles to London, and in dozens of colleges and universities throughout North America. These photographs are from the UBU Rep production.

Characters

THE READER
M. WOOLF
LITTLE RED
GRANDMÈRE

Left to right: M. WOOLF, LITTLE RED RIDING HOOD. (*Photo by Ole Hein Pedersen*)

M. WOOLF: Do you mean, dear grandmozzer, zat I cannot embrace you, encompass you, put my, uh, mouse, mouf, mout, I <u>can</u>not say zis word but you know what I mean—ze area below my nose—cannot kees your beautiful wizzered cheek?

Left to right: M. WOOLF, GRANDMÈRE. (*Photo by Ole Hein Pedersen*)

M. WOOLF: Mesdames et messieurs. A small confession. I love to devour lettle cheeldren. (*smack smack drool*) Oui, monsieur, I assure you I speak only ze truth. Devouring lee-tle cheeldren is my mission in life. Mon destin. I do not choose it, it chooses me.

THE UNIVERSAL WOLF

a vicious new version of "Little Red Riding Hood"

A little proscenium stage with red velvet curtains. It sits on the larger stage like a telephone booth or a police box — and carries with it the same sense of endangered isolation. Audience STAGE RIGHT *is a table and chair.*

The READER *sits in the chair waiting to begin the play. The* READER *will read all the stage directions that the actors can't, won't, or don't do. The* READER *will also create the voices of the structuralists, the bird, the post-structuralists, the audience, the stagehands, and* LITTLE RED RIDING HOOD'S *mother. The* READER *is very lightly miked.*

THE UNIVERSAL WOLF: *a vicious new version of* "Little Red Riding Hood" *by* JOAN M. SCHENKAR.

Part I

LITTLE RED RIDING HOOD *appears on the stage apron in a field of wild flowers, carrying a wicker basket. Since the play has not yet begun, her presence is a little insubstantial.*

LITTLE R: Oooooo. How pretty. How pretty.

From offstage, an exclamation: "!!!!"

LITTLE R: I'm coming, maman.

Another exclamation: "!!!!"

LITTLE R: I'm <u>coming</u>, maman. I have just to collect one last item for dear grandmother's little basket. (*cheep cheep*) Here birdie birdie. Come birdie birdie. How good you would look in a pâte brisée. (*cheep cheep*) Here birdie birdie. Come birdie birdie. Perhaps you would be more comfortable in a tarte tatin? That's right birdie, perch yourself on my finger. (*cheep*) What a lovely little birdie. (*cheep cheep cheep*) (*to the audience*) Now watch this. This, too, will be lovely.

LITTLE RED RIDING HOOD *wrings the birdie's neck—"cheep cheep URK"—and exits, laughing an insupportably silvery little laugh.*
The house lights go down. A hairy paw parts the tiny velvet curtains. Voila! The head of a wolf emerges! Authentic teeth, authentic fur, authentic everything. Except the accent, which is the accent of Maurice Chevalier.

M. WOOLF: Bon soir, mesdames at messieurs. Bon soir. (*sings*)

> I am ze Wolf Aoow Aoww
> I am ze Wolf Aoow Aooow
> I am ze 'orrible terrible
> Creature zat lurks in your
> Dreams when you scream
> In your bed are you dead?
> I am ze Wolf
> Aowww Aowww

Bon soir. I am M. Woolf, a votre service. (*snarrl yeowll, snap, snap, drool*) Oh, excusez-moi, pardon, pardon. Forgive me, mesdames at messieurs. I 'ave a 'ard time to keep control when it comes to ze saying of my last name. Wiz your permission I will try it anozzer time. Woo Wooo . . . woooo . . . Woooolff! (*snarrl, yowl, yeeowll*) A thousand pardons again good people. (*a silk handkerchief dries the jaw*) It is such an inflammatory last name, non? So, 'ow do you say, provocatif? But it 'as a certaine ring, do you not agree? A résonnance of long white teeth and croque-messieurs made wiz ze fingers of five year old cheeldren. (*snarrrl, arrrl, arrrl, snap!*) Nom de dieu! I see I can keep nozzing from you tonight, good people. (*a toothy grin, a resettling of intentions*) Mesdames et messieurs. A small confession. I love to devour leetle cheeldren. (*smack smack drool*) Oui, monsieur, I assure you I speak only ze truth. Devouring leetle cheeldren is my mission in life. Mon destin. I do not choose it, it chooses me. For petit déjeuner I like ze five year olds (*smack smack*), for lunch ze nine to twelves, and for mon diner ze teenagers are always appropriate. And because, like all ze moderne French (*left paw on left hip*), I am structuraliste, ze meaning of my obsession wiz cheeldren 'as no meaning for me. I eat cheeldren raw and I eat zem cooked. Ça y est.

The image of Claude Lévi-Strauss appears behind M. WOOLF. *It holds up an enormous carte de visite labeled* MYTHS ABOUT THE ORIGINS OF COOKING, *then gently fades away.*

M. WOOLF: I can substitute one child for anozzer, I can change <u>zere</u> names, I can change <u>my</u> name (*a graceful shrug of lupine shoulders*). It is all ze same to me, so long 'as I 'ave my leetle collation.

The image of Roland Barthes appears in an armchair, deliberately crosses its legs and says: "An eminently structural object is created by two modest actions: substitution (one part replaces another as in a paradigm) and nomination (the name is in no way linked to the stability of the parts)." *The image uncrosses its legs and is instantly replaced by the velvet curtain.*

M. WOOLF: You see good people. It is merely a question of application. Ze right part for ze right part. Ze bon dieu gave me zees lovely teeth—ze better to eat leetle limbs wiz—and (*a hairy paw taps a canine*) Aowwww! Oh zat hurrts! Pardon! Aooowww! Aooowwrrr! Zis tooth must be replaced! (*the silk handkerchief comes out and dries the jaw*) To continue, bon gens. You are 'ere tonight to witness the re-enactment of a leetle meet. Mit? Meeth? I <u>cannot</u> say zis word but you understand me, non? I come to you in a mytology. Zere are many people in zis room right now who think zey know how my small story will end. Eh? Am I right? Of course I am right. You see (*mouths the words, he's not going to lose control*) M. Woolf, you think fairy tale. And <u>zen</u> you think of ze Little Red Hood wiz 'er cape and 'er basket and 'er benign grandmozzer in bed. Suddenly ze image of M. Woolf wiz 'is teeth (*a copy display of dentition*) appears on ze screen of memory. Quel horreur! Eh? And <u>zen</u> you remember ze 'appy ending of your violent American childhoods. Ze brave Woodsman comes wiz 'is gleaming axe and commits an 'orrible vivisection upon ze suffering protagonist. Well <u>zat</u> was version of ze brothers Grimm. Ze <u>German</u> version. Germans love to—'ow you say—compensate for zere national crimes and terrible cameras wiz 'eroic avoidances of ze <u>real</u>. But we French—anozzer style entirely. We French always—'ow do your American gangsters call it—face ze musique.

The image of Alain Robbe-Grillet appears looking thru a pair of binoculars. It says "Metaphor is never an innocent figure of speech," *then drops its binoculars and vanishes.*

M. WOOLF: And so tonight good people you will see ze French version of ze Little Red One. Tonight we will remove entirely ze concept of ze Woodsman from ze narratif and—'ow do your American landlords call it—<u>renovate</u> zis little story. For wizout ze Woodsman, wizout ze 'eroic male, zis simple tale returns to its sixteenth-century spirit—bestiale, brutale, and très très primitif. Tonight, mesdames et messieurs (*flourish of an imaginary cape*) M. <u>Woolf</u> (*snarrrl, yowl, owl, howwwll*) will be ze only male on ze stage!!

The image of Julia Kristeva appears holding a glass of chartreuse. It sips and says: "Narrative is, in sum, the most elaborate attempts of the speaking subject to situate his or herself among his or her desires or taboos, that is at the interior of the Oedipal triangle . . . oooops!" *The glass falls to the floor, the image disappears. The velvet curtains fold around* M. WOOLF *and, in the place where his teeth just were, the charming face of a charming* LITTLE RED RIDING HOOD *appears. Curls, big eyes, dimpled cheeks, cupid's mouth, cleft chin, the works. The face is framed by a red velvet hood and smiles insupportably.*

LITTLE R: Bon soir, tout le monde. I am Little Red Riding Hood, preparing to visit the house of my dear grandmother in the middle of the deep, dark, Bois de Boulogne. My grandmother (*a toss of the curls*) is the extraordinary person who gave me this little red hood which I wear everywhere and by which I am everywhere known (*another insupportable smile*). You will notice that I speak American quite perfectly. But you must not feel badly about that. I have two languages and you have only one. This is life. This is also the result of the superior training all French children receive in their little lycées—where it is understood that Americans can speak no language but their own. For language, as everyone knows, is an ability limited to the happy few—most of whom dwell in my country. The happy few . . . the happy few. This is a phrase I once read and liked very much. The "happy few." It makes me think of my dear grandmother as well as myself for my grandmother is also a very unusual person . . . (*an insupportable smile*).

From offstage, a question "??"

LITTLE R: Yes, maman. I do have my little wicker basket.

Another question: "??"

LITTLE R: No maman. Grandmère asked for fresh meat and five bottles of blackberry wine.

An exclamation: "!!!"

LITTLE R: Grandmère does not have a problem with blackberry wine, maman. She loves blackberry wine.

Another exclamation: "!!!!"

LITTLE R: Maman. Grandmère is a professional woman and would be very sorry to hear you speak about her in this way. Especially to me. (*to the audience*) My mother, unfortunately, is not a spiritually-inclined person. Quand même, she is my mother and for that I must respect her.

A statement: "."

LITTLE R: No maman. You can be sure that I will not put my foot off the path to grandmother's house.

A question and an exclamation: "?!"

LITTLE R: Yes maman. I do remember hearing stories of Big Bad M. Woolf.

Snarrl, Owll, Howlll, Yeowl, Arff! is heard from behind the curtain. A stagehand screams: "Hold his <u>paws</u>, fa chrissake! Hold his jaws!! I never <u>seen</u> a stage wolf be-have like that! <u>Grab</u> the sonofabitch, willya, <u>it's</u> <u>not</u> <u>his</u> <u>cue</u>!! Aooooooowwww!"

LITTLE R: Believe me, maman. Though I have not the smallest idea of what M. Woolf looks like, his presence is so real to me that I imagine I can hear him howling outside our door at this very instant. Can <u>you</u> not hear him, maman? I am certain it is M. Woo . . .

M. WOOLF *bursts thru the curtains, his fur very disturbed. The heads of* M. WOOLF *and* LITTLE RED RIDING HOOD *appear simultaneously for a nanosecond, there is a (dramatically) unrealized "incident," and the little head of* LITTLE RED *quickly withdraws.*

M. WOOLF: Woolf! (*arf arf snarrl*) Woolf! (*arll yeowl yargh*) Oh pardonnez-moi, mesdames et messieurs. It is ze sound of my own name zat rouses ze beast in me. I meant, naturellement, only to complete ze charming child's sentence wiz ze word . . . (*wurgh! worf! wlugh!* M. WOOLF *stifles himself with a right paw*). Please! Please! Charming Child! Come back I beg of you! Non? She is disconcerted for ze moment, ladies and gentlemen, but I assure you zere is more to 'er story. You 'ave not seen ze last of ze Little Red One, I promise you zat. What? What do you say, madame? You 'ave no sympathy wiz my little faux pas, madame? You cannot yourself imagine losing control, you think it is not in you to 'owl and yeowl like M. W . . . like me. Hah! It <u>is</u> in you, madame. Listen to ze sounds your own stomach makes ze next time you are 'ungry. Growl 'owl 'owl is what you will 'ear. Ze beast within, ze (*mouths the word*) wolf inside. Make no mistake, madame. Zere is a wolf in you and 'e wants to get out.

Howwl! Yeowl! Yeeowwll! M. WOOLF *outdoes himself in the vocal department. A burly arm thrusts thru the curtains, hammerlocks* M. WOOLF's *neck, and drags him offstage.* "Awright, awright, I <u>got</u> the sonufabitch, but I don't know how long I can <u>hold</u> him."

The image of Jacques Lacan appears in academic garb, smoking a pipe. It as-sumes a speaking position, attempts to remove the pipe from its mouth, fails com-pletely, and dissolves in embarrassment.

A childish, dimpled, waving hand appears thru the curtains.

LITTLE R: Hello again, good people. Tout va bien. I am back and maman is resting. (*a slight, duplicitous smile*) To be accurate (*a bright smile*), maman is fainted. She insisted to believe that it was really the Big Bad Wolf who brushed past me in the doorway just now, and frightened herself into fits. In any case, she is now, as you phrase it in Hollywood, out of the picture — so I can share with you the <u>very</u> naughty thing I am about to do (*a coy, coy, giggle*).

In the audience we hear rude sounds in the gustatory mode — lip smacks, drools, a few low, appetitive whistles. LITTLE RED RIDING HOOD *stamps her little red riding foot.*

LITTLE R: No no <u>no</u>! Not <u>that</u>! <u>Shame</u> on <u>you</u>. And <u>you</u>. And <u>you</u>, sir. And that man <u>there</u> in the raincoat who just made a crude gesture at me! Such a thing would <u>never</u> <u>ever</u> happen in my own country. <u>Never</u>!

From the back of the hall: "Salope!" LITTLE RED *resettles with effort.*

LITTLE R: What I was referring to as "naughty," good people, was my excursion thru the deep, dark, Bois de Boulogne, for the walk to the house of my grand-mother is full of horrible dangers. There is a perpetual rotation of picnickers, vendors, and unattached males watching for evil opportunities. Quand même, a walk once a week in the Bois fills me with fresh air and favorable feelings. And from time to time, I come upon the charming Woodsman of the Bois, leaning on his <u>remarkably</u> shaped axe—who always has a kind word for a little girl in a red hood bringing a basket of comfort to her dear grandmother.

From the back of the hall: "Salope!" *again. Also:* "Dwarf! Dwarf! <u>Lesbian</u> dwarf!" LITTLE RED's *embouchure tightens firmly. Someone in front shouts:* "Where's the <u>wolf</u>?" *Snarrrl! Yowl! Yyrrr!* "My cue," *says* LITTLE RED *and she hastens on her way as a hairy snout once again thrusts itself thru the curtains.* "<u>My</u> cue," *says* M. WOOLF. "Mon <u>entrance</u>, mesdames et messieurs." *Snarrl! Owl! Urg!* M. WOOLF *is <u>aggrieved</u>.*

M. WOOLF: <u>Forget</u> ze woodsman, dear people, <u>and</u> 'is axe. Banish ze brawny 'ero from your mind. We 'ave dissolved 'is function by removing 'im from zis narrative. Zere is at present no one to rescue and no one to <u>be</u> rescued. Ze danger in zis leetle story is now a much more subtle matter. Am I right? Of <u>course</u> I am right. Ze narrator is <u>always</u> right. Now for ze worthless woodsman we 'ave substituted zis wonderful chart.

A hairy arm inserts a large white bristolboard thru the curtains. The board is fastened to a stick and appears to be completely blank.

M. WOOLF: We 'ave substituted zis chart for ze negligible woodsman, good people, because we French do not ever remove something wizzout replacing it. And, in any case, wizzout ze false 'ero, Little Red Riding 'ood's little red story begins to resemble—may I say it good people?—ze most mysterious encounter given to ze entire race of 'umans. (*a dramatic flourish of the paw towards the bristolboard*) Wizzout ze woodsman, my friends, ze story of ze Little Red One comes to approach zat terrible collision of 'umanity and 'opelessness known as Le Néant. Nozzingness. Absolute Existential Zero!!!

And the bristolboard is rotated on its stick to reveal what is printed on its backside in big red letters punctured and dripping cocktail sauce: ZERO. *Hideous shrieks from the audience.*

M. WOOLF: Mon Dieu! Madame! Madame! Au succours! Au succours! Somebody must 'elp ze poor fainted lady in ze first row! And ze fainted ones in ze fifth, seventh, and ninth rows! And there in the aisle a gentleman is 'aving a 'orrible serious 'eart attack! Sssshhhh! Ssssshhh! Good people. Shrieking is of no use in zis situation and merely interrupts my attempt to deconstruct ze narrative and penetrate its mysteries. Silence mesdames! Control yourselves messieurs! Think of your mothers!

The image of Julia Kristeva appears with a glass of armagnac. The image grips the glass tightly and says: "By maternal I mean the ambivalent principle that derives on the one hand from the species and on the other from a catastrophe of identity." *The image disappears, followed more slowly by the armagnac.*

M. WOOLF: Look again at zis sign, good people and tell me what you see. A smooth (M. WOOLF *says smooze*) white nacreous surface, eh? Not unlike ze concept of Existential Blank. And notice ze sharply cut edges of ze board— 'ow it recalls ze serious side of an axe—eh? And ze wooden 'andle 'ere—a representation both of what ze removed woodsman chops wiz <u>and</u> of what 'e chops. Zis sign, ladies and gentleman, is not merely a sign. It is a SIGN and we must take it <u>very</u> seriously. (*The ears of* M. WOOLF *prick up*) Aha! My big ears 'ave just detected sounds of ze Little Red One picking forbidden flowers. Ssshh. Ssshh. If you are very quiet you can 'ear 'er too. (M. WOOLF *assumes his most factitiously welcoming smile*)

Tum te tum. Offstage LITTLE RED *is singing.*

LITTLE R: I pluck the flowers
    For Grandmère
    I bottle the buds
    For her drink
    I gather berries
    For Grandmère
    And crush them
    And squeeze them
    And dirty the sink
    For my grandmère loves to see dying
    Little ones struggling in pain
    Puppies in ponds
    Cats flat on the road
    Bunnies in traps
    A badly squashed toad
    Are part of her fav-o-rite view
    For ma chère
    Grandmère

    (*and here* LITTLE RED *glares straight at the audience*) I'd even kill <u>you</u> and <u>you</u>.

M. WOOLF: Et voilà, mesdames. Regardez messieurs. Is it not as I said?

LITTLE R: Oh my oh my. How very familiar you look, monsieur. And yet you are not the Woodsman with the remarkable axe. No no you are certainly <u>not</u> the Woodsman I know. But perhaps you are <u>another</u> Woodsman? A . . . (*she looks closely*) hairier, damper Woodsman?

M. WOOLF *makes a surreptitious attempt to smooth his arm fur, then whisks his handkerchief across his dripping lower jaw. He summons a reliable smile.*

LITTLE R: And if you <u>are</u> another Woodsman, monsieur, you will know the path to the house of my dear grandmother and you will direct me to it. (*and here* LITTLE RED *quavers a bit*) For I seem, good M. Woodsman, to have . . . just a little . . . lost my way.

M. WOOLF: Lost, chère mlle? Lost? Oh do not say it. Though these woods are deep, dark, and threatened with meaninglessness, you are surely not lost. For, charming child (*an assessing glance*) in the 11 to 15 year old category, you have found <u>me</u>! Me! Moi, M. Wooo (*the* WOLF *grabs his snout and censors himself just in time*) Woods. Ready, willing and able to shine ze bright light of my attentions on your leetle probleme.

M. WOOLF *broadens his smile and a little string of saliva appears at the* STAGE RIGHT *corner of his lower jaw. From the seventh row of the audience comes a warning*: "Dwarf, dwarf, ya <u>dumb</u> <u>dwarf</u>. He's gonna <u>eat</u> you."

LITTLE R: You are not, then, a Woodsman, kind sir? You are only M. Woods?

M. WOOLF: Ah, charming child. Your beautiful youth must be ze excuse for your ignorance. Zere is no longer a woodsman in your leetle story. Ze woodsman was a crude protuberance, an ugly thorn in ze primrose path of our leetle meet. Meeth. Myt. You know what I mean. A fiction with résonnance. No, zere ees no woodsman, charming child, zere ees only me, alone in all zis wooded space to guide you.

The image of Gaston Bachelard appears with a postal sack on its back. It removes a card from the sack and reads in a whisper: "Space has always reduced me to silence," *then disappears.*

LITTLE R: But I <u>insist</u> upon a woodsman! I <u>depend</u> upon a woodsman! <u>I must have a woodsman</u>!

M. WOOLF: Dear child—in an <u>exceptionally</u> succulent stage of development— not only is ze woodsman absent from zis recital but I shall personally see to it (*and here* M. WOOLF *smiles a smile of unimaginable wickedness and moisture from his salivary glands finally passes the point of control*) zat we do not 'ave even a sweet old grandmozzer to obstruct our wonderful duet. Your grand-mozzer will be replaced wiz something <u>simpler</u>—something—on ze order of zis placard. (*and* M. WOOLF *points to the dripping* ZERO)

LITTLE R: That is <u>ridiculous</u>, M. Woods! There is <u>no</u> <u>question</u> of replacing my remarkable grandmère! Why in her youth grandmother dearest was a <u>serious</u>
<u>professional</u>—the only female butcher in the Bois de Boulogne! (*proudly*)
Most of the tiny mammals of the Bois have ended their lives on chère grandmère's butcher block. And now, <u>now</u> that she is <u>retired</u> you wish to <u>replace</u>
her?! No, no M. Woods, my dear grandmother will <u>never</u> be replaced!

M. WOOLF: (*a paw raised in placation*) I positively take your point, charming
child. So, ze old relative 'as a good eye and a steady 'and, zen?

LITTLE R: Better than that, M. Woods. Dear grandmother has a remarkably hard
heart. It's a quality which replaces almost every other quality. But, M. Woods,
dear <u>grandmother</u> will not be replaced <u>so</u> <u>just</u> <u>get</u> <u>over</u> <u>it</u>!

M. WOODS: I take your point again, charming child. And by ze way, your com-
mand of ze American vernacular is superbe. (*slyly*) I understand zis ability
missed your poor mother entirely.

LITTLE R: I <u>have</u> heard that, M. Woods. I <u>have</u> heard that maman lacks a certain
. . . oh . . . (*shrugs*) . . . you know . . .

M. WOOLF: (*top of his form*) Ah, my dear child. Zere are things I could tell you
about your poor mozzer, things only a man of my generation could know—
but non, non I <u>must</u> not. I <u>will</u> not. I <u>shall</u> not.

*The image of Pierre Louys appears in a Paul Poiret evening gown. It drops a
shoulder strap and says: "I will reveal something but not more than is permit-
ted."—then shimmers away.*

M. WOOLF: And now, charming child, let me encourage you to collect a few
more forbidden blooms for your noble grandmozzer. For I see zat ze bouquet
you 'ave assembled for ze old paragon is a little scanty.

LITTLE R: Scanty, monsieur? Is it possible?

M. WOOLF: It ees, darling dryad. As you say, everyone in zis deep, dark, forest
knows ze reputation of your extraordinary grandmozzer and no one would be-
grudge 'er a full bouquet. So take zis leetle corsage from me (*and* M. WOOLF
hands her a blighted blossom), pin it to your cape, and pick ze proscribed
posies. Go on, go on! Enjoy yourself! And when you 'ave finished, <u>zat</u> is ze
way to Grandmozzer's 'ouse. (*and* M. WOOLF *turns to the audience with a vil-
lanous whisper*) In ze meantime, I shall snatch zis delectable morsel's leetle
basket, arrive at Grandmozzer's dwelling, and swallow ze old monster toute
entière. Cap, spectacles, ze knitting and, if necessary, argh, ze needles.

LITTLE R: Well, M. Woods. There is justice in what you say. I would not care to
approach grandmother dearest with anything less than the best. But I must
begin now—for I see that the shadows are getting longer.

A large shadow suddenly extends itself across both M. WOOLF *and* LITTLE RED RIDING HOOD—*and just as suddenly retreats.*

LITTLE R: (*to the audience*) And while this strange man, deluded by my clever story, imagines me picking flowers in a field, I shall run as rapidly as dignity permits to the house of my dear grandmother, using a short cut known only to me. For in this M. Woods I am smelling a rat. I do not like the way his mouth consistently drips moisture—though, to be sure, I am too polite to say so. (*to* M. WOOLF) Au revoir, M. Woods. I am on my merry way. Au revoir. (*and she forgets her basket as she backs out between the velvet curtains*)

M. WOOLF: (*wiping his mouth on his sleeve and surreptitiously slurping up the overflow*) Slurp slurp. Au revoir, charming child. And 'ow do zey say in American vacationlands, take your time my leetle one. Take your time. Ze forbidden flowers cry out for your attentions. (M. WOOLF *whirls 'round to the audience, a different wolf now, every one of his teeth available for viewing*) Aooow aaow aooooww! Ze leetle hors d'oeuvre 'as left 'er basket to assist me in my impersonation! M. Woolf 'as prevailed! Ha! HA! Grandmozzers beware! Leetle girls BEWARE! M. WOOLF (*Aooooow!*) is on ze loose once again!!!!!!

The same large shadow that fell across M. WOOLF *and* LITTLE RED *falls again, this time accompanied by a piercing electronic chord. The lights darken ominously.*

End of Part I

Entre-acte

The curtains part once again. It is M. WOOLF—*quiet, focused, pleasant, and quite dry. From offstage we hear the stagehands:* "Jesus-god it took two towels to get that wolf's jaw cleaned off! The producer's gonna <u>croak</u> when she sees the laundry bills on this show!" "Are you kidding? I hadda stuff a washcloth under his <u>tongue</u> so he wouldn't drool all over the <u>dresser</u>!" "He's not human, he's just not human." M. WOOLF *advances ingratiatingly.*

M. WOOLF: I forgot! I forgot one leetle thing, good people. One tiny leetle thing to show you before ze Red One appears wiz yet anozzer side of 'er endless story. Ladies! Open your purses! Gentlemen! Search ze floor! I want ze entire audience to retrieve its programs from wherever zey 'ave been concealed! I will now ask you to . . . 'ow do your American scholars call eet? . . . interact wiz ze texte! 'Ave we all found ze beautiful programmes? Bon. Turn to ze block of texte on page 5. You weel notice zat eet comes <u>after</u> ze inflated biography of ze playwright and <u>before</u> ze pitiful pleas for money by ze theatre. On zis page 5, you weel find ze structurally correct version of my story. My story in its primal state <u>before</u> ze 'orrible intrusion of ze stupide woodsman. Lights, M. le technicien! Lights eef you please! Of course ze lighting technicien might well be a woman, but in zis dim atmosphere eet is impossible to discern ze gender of <u>anything</u>.

At this moment, the image of Teresa de Lauretis appears in full doctoral costume, holding a diploma and weeping. The image raises its right hand and says: "The female sex is invisible in psychology and in semiology it does not exist at all." *The house lights come on and Dr. de Lauretis vanishes.*

M. WOOLF: Raise your textes to ze light my dears, prepare your minds for a shock, and read. <u>Read</u>. To yourselves of course. But <u>read</u>.

Audience reads the following text:

Page 5

So the wolf took the path of the pins and arrived first at the house. He killed grandmother, poured her blood into a bottle, and sliced her flesh onto a platter. Then he got into her nightclothes and waited in bed.

"Knock, Knock."
"Come in, my dear."
"Hello, grandmother. I've brought you some bread and milk."
"Have something yourself, my dear. There is meat and wine in the pantry."
So the little girl ate what she was offered and as she did, a little cat said,
"Slut! To eat the flesh and drink the blood of your grandmother!"

Then the wolf said, "Undress and get into bed with me."
"Where shall I put my apron?"
"Throw it on the fire; you won't need it anymore."

For each garment—bodice, skirt, petticoat and stockings—the girl asked the same question; and each time the wolf answered, "Throw it on the fire; you won't need it anymore."

When the girl got in bed, she said, "Oh, grandmother! How hairy you are!"
"It's to keep me warmer, my dear."
"Oh grandmother! What big shoulders you have!"
"It's better for carrying firewood, my dear!"
"Oh grandmother! What long nails you have!"
"It's for scratching myself better, my dear!"
"Oh grandmother! What big teeth you have!"
"It's for eating you better, my dear."

AND HE ATE HER.

M. WOOLF: (*looking around the house*) Is zere anyone who 'as not finished? Good. Is zere anyone who missed ze four beautiful words in ze last sentence? "And he ate her?" Good. You now 'ave all ze facts you need. Let ze carnage begin. (*and* M. WOOLF *makes a surprisingly dignified exit*)

End of the Entre-acte

Part II

The curtains open wider than they ever have on the same little stage. It is now GRANDMOTHER's *house and the decor is that of a retired butcher who might at any moment resume her career. We see chopping blocks, a full set of Sabatiers, and various small mammals hanging by their hindquarters in gruesome disarray.* GRANDMOTHER *sits in a rocking chair with cap, spectacles, two outsize needles (but no knitting), and a bottle of blackberry wine. She rocks and sips and sings her Grandmother Song.*

GRAND M: They think that I'll knit by night
           They hope I'll crochet by day
           They want their socks mended
           Their sad problems ended
           Well it won' t be by me
           Hee hee
           Hee hee
           No it won't be by me
           Not by me.

A loud knocking sound KNOCK KNOCK *interrupts* GRANDMOTHER's *big aria. From offstage we hear:* "Grandmother dearest grandmother! Open the door. Oh please please please please please open the door!!"

GRAND M: It's Little Red Riding Hood. For godsake Little Red Riding Hood! Are you blind? (*to the audience*) She must be blind. The door is open. RAISE THE LATCH. (*knocking continues*) For godsake Little Red Riding Hood. Are you deaf? (*to the audience*) She must be deaf. The latch! RAISE THE LATCH!

LITTLE R: (*entering*) I raised the latch, Grandmère . . .

GRAND M. Smart girl. (*to the audience*) She's coming along.

LITTLE R: . . . and I ran all the way thru the Bois de Boulogne (*pant pant*) to advise you (*pant pant*) of the arrival of a very suspicious gentleman with moisture around his mouth.

GRAND M: That will be the wolf, Little Red Riding Hood. I know this story very well.

LITTLE R: (*marveling*) The moist man with fur on his hands was M. <u>Woolf</u>! <u>That</u> was M. WOOLF!!

GRAND M: Sometimes I fear the girl has inherited more traits from her mother than from <u>me</u>.

LITTLE R: Do not say it, grandmother dearest! I beg you.

GRAND M: Well sit down and drink with me granddaughter and we'll discuss why I forgot about your visit and what to do about the possible new monsieur.

LITTLE R: I am too young to drink, grandmère. Maman says it is drink that has dissolved your memory.

GRAND M: Drink is the proper partner for meat, Little Red Riding Hood, and it is meat that makes a memory. Or so we butchers always say. (*gulp gulp*) Now describe the strange monsieur for me. I must see him before I can deal with him.

LITTLE R: (*carefully*) He was . . . hairy . . . damp . . . unctuous . . . and full of fine phrases.

GRAND M: It's the wolf, alright.

LITTLE R: <u>Really</u>, grandmother dearest. That was <u>really</u> M. Woolf?!!

GRAND M: Oh for gods<u>sake</u> Little Red Riding Hood.

LITTLE R: Well, then, grandmère. M. Woolf is coming to eat us both and with my little basket, too, which in my haste I abandoned.

GRAND M: <u>My</u> little basket you mean. (*avariciously*) What's in it? <u>Fresh</u> <u>meat</u>? Did you put <u>fresh</u> <u>meat</u> in my basket?

LITTLE R: Six bottles of blackberry wine, some wilting flowers, and one deceased songbird at the bottom, dear grandmother.

GRAND M: Six bottles! Good for you granddaughter! I detest cut flowers, as you well know but the bird is a <u>wonderful</u> touch. I'll pop him in a pâte brisée. If I remember. Now in just a moment that <u>awful</u> wolf will be at the door trying to imitate <u>you</u>, Little Red Riding Hood.

LITTLE R: Is he <u>that</u> stupid grandmother dearest? Or does he think <u>you're</u> that stupid?

GRAND M: That is how the story goes, Little Red Riding Hood. At least I <u>think</u> that is how the story goes. My memory is as full of holes as a hairnet.

LITTLE R: It's the wine, isn't it grandmère?

GRAND M: (*taking a slurp*) It's the <u>meat</u>, Little Red. It's been days since I've had <u>fresh</u> <u>meat</u>. (*looks at the bottle*) Of course, every pleasure has its penalties. (*glug glug glug*)

LITTLE R: Well, but dearest grandmère, what are we to <u>do</u>?

GRAND M: (*taking a slug*) I'm <u>thinking</u>, Little Red.

LITTLE R: You're <u>drinking</u>, grandmère.

GRAND M: The one supports the other (*glug glug*). Or so we butchers always say.

LITTLE R: Thank heaven, chère grandmère, that I do not have your responsibilities.

GRAND M: Ha HAH! I've <u>got</u> it! The <u>perfect</u> <u>solution</u>!

LITTLE R: Oh grandmother. You are certainly the cleverest old person in the Bois de Boulogne! Tell me your solution!

GRAND M: (*raises her head to speak, but memory fails*) Woops, it's gone! The idea has flown my mind like a bird from a bough! (*to herself*) Must be a protein deficiency. (*to the audience*) Old age is a <u>miracle</u> of selective consciousness. A <u>miracle</u>.

LITTLE R: We are lost! We are lost! Maman was right! You have drunk your mind away!

GRAND M: Stop that gibbering you brainless child. <u>No</u> one is lost! A <u>solution</u> is lost, that is all. And in one minute, I will have another. (*to the audience*) Old age is very resilient.

GRAND M *begins to think very hard while* LITTLE R *advances in an irritating way, allowing her corsage to come in contact with* GRAND M*'s allergenic zone.* GRAND M *sneezes explosively and we hear an offstage* KNOCK KNOCK. M. WOOLF: (*violently falsetto*) "Grandmère oh grandmère. It is Little Red Riding Hood come to visit. Grandmère oh grandmère please let me in. Aooww."

GRAND M: (*sneezing*) An idea! I have an idea! Your corsage has sharpened the blades of my intelligence! Into the armoire Little Red Riding Hood and don't let me hear you breathe! You will find a well-honed axe on your right hand side. Achoo! Ha ha! Achoo! These sneezes will save our lives!

LITTLE R, *hyperventilating, scrambles into the armoire just in time to avoid the entrance of* M. WOOLF ("Grandmère oh grandmère"), *heavily costumed in a cerise tablecloth and a cottonwool bib. In this disguise,* M. WOOLF *could fool no one.*

GRAND M: Ah my darling little girl. My own daughter's child laden with goodies for her short-sighted and arthritic relative. What's in the basket, kiddo, I'M HUNGRY.

M. WOOLF: Oooh dear grandmozzer. I was in such a hurry to arrive zat I forgot to look in ze basket. (*he flips quickly thru the top layer*) But you weel immediately find plaisir in zees lovely flowers which I labored to gather for you.

GRAND M: Have you dropped an oar in the water, Little Red Riding Hood? You <u>know</u> I'm violently allergic to <u>anything</u> that grows. ACHOO ACHOOO ACHOO. Why the moment I come into contact with chlorophyll (*and here she touches a leaf*) I break out in hideous pustules, boils filled with slime, wens, warts, carbuncles, and large purple spots! Look! Look! And anyone who touches me suffers the very same affliction.

M. WOOLF: (*pulling back in horror*) Do you mean, dear grandmozzer, zat I <u>can</u>-not embrace you, encompass you, put my, uh, mouse, moufe, mout, I <u>cannot</u>

say zis word but you know what I mean—ze area below my nose—cannot kees your beautiful wizzered cheek? Your neck full of exquisite veins running in blood? (M. WOOLF's *bib fills with saliva*)

GRAND M: ACHOO Little Red Riding Hood ACHOO. Do you remember what happened the last time you approached me with a bouquet in hand?

M. WOOLF: Uh . . . I am a leetle vague on that subject, dear grandmozzer.

GRAND M: Why, we had to rush you right to the hospital, Little Red Riding Hood. Your lips swelled up like soccer balls, your eyes looked like fresh pamplemousse, even your ears were affected. (*peers*) Why Little Red Riding Hood, I believe your ears are <u>still</u> affected. How very large they look.

M WOOLF: The better to hear you with, ancient relative.

GRAND M: And your mouth. Surely you have had some serious dental work since your last visit? Your teeth seem twice as large as they once were.

M. WOOLF: No no dear grandmozzer. I assure you my teeth are in a terrible condition. (*touches them*) Aooww.

GRAND M: And your nose, dear child. What happened to your nose?

M. WOOLF: Eet is ze way of adolescence, grandmozzer dearest. You know how quickly one feature can outstrip anozzer in ze process of growth. And now I can smell you so much better. Snif snif. Snif snif. I can smell you <u>and</u> something else. Are you certain we are quite alone, dear grandmozzer? Snif snif.

GRAND M: I was expecting no one but you, granddaughter ACHOO ACHOO and now you have entirely forgotten my basket of presents which was so terribly important to me, living alone as I do so entirely and without consolation. SOB SOB.

GRAND M's *loud, false sobs touch* M. WOOLF *as real emotion never could.*

M. WOOLF: (*to the audience*) Oh my goodness, I deed not calculate affects of my avidity on ze old woman. Zis touches me very much, very much indeed. (GRAND M *sobs louder*) I sink I must kill ze poor thing quickly to put 'er out of 'er extreme misery. (GRAND M *instantly cries more softly*) But 'ow can I kill 'er if I cannot <u>touch</u> 'er?

GRAND M: Boo Hoo Hoo. Alone! Forsaken! Undernourished!

M. WOOLF: Eet ees clearly time to reveal myself and accomplish ze classical deed, but all zis emotion is, 'ow you say in American business circles, keeling my appetite for power.

GRAND M: Poor poor poor grandmother with nothing but a distant daughter, an ingrate grandchild, and a dull collection of carving knives! Boo! Hoo! Hoo!

M. WOOLF: Really, I cannot tolerate zis display of emotion. Grandmozzer dear grandmozzer! Cease your crying! Desist from your depression! See! See! (*he holds up the basket while rummaging thru it*) I have brought you 1, 2, 3, 4, 5, 6, six bottles of, of zis maroon liquid to drink. And beneath them . . . Argh! A dead hen of some sort.

GRAND M: I believe that's a songbird, Little Red Riding Hood.

M. WOOLF: Whatever it is, dear grandmozzer, I am certain it will make someone a very good meal. (M. WOOLF *begins to drip a little*) Now dry your dreadful tears and think about cooking.

GRAND M: I'd rather think about drinking, darling granddaughter. Your foolish flowers have begun to raise welts on my skin. See here and here.

M. WOOLF: Mon dieu! Could ze old dragon be correct? Her forearm looks anyway like a bas-relief map of the Pyrénées. (*to* GRAND M) Grandmozzer dearest. Eet ees true, zen. You are poisonous to ze touch?

GRAND M: Lay a hand on me, Little Red, and that hand will never again be the same.

M. WOOLF: Heureusement, my appetite is momentarily suppressed by ze old ladies' histrionics and, besides, I 'ave already confessed it, my serious preference is for prepubescent cheeldren. SLURP DROOL. Mon dieu! Mon bib! Uh, grandmozzer. Whatever can I do to offer you consolation for zis hideous condition?

GRAND M: Open a bottle for me Little Red and allow me to drown my misery in fermented blackberry juices.

M. WOOLF: Eet seems a small sing to ask, dear grandmozzer, 'ere you are. (*hands her a bottle*)

GRAND M: Salut salope. (*glug glug glug*) Ahhh. Much much better. But when thirst is satisfied, hunger begins to speak. Or so we butchers always say.

LITTLE R *sneezes in the armoire.*

M. WOOLF: (*freezes in a predatory attitude*) Aha! Grandmozzer. Zere is someone in your armoire.

GRAND M: Is it possible?

M. WOOLF: Years of serious training 'ave allowed me to identify ze smallest sound of prospective prey. Eef only I could 'ear it again.

LITTLE R: ACHOO ACHOO.

M. WOOLF: Merci.

GRAND M: (*to the audience*) The little fool is allergic to mothballs.

LITTLE R: ACHOO ACHOO ACHOO.

M. WOOLF: Oh merci merci. Now zat, eef I am not mistaken, is a female sneeze in ze 11 to 15 year old category. It is a blond sneeze, moreover, and more zan likely ze sneeze 'as blue eyes. Am I warm, dear grandmozzer.

GRAND M: You're running a temperature, Little Red Riding Hood.

M. WOOLF: I can only conclude, dear grandmozzer, zat in your armoire is concealed a dreadful, female imposter, 'oping to supplant me in your abundant affections.

GRAND M: Could it be M. <u>Woolf</u>, Little Red? Could it actually be the <u>big</u>, <u>bad</u>, <u>wolf</u> and could that <u>wolf</u> be a <u>female</u>?!!

M. WOOLF: Aoww. Aowwww. Even my name uttered by anozzer person affects me 'orribly. Woooooolf! Woooooolf! Aoooww! Aooowww! Pardon dearest grandmozzer. I am overly excited. I sink we might 'ave located ze terrible M. (*whispers*) Woolf in your armoire. I must enter and vanquish him. Or 'er, in zis case.

GRAND M: Go right ahead, darling granddaughter. I will sit here with my bottle and my needles and my knives at the ready.

M. WOOLF: At last! At last! My appetite will be satisfied! At last! Justice for ze Wolf! Aaaaooowwww!!!

M. WOOLF *enters the armoire and* GRAND M *shouts* "On the <u>right</u>, Little Red. Remember the axe is on the <u>right</u> and the blade is <u>sharp</u>." *And then* GRAND M *locks the armoire. We hear* LITTLE RED: "Where did you say that axe was, grandmère?!! On the left?" *and horrible sounds of battle:* "Take that! Beast!" "Aooww aowww." *Fur, blood, and tufts of blond hair drift, spurt, and blow out of the closet. Suddenly all is silent.* GRAND M *approaches the closet and opens the door.* LITTLE RED RIDING HOOD *steps out, bloody axe in hand, hood seriously askew.*

LITTLE R: I <u>did</u> it, grandmother dearest! I hacked the horrible M. Woolf into small steak-like pieces and, what is more, I did it at close range in a closet with a <u>very</u> dull instrument.

GRAND M: I could have <u>sworn</u> I had that axe sharpened.

LITTLE R: Alcohol, grandmère, has completely destroyed your mind. (*begins to boast and strut*) And not only, chère grandmère, did I accomplish this heroic deed under the very worst of conditions—to which you <u>heartlessly</u> exposed me—but I was even able to turn one of M. Woolf's own <u>signifiers</u> against him. To repeat, grandmère, I, Little Red Riding Hood, have <u>deconstructed</u> the Big, Bad Wolf.

GRAND M: (*sarcastically*) Oh brava brava granddaughter. What a blow, what a blow. Now, give me the axe, take this kettle, and catch what remains of the wolf's blood—and we will have sausages as well as songbirds for our breakfast.

LITTLE R: Ah, a boudin noir. I will do it with pleasure, dear grandmère. Your cooking has always been a lighthouse in the stormy seas of my childhood. Though to be frank, I think you use more wine in your sauces than is strictly necessary. (*she smiles her insupportable smile and reenters the closet*)

GRAND M: I don't know if I can support another decade of that smile.

LITTLE R: (*from the armoire*) Tee hee.

GRAND M: I don't know why I should put up with another year of that voice.

LITTLE R: (*from the armoire*) Ooooooo. Yuck.

GRAND M: I don't think I can stand another second of that attitude.

LITTLE R: (*from the armoire*) Oh grandmère you would not believe the mess M. Woolf has made in your armoire. Really, it is too awful.

GRAND M: (*stroking her needles*) It wouldn't be infanticide. Not at her age. She's just at the point where I might even be congratulated for . . . (*a trickle of blood flows out from under the armoire door*) My my. Once the blood starts flowing, there's no telling what direction it will run in. Or so we butchers always say. Heh heh heh. Appetite comes with eating. Another thing we butchers always say. Heh heh heh. Come out! Come out my dear! You've collected quite enough blood now. Come out and join your aged grandmother for a little nap before cooking. Or eating. Whichever applies. Heh heh heh.

> GRAND M's *teeth seem to lengthen as* LITTLE RED *emerges with the kettle of blood.*

LITTLE R: Here is your full kettle, chère grandmère, but I fear there is as much saliva as blood in it. M. Woolf was not a very fastidious animal and in the closet the two fluids just seemed to run together.

GRAND M: Put it down here, Little Red Riding Hood, and take off your cloak. I feel overcome by an immense fatigue.

LITTLE R: It's the wine, I'm afraid. And your very great age, grandmère.

GRAND M: (*to the audience*) Really, I marvel at the wolf's self-control. How could he not kill her immediately. Alright, Little Red, hop into bed, next to the wall where you will be warmed and protected.

LITTLE R: (*to the audience*) Did I not tell you what a remarkable woman my grandmother was?

GRAND M: That's right, little one. In you go. Hee hee hee.

> *Suddenly the spirit of Djuna Barnes appears in the famous profile portrait by Berenice Abbot. The spirit points to the bed and says with an evil intention:* "Children know something they can't tell. They like Little Red Riding Hood and the Wolf in bed together."

GRAND M: Now let me sing you a little slumber song. Something I used to sing for you when you were a very <u>little</u> Little Red Riding Hood.

LITTLE R: (*yawning visibly*) Oh grandmother dearest. Maman says you never got thru a lullaby in your whole life. You were always far too gone in alcohol, Maman says. (*yawn*) My, there is nothing like murder to relax the limbs and senses.

GRAND M: <u>Now</u> you sound like my own real granddaughter. At <u>last</u> you sound like a real Hood. It's quite late, of course, <u>too</u> late really, but it's very nice to hear.

LITTLE R: And is Hood your surname as well, chère grandmère? I've never really known <u>what</u> name you choose to go by. (*yawn*)

GRAND M: Hood is really more of a condition than a name, Little Red. Now close your little eyes and grandmother will sing you a lullaby to finish the day.

LITTLE R: Yawn. Where is the blood, grandmère? Where is the blood I extracted from M. Woolf? Yawn.

GRAND M: It is just here in the kettle under the bed, Little Red. Waiting to be used for a court bouillon.

LITTLE R: And the limbs of M. Woolf? And all that ugly fur?

GRAND M: All will be taken care of, I assure you my darling. I have a use for everything. Now close those little eyes and let grandmother sing you to a final sleep.

LITTLE R: Final, chère grandmère? What do you (*yawn*) mean by final?

GRAND M: Close your eyes, Little Red Riding Hood, and listen.

> Life is grotesque
> A terrible thing
> Love is a joke
> Choked by a ring
> The Wolf is alive
> Under everyone's bed
> And you would be better off DEAD
> Little Red
> You would be better off DEAD.

LITTLE RED RIDING HOOD *is snoring gently by lullaby's end.*

GRAND M: Now let me see. Where was I? Ah yes, the blackberry wine. A perfect accompaniment to meat. <u>Certain</u> kinds of meat. Or so we butchers always say. Now where are my knives and my knitting needles?

As the lights dim, GRANDMOTHER *is backlit in murderous silhouette, plunging her sharpened needles over and over and over again into the increasingly lifeless form of* LITTLE RED RIDING HOOD.

Suddenly, the image of Roland Barthes appears, driving a laundry truck. It circles the set once, steps out of the cab, tries to make sense of the scene it sees, shudders, thinks, shudders again, shrugs its shoulders, remounts the truck, and drives off. From offstage we hear the sounds of the stagehands killing each other in bloody battle over the meaning of what we've just seen. Cries of: "Structure! I'll give you structure! POW!" *and* "What do you <u>mean</u> the wolf was the protagonist! BLAM!" *echo thru the set.* GRANDMOTHER, *back in her rocking chair, plies her yarnless needles as the battle sounds roll over her and blood from the bed stains the floor around her chair.*

The set goes slowly and deliberately to black.

Finis

BURNING DESIRES

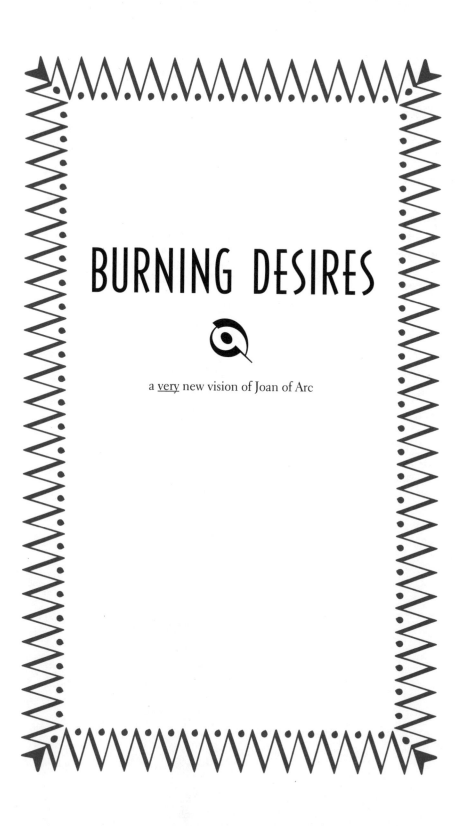

a <u>very</u> new vision of Joan of Arc

BURNING DESIRES had its first showing at New Dramatists, New York City, directed by Liz Diamond, in 1995–6.

Cast

Characters	Speech
DR. GEORGE DARK	Upper middle class American
MRS. MARTHA DARK	Upper middle class American
ADULT JOAN	Illuminated American
YOUNG JOAN	Teenage American
JOHN & JOHN DARK	American
DIANA	Greek-accented American
MARLENE DIETRICH	International
GERTRUDE STEIN	Stream-of-conscious American
EMILY BRONTË	Yorkshire-flavored English
EMILY DICKINSON	New England
PRINCESS ANGELINE	Salish Patois
PRINCE DWAYNE	Salish Patois
GILLES DE RAIS	Teenage French
THE BONFIRE GIRLS	Teenage American
THE BOY SCOUTS	Teenage American
THE SURGEONS	American
THE SALISH	Salish Patois

BURNING DESIRES

a <u>very</u> new vision of Joan of Arc

Part I

Mise en scene: **SEATTLE IN THE** 1950's. *The stage should be divided into two playing areas: the* OUTSIDE, *which is always various parts of* VOLUNTEER PARK *including a* DESERTED BEACH *and the* LONGHOUSE OF A SALISH INDIAN TRIBE, *and the* INSIDE, *which is always various parts of the* DARK HOUSE *including the* MATER-NITY WARD *of a 1940's Seattle Hospital, the* DARK FAMILY LIVING ROOM, YOUNG JOAN'S BOUDOIR, *the* BONFIRE GIRLS' RECREATION ROOM, *the* LABORATORY OF DR. DARK, *and whatever other terrain is needed.*

Whenever necessary, actors should double and triple (but not cross-gender) their roles. Ten actors are enough.

Everything that can be represented physically, should be represented physically. When it is impossible or ridiculous to use an actor or a prop, use rear-projections or film. This is a fast show, sports-car fast in the scene changes. If there is a prosce-nium, it should suggest a rainbow.

Completely black stage.

Sound of precipitation as the Audience enters the house.

Lights up on the Audience, which takes out its programs and begins to read the first scene. <u>Silently</u>.

The first scene. (Printed in the Audience's programs.) **PLAYWRIGHT'S STUDY.** *A desk, a chair, some books.*

MARLENE DIETRICH, *looking like herself (<u>more</u> so, if possible), sits leggily on the edge of a large desk, waving a contract like a fan in the face of the female* PLAYWRIGHT.

MARLENE: This is how we do things in pictures, darling. Everything in the contract. That should appeal to you as a writer, no?

SCHENKAR: (*straight into the audience*) I don't know how Marlene Dietrich got
to be my Literary Agent. Can you imagine? I mean I had expected maybe . . .
Jane Austen. Dorothy Parker in a pinch. But <u>Marlene</u> <u>Dietrich</u>?!!!

MARLENE: Pick up that pen darling. The signature goes right here at the bottom.

SCHENKAR: After a while, I came to see the logic in this lustrous creature sitting
on a corner of my desk, shaving her legs, doing her makeup, giving me advice.
She knew all the tricks writers use to postpone working . . .

MARLENE: I know what you're thinking and you can clean out the refrigerator
later. Much much later.

SCHENKAR: . . . and she took the job of inspiring me <u>very</u> seriously.

MARLENE: Now why don't you finish that monologue, darling. And do something about your hair.

SCHENKAR: I began to take her cruising in my sportscar.

MARLENE: (*rolling her eyes*) How I <u>hate</u> riding in tiny automobiles . . .

SCHENKAR: I was so dazzled by her radiance that I found her slipping between
the sheets of my work . . .

MARLENE: (*holding her head*) Kitsch, darling. That is ab-so-lute kitsch! No writer
should <u>ever</u> do kitsch! (*smooths* SCHENKAR's *cheek*) And, darling. Believe me.
A little make-up wouldn't hurt.

SCHENKAR: (*a little hurt*) Unfortunately, my Agent was allowed to criticize as
well as inspire.

MARLENE: Ach! Liebchen! You wouldn't believe the responsibilities I have.
Even if I could speak about them. Which I cannot. (*seductively*) And by the
way, I hope this new play has a part for me. (*muses*) Perhaps a saint. I've done
too many whores, darling.

SCHENKAR: (*a revelation, she picks up her pen*) A saint . . .

End of first scene.
*Lights up on the Audience. Crowd sounds, recorded, the buzz and hum of a
rapidly filling theatre. The Audience should be temporarily deceived into thinking
the sounds are coming from* <u>them</u>.
    VOICES *of a couple,* DR. GEORGE *and* MRS. MARTHA DARK, *making their way down
a crowded row in the theatre, interrupting the Audience as it reads the first scene.*

VOICES: "Excuse me."

"Pardon me madam."

"Sorry sir."

"Be careful George, that's a hat."

"That's not a hat that's my foot.

"Watch out, watch out."

"God I hate crowds," etc. etc.

A little smoke begins to drift across the black stage.

MARTHA: I smell smoke, George. There's smoke in here.

GEORGE: You are always smelling smoke, Martha.

MARTHA: Not in a movie theatre, George. I never smell smoke in a movie theatre.

*An insistent crackling sound. The black stage begins to burn and smolder like
cigarette paper.*

MARTHA: George. I hear something.

GEORGE: I hear it too.

MARTHA: It sounds like paper crackling GEORGE. It sounds like . . .

GEORGE: FIRE.

AUDIENCE: FIRE! FIRE! FIRE! FIRE!

*The black stage is engulfed in smoke. The title "Burning Desires" burns in flames
thru the darkness, just in time to prevent the Audience from stampeding the exits.*
Suddenly the adult, present-day JOAN OF ARC *is revealed on stage at the wheel of
a white 1957* TRIUMPH *convertible with a serious exhaust problem.* JOAN, *swathed
in exhaust smoke, alight with spiritual flames, sits in the car like a stunt driver.*

JOAN: (*brushes cinders off her shoulder, waves away the exhaust, and conspicu-
ously lights up a Gauloise*) This is the story of Joan of Arc and how she came
to be born into a new fate. It's been my story for a long time and now it's going
to be yours. Listen to me carefully. I have never told it like this before.

Appropriate visuals for JOAN's *story appear—all of them depicting an exquis-
itely ordered city of Seattle, painted in 50's pastels—with backdrops as emerald
and fictitious as an Irish Spring.*

JOAN: Here is Seattle, Washington, long before it was discovered by the rest of
you. It's 1957 or '58 right now and a light rain is falling. (*she opens a small um-
brella and raises it above her head*) The story—my story—will begin here. In
1958 everyone in Seattle is smoking Newports or Marlboros and driving
Buicks with Powerglide transmissions.

(*Armies of smokers in Buick convertibles broach the bridges of Seattle.*)

JOAN: All the men go to work and get haircuts.

(*A thousand electric razors buzz the backs of a thousand male necks.*)

JOAN: All the women keep house and visit the beauty parlor.

(*A hundred hair dryers in a hundred hair salons rev up to "hi."*)

JOAN: The boys play baseball.

(*Boys beat each other with bats on a baseball diamond.*)

JOAN: The girls do synchronized swimming.

(*Girls in matching petaled caps swim notably out of order.*)

JOAN: The Beatniks are safely in San Francisco.

(*Cafés wih no customers.*)

JOAN: Family values prevail.

(*A family snarlingly adjusts itself for a group photograph.*)

JOAN: And everywhere in the city, the rain falls without ceasing.

(*A torrential downpour.*)

JOAN: Fireplaces fizzle,

(*Rain pours down a chimney, completely extinguishing the fire in a family room.*)

JOAN: barbeques smolder,

(*An entire Shriners' picnic looks dumbly at a damp raw pig.*)

JOAN: arsonists lose heart,

(*A pyromaniac weeps over water-logged matches.*)

JOAN: even smokers can't keep their cigarettes lit in the downpour.

(*Cigarettes all over town go out mid-puff.*)

JOAN: You couldn't start a fire in Seattle to save your life—or to take someone else's.
   It's the perfect moment for the reappearance of Joan of Arc. This time, she might not burn.

Montage of 40's images of statues and paintings of JOAN OF ARC—*all in the final agonies of martyrdom* . . .

JOAN: Before the infant Joan Dark was born in Seattle, Washington, it rained in the city for three whole months . . .

Sound of torrential rains comes up under the last few words and quickly rises to Hurricane Andrew level. A crack of lightening in the form of a fleur-de-lys, an amazing succession of high cumulus formations, instant night, and the strangest configuration of stars and planets since the Book of Revelation was made public. Blackout.

Lights up: JOAN'S BEDROOM *which, in this scene, doubles as a* WORLD WAR 2 MATERNITY WARD. *Everything green and grey, wartime shortages everywhere apparent. Lights are flickering as an infant (baby* JOAN) *is delivered from a white-sheeted mound of moaning womanhood by a* DOCTOR *and an indifferent* NURSE.

DR.: Here it comes, nurse. Here it comes. Get ready. We don't want you to drop <u>this</u> one.

The INFANT *appears, smiles, glows phosphorescently, and lisps a line from one of the shorter Emily Dickinson poems. No one notices the poetry, but the seedy* NURSE *(who's palming a Pall Mall) fumbles the* INFANT *in shock when a flock of white doves attacks the* DOCTOR *as he approaches the baby's umbilical cord with a nasty surgical tool. The* DOCTOR *cowers in a corner, beaten back by the whirring wings of the enraged birds.*

The newborn INFANT *speaks distinctly to the* DOCTOR:

JOAN: I don't <u>yike</u> you.

DR.: *(trying to get the* NURSE's *attention)* Nurse! Nurse! Jesus <u>Christ</u>, Nurse! The baby just <u>said</u> something!

The room is suddenly bathed in golden light and all eyes turn to the window as the crummy NURSE *holding* BABY JOAN *points to the spreading sunshine.*

NURSE: Look Doctor! For godssake! <u>Look</u> at that! The sun's out! You can see the goddamn mountains! You can see the goddamn <u>trees</u>! It's a <u>miracle</u>! It's a <u>real</u> <u>miracle</u>! *(she holds the* INFANT JOAN *in one arm and smokes her Pall Mall furiously with the other)*

A fabulous rainbow enters the room and points to the glowing, crowing INFANT JOAN. *The* NURSE, *shocked again by the rainbow in the act of lighting another cigarette, and again missing the <u>real</u> miracle, drops little* JOAN *on the floor.*

NURSE: Ooooops.

Blackout.

Lights up: the DARK HOUSE. *The heads of* DR. GEORGE *and* MRS. MARTHA DARK *in profile in a large frame. They are both smoking energetically. She smokes Kents, he smokes Chesterfields. The frame hovers over* CHILD JOAN, *age 7 or 8, upstage in her pink and white and blonde-wood* BEDROOM. *She is constructing, with great meticulousness, a somewhat ecumenical altar featuring the Baby Jesus and his Mother, the black Madonna of Poland, Mary of Medjugorje, an enormous Star of*

David, framing a particularly violent interpretation of Jael and her Nail, a statue of Kuan Yin, a statue of Kali the Destroyer, and pictures of Emily Dickinson, Emily Brontë, Gertrude Stein, and Diana of the Ephesians, with drawn bow.

LITTLE JOAN *hums liturgical music happily as she works. Occasionally she performs small miracles.*

MARTHA: George. I never thought we'd have a religious child. I thought many things, George, when I found myself pregnant for the first time. Believe me, between the vomiting and the headaches, I thought many things. But I never thought the outcome would be religious. We should have sued the nurse who dropped her, George. We should have sued the <u>hospital</u>.

Lights up: LITTLE JOAN *kneels before the statue of the goddess Diana.* LITTLE JOAN *holds a large, lethal peashooter.*

LITTLE JOAN: (*with immense feeling and a slight lisp*) Oh goddess Diana. Help me to be as gweat a shot as you are. Help me to hit that wittle bastard Billy Jensen wight in the eye.

Lights up: GEORGE *and* MARTHA *some years later. Same position, same cigarettes, same frame.*

MARTHA: She's doing her <u>home</u>work, George, <u>that's</u> what she's doing. You know she studies night and day.

Lights up: JOAN'S BEDROOM. JOAN, *a lovely 12 year old, is on her knees before her altar, speaking to the images. As she addresses each one, it illuminates and seems to breathe.*

JOAN: Emily Dickinson, thank you for that poem. Even my English teacher didn't understand it.

MARTHA: How <u>else</u> do you think she gets those perfect grades, George. She stays in her room and she does her <u>work</u>. I only wish her <u>brothers</u> were that conscientious.

JOAN: (*still on her knees*) Emily Brontë, I never could have finished that map of the moors without your guidance . . .

Lights up: GEORGE *and* MARTHA.

GEORGE: In her room all day long Martha? That's not normal. I just hope she's not . . . (*whispers the word*) <u>praying</u> again Martha. I just sincerely hope she's given up <u>that</u> habit for Lent.

Lights up: JOAN *in prayerful attitude.*

JOAN: Gertrude Stein. That gym suit you picked out for me scared the <u>hell</u> out of the volleyball coach. (*big grin, as she reassumes her devotional posture*)

Lights up: GEORGE *and* MARTHA *some years later. Same position, same ciga-rettes, same frame. Arrows whiz around* GEORGE.

GEORGE: Why the bow, Martha. Why the <u>bow</u> and <u>arrows</u>. Other girls her age <u>knit</u> or belong to <u>swim</u> teams. Why the goddam <u>bow</u>?

Lights up: **JOAN'S BEDROOM.** JOAN *age 15 on her knees before her altar. She wears a bow and quiver.*

JOAN: Oh goddess Diana. Give me some guidance. Tell me how to use my pow-ers. I'm just a <u>teen</u>ager, for cripesssake.

Lights up: MARTHA *and* GEORGE.

MARTHA: She told me the bow was historical, George. She said the Goddess Diana and all the Amazons used it in the old days and to tell the truth George, actually (*highly embarrassed*) . . . I think the way she wears it . . . looks . . . sort of . . . <u>cute</u>.

Lights up: JOAN *unobserved by her parents, bow drawn, arrow knocked and pointed straight at her father's framed heart.*

JOAN: (*sotto voce*) Is this what you want me to do Diana? Shoot at <u>him</u>? (*straight to the Audience*) I'm having trouble translating from the ancient Greek.

GEORGE: (*purpling*) Aaargh. <u>Cute</u>. For <u>god</u>ssake Martha, Joan is running around this city with a <u>bow</u> on her shoulder and a <u>quiver</u> on her back! I'm taking her athletic privileges away Martha! I'm taking her <u>sportscar</u> away!

MARTHA: Oh look George. It's raining again.

GEORGE: What do you mean raining <u>again</u> Martha. It's just <u>raining</u> <u>harder</u>, that's all. Unless the rain attains a certain velocity around here, we don't even <u>ac-knowledge</u> it. (*finally sees the arrow stuck in the doorjamb*) What is that girl up to <u>now</u>, Martha.

MARTHA: She's driving to her first Bonfire Girl meeting George. She wanted to join the Brownies but I didn't care for the uniforms.

Lights up: YOUNG JOAN *in her smoking* TRIUMPH *quiver on her back, appears to drive thru the rain like a pro. A flock of doves flutters around the* TRIUMPH.

GEORGE: (*still in his frame*) Bonfire Girls. <u>Hah</u>. I'm surprised she didn't try for the <u>Boy</u> Scouts.

Lights up: ADULT JOAN *in the* TRIUMPH. *Big drag on her Gauloise.*

JOAN: Of <u>course</u> I tried for the Scouts. They didn't want me.

Lights up: **NANCY DETWILER'S BASEMENT.** *Another part of the stage. A* BON-FIRE GIRLS *meeting is in progress. The girls are in full regulation uniform—a hideous confusion of Girl Guide and Kwakiutl Indian—and they look ridiculous.*

They're making up each other's faces, perming hair, dancing with each other. Cigarette smoke is everywhere apparent and there's a smoldering fire in the rec room fireplace. The BONFIRE GIRLS *take turns feeding it with anything at hand—books, small pieces of furniture, the family poodle, etc. A solid atmosphere of juvenile delinquency prevails.*

JOAN: (*recoiling slightly at the sight of the fire, she whispers*) Is this where I'm supposed to be, Diana?

VOICE: (*celestial, cool*) Wherever you are, Joan dear, is where you're supposed to be. Hang on to your bow.

A *chorus of* BONFIRE GIRL *voices howl:* "Shuddup I can't hear the music," "Christ Jeanie you spilled the beer," " Oh god don't tell me <u>she's</u> the new member," "Feed the fire," "Feed the <u>fire</u>! "FEED THE FIRE!"

NANCY: (*emerging from behind a cloud of smoke*) <u>I</u> am Nancy Detwiler, <u>these</u> are the Bonfire Girls, and <u>this</u> (*points to the carnage*) is what we do at meetings.

JOAN: It's nice to . . .

CINDY: Anybody got a Newport?

JOAN: . . . meet you.

GRETCHEN: Where's the wine, Nancy?

NANCY: (*gestures towards the record cabinet*) Behind the Julie London albums.

CINDY: Jeez it's only half full.

NANCY: I had a hard week Cindy, OK?

The BONFIRE GIRLS *sit in a circle, passing the jug, lighting up, sewing fake Indian beads on each other's uniforms.*

GRETCHEN: (*to* JOAN) Pass those beads quick willya. I just saw Nancy's mother out there (*points out the picture window*) rooting up the rhododendrons.

ANNE: She's looking for cigarette butts.

NANCY: Oh <u>Christ</u>!

CINDY: That's all we need another inspection.

JESSIE: The whole damn troop's on probation for swearing anyway. Throw me some blue ones.

GRETCHEN: <u>Jeez</u> these things are ugly.

CINDY: I bet the <u>real</u> Indians burned their beads.

NANCY: Turn up the music. I can't hear a thing.

NANCY'S MOTHER *appears wearing an Indian headress. She is unheard because of the music.*

MOTHER: Yoo hoo Girls. <u>Girls</u>. It's troop inspection time. Girls. Hellloooo. Have we practiced our fire-starting yet? (*she waves frantically*)

GRETCHEN: (*screaming*) Are those real arrows Joan or what.

VOICE: (*it's* DIANA's *voice*) Show them, Joan dear. Show the little savages what is real.

JOAN: (*responding to* DIANA's *cue with a confident grin*) You bet they're real, Bonfire Girls. Watch my form on this one. (*takes out an arrow, nocks it, whirls around and lets it fly into a dartboard 6 inches from the right ear of* NANCY's MOTHER)

MOTHER: JESUS CHRIST! (*drops her shopping bag and war bonnet*) It's an <u>Indian</u>! (*runs out the door*)

ALL: (*in concert*) WOW. You damn near killed Nancy's mother!!

VOICE: Well done, Joan. Though you were a centimeter south of the bullseye. (JOAN *cocks her head, listening*)

NANCY: (*nastily, she's jealous*) Did I mention that Joan hears voices?

CINDY: Voices, that is so <u>weird</u>.

CAROLINE: Like <u>whose</u> voices? Like Dion and the Belmonts? Like Frankie Avalon's? Like <u>whose</u>?

JOAN: <u>Women's</u> voices. You know. Writers . . . movie stars . . . <u>goddesses</u>.

ALL: (*in concert*) <u>GODDESSES</u>!!

JOAN: (*very frank and straightforward*) Well I haven't actually contacted Venus <u>yet</u> . . . but the Goddess Diana speaks to me every day and lately Emily Brontë and Gertrude Stein and Marlene Dietrich have been whispering . . . (*slight pause, as tho' listening to instructions*) Uh-oh. I'm not supposed to mention this.

CINDY: Yeah I <u>bet</u> you're not. Hey Nance (*she's getting drunker*). Who does Joan remind you of?

JULIE: (*also tipsy*) Catherine of course. Why'd we let ole Catherine in?

GRETCHEN: (*sotto voce*) Why'd we let <u>Joan</u> in?

NANCY: <u>My</u> mother plays golf with <u>her</u> mother that's why.

CAROLINE: Where the hell <u>is</u> Catherine anyway?

JULIE: She's prob'ly in the john.

CINDY: As usual.

JULIE: Fixing her hair.

NANCY: Or her face.

JULIE: Forget the hair.

CAROLINE: Forget the <u>face</u>.

CATHERINE of New Rochelle appears all in white, uniformless, hideously frilly, revoltingly feminine, phony as a romance novelist. (A suburban New York accent would be nice.)

NANCY: (*announcing*) Catherine. Of New Rochelle. Wherever <u>that</u> is. (*sotto voce*) My mother plays golf with <u>her</u> mother too. (*to* CATHERINE) Meet Joan Dark.

CATHERINE: (*languidly*) Oh really.

NANCY: Joan has something in common with you Catherine.

CATHERINE: (*languidly*) Oh really.

VOICE: (*of* DIANA) You <u>don't</u> have anything in common with her, Joan dear, but go ahead. Make the contact. It's part of your destiny.

There is a pause as JOAN *and* CATHERINE *look at each other,* JOAN *in anticipation of a confidante,* CATHERINE *measuring a rival.*

CATHERINE: I promise you, Bonfires. This will <u>never</u> work.

Blackout.

Lights up: CATHERINE'S BEDROOM. *Which is* JOAN'S BEDROOM *tricked out with revoltingly frilly appurtenances, and splashed with pastels.*

CATHERINE: I <u>really</u> don't think this is such a <u>wonderful</u> idea Joan.

JOAN: I have to know Catherine. I have to know if your White Lady is the same as my Goddess Diana or my Emily Brontë or my Marlene Dietrich. And I'm prepared to stay up all night to find out.

CATHERINE: Well I'm <u>sure</u> I haven't a <u>clue</u>. My White Lady appears in my room every night in a <u>halo</u> of radiance and an <u>elegant</u> wedding gown and she <u>never</u> says a word about archery or poetry or Hollywood movies. (*practiced pause*) She <u>never</u> says a word about <u>anything</u>.

JOAN: (*genuinely excited*) Gee. A wedding gown. I wonder what the Goddess Diana would think of . . . (*Pauses as tho' listening*) Uh oh. Oh. Really Diana? And St. Marlene agrees? (*wincing*) Isn't that a little . . . <u>harsh</u>?

Blackout.

Lights up: ADULT JOAN *in her* TRIUMPH, *high above the city of Seattle. She appears to be driving slowly.*

Lights up: YOUNG JOAN *is dimly seen, still in* CATHERINE'S BEDROOM.

JOAN: Catherine. We've been here the whole night and your White Lady never showed up <u>once</u>. (*disconsolately*) The Goddess Diana was <u>right</u>. I don't have <u>any</u>thing in common with <u>any</u>body!

Blackout on BEDROOM.

PRESENT-DAY JOAN *pauses at the top of* QUEEN ANNE HILL.

JOAN: After the incident with Catherine, I began to drive the streets of Seattle, looking for a clue to my waiting fate. I knew I was being prepared for something—the Goddess Diana had dropped a few hints about destiny—but my other voices were silent on the subject. (*big drag on a Gauloise*) Meanwhile, and <u>very</u> suddenly, the Goddess Diana withdrew from my life.

Lights up: YOUNG JOAN, *disconsolate, sits in* VOLUNTEER PARK.

VOICE: (*of* DIANA) I'm going away Joan dear. On a honeymoon trip. With a Greek poet. You'd love her work. It's time for someone more worldly to take over your education. (*calls*) Oh Marlene. Marlene Dietrich . . .

JOAN: (*merges her voice with* DIANA's) Marlene. St. Marlene Dietrich. The Goddess Diana has deserted me for a <u>woman</u>.

MARLENE: (V.O.) Not a woman, darling. A <u>genius</u>. Diana left you for the poet Sappho. Now get in that car, liebchen, and <u>drive</u>.

Lights up: ADULT JOAN *in her* TRIUMPH.

JOAN: Who could refuse a suggestion from Marlene Dietrich? I drove thru the city. I learned as I drove.

JOAN: The city I saw was a place of lush gardens and emerald lawns . . .

(*in a lush garden a band of boys tries to steal* YOUNG JOAN's *TR-3; she jujitsus each of them over her shoulder; they land on an emerald lawn. In the background, several* BONFIRE GIRLS *are trying to ignite a lovely bed of tulips.*)

JOAN: . . . of sparkling waters and constant cloud covers.

(*the Seattle Fire Department hoses thousands of gallons of sparkling water on an enormous fire at The Kline-Gallen Home for the Aged;* YOUNG JOAN *methodically and repeatedly emerges from the billowing smoke with a rescued old person in her arms, on her back, or in a borrowed wheelchair. A troop of* BONFIRE GIRLS *stands by, concealing torches, and watching the flames with real excitement.*)

JOAN: A church-going city.

(in front of a Cathedral a BOY SCOUT *pushes a* BONFIRE GIRL *to the ground. The* BONFIRE GIRL *punches the boy thru the Cathedral's open door.)*

JOAN: A city so clean that garbage cans were forbidden within its limits. At least you never <u>saw</u> garbage cans in Seattle.

*(*BONFIRE GIRLS, *impersonating good citizens, light trash fires for fun.)*

YOUNG JOAN, *the* JOAN OF 1958, *now replaces* ADULT JOAN *in the* **TRIUMPH** *and in the narration.* ADULT JOAN *relinquishes both positions with grace and good humor.*

JOAN: I used to spend a lot of time—before St. Marlene Dietrich and her friends came to me—wondering how to reconcile the city of Seattle to itself. But after the visits started, my mind began to move in other patterns. My mind began to . . . <u>receive</u>.

Blackout.

Lights up: **JOAN'S BLONDE WOOD BEDROOM:** MARLENE DIETRICH *applies makeup in front of the mirror,* GERTRUDE STEIN *sits on the altar smoking a cigar,* EMILY BRONTË *and her dog* KEEPER *are in a sort of ecstatic arrest at the writing table.*

Lights up: **DARK HOUSE.** YOUNG JOAN *pauses in front of the door, listening for something. She hears it, a beatific expression transforms her face, and she enters the house.*

Lights up: **JOAN'S BEDROOM.** MARLENE DIETRICH *and* GERTRUDE STEIN *are casually lounging about;* EMILY BRONTË *is still entranced at the writing table, and* EMILY DICKINSON *is invisible and reciting in the closet.*

EMILY D: Wild nights! Wild nights!
　　　　Were I with thee
　　　　Wild nights
　　　　Would be our ecstasy!

GERTRUDE: *(facing the closet, hands on hips, she looks like a teakettle)* Jesus <u>Christ</u> doesn't that woman ever come out of the closet.

MARLENE: Now Gertude Stein. Darling. You know how shy she is.

EMILY B: *(suddenly alert)* <u>I</u> am shy, Marlene Dietrich. Emily Dickinson is completely <u>daft</u>! *(sinks back to her trance)*

GERTRUDE: *(turns approvingly)* Good for you Emily Brontë I had no idea English writers could be so colloquial.

Bump at the door.

GERTRUDE: <u>Now</u> what.

MARLENE: Ach gott. It's Joan's brothers. The little Nazis are surveiling the room. I smeared lipstick on the door lock and their eyes have been bright red all week.

GERTRUDE: (*rubbing her hands together*) Oooo what about a hatpin thru the keyhole or (*scans the vanity*) a squirt of your special perfume Marlene a shot of alcohol in the eyeballs oughtta do <u>some</u>thing for the little dwarves.

MARLENE: The perfume is only lethal to <u>grown</u> men, Gertrude.

GERTRUDE: Well they'd better not get in <u>my</u> way that's what I've got to say and that's <u>all</u> I've got to say.

MARLENE: (*suavely reproving*) The important thing, Gertrude darling, is whether or not the boys get in <u>Joan's</u> way.

EMILY B: (*coming momentarily out of a trance*) Gertrude. Marlene. Tell me the names of these savage children.

MARLENE: John.

GERTRUDE: (*in glum repetition*) And <u>John</u>. John and John. John and John. John and John. (*brightens*) That sounds just like something <u>I</u> might have written.

Blackout.

Lights up: **DARK FAMILY LIVING ROOM.** GEORGE *and* MARTHA, *smoking furiously.*

MARTHA: We shouldn't have named them both John, George. I'm telling you, we should never have done it. It's very bad for their psychologies.

GEORGE: Well, I certainly wasn't going to name them after <u>me</u>, Martha. Being a junior is a <u>terrible</u> thing. <u>Just</u> <u>terrible</u>. I should know. (*broods*)

MARTHA: No one said you had to name them George, George. I don't even <u>like</u> the name George.

GEORGE: Just how many boys names <u>are</u> there, Martha.

MARTHA: There's Douglas, George. There is certainly always Douglas.

The two JOHNS *burst in. One* JOHN *always addresses* GEORGE, *the other speaks only to* MARTHA.

JOHN: Mom!

JOHN: Dad!

JOHN: Lookit Mom!

JOHN: Lookit Dad!

2 JOHNS: We caught another cat.

JOHN: And we found its liver Dad.

JOHN: And its kidneys Mom. Look.

JOHN: And its dick Dad. We found its dick. It was right where you said it would be.

GEORGE: (*fondly, sternly*) Boys. Boys. I appreciate your interest in anatomy but . . . (*lifts cat by the tail*) Oh my. That seems to be the Sternoff's cat. How many times have I told you not to touch animals that are <u>owned</u>.

JOHN: (*hiding the cat collar behind his back*) Its collar was gone Dad.

JOHN: We didn't know it was <u>owned</u> Mom. We wanted to see what was <u>inside</u>.

JOHN: It was like educational Dad.

GEORGE: Boys. Boys. A little knowledge is a dangerous thing.

JOHN: What does Dad mean by that Mom.

MARTHA: I haven't the faintest idea John. And <u>John</u>, you know perfectly well what the Sternoffs cat looks like . . . uh, looked like. It was a Jewish cat and <u>Jewish</u> cats have very distinctive markings. Now boys if you so much as touch one more neighborhood animal, Jewish or non-Jewish, I will lock up your bikes for the entire summer and that is a very firm promise.

JOHN: Awww Mom.

JOHN: Geez Dad.

GEORGE: (*sotto voce*) It's an <u>idle</u> promise Martha. You <u>know</u> it's going to rain all summer long.

MARTHA: (*sotto voce*) It's <u>not</u> an idle promise George. These boys are so stupid they <u>ride</u> in the rain. (*viva vice*) Now why don't you go play with your sister. Joanie has such a nice way of playing. So. . . . quiet.

JOHN: We don't want to play with our sister Dad.

JOHN: Our sister is nuts Mom.

JOHN: She stays in her room all day long Dad.

JOHN: How come Joanie gets her own room and we don't.

JOHN: She's a <u>girl</u> dumbell. Girls always get their own rooms. So they can practice their archery.

JOHN: And talk to people who aren't there. Well <u>sometimes</u> they're there.

JOHN: And read stuff in other languages.

JOHN: And pray Mom.

JOHN: And <u>pray</u> Dad.

JOHN: I just <u>said</u> that, flatnose.

JOHN: Well she prays a <u>lot</u> John.

JOHN: I <u>said</u> that zitface.

GEORGE: Joan is . . . <u>talking</u> to people now?

JOHN: Older women, Dad.

JOHN: And they're talking <u>back</u> peabrain.

GEORGE: (*to* MARTHA) Uh-oh. This is a new development Martha.

MARTHA: And it hurts me very much George. Very much indeed.

GEORGE: Well it hurts me too, Martha. I've been X-raying that girl for <u>years</u>. No doctor-father wants to sign the commitment papers that will wire his daughter to a hospital gurney and electroshock her into the 1950's for godssake.

MARTHA: There you go again George. Just totally thinking of Dr. Dark. Our only daughter, <u>George</u>, is confiding in women who aren't <u>related</u> to her. Now how do you think that makes her <u>mother</u> feel.

GEORGE: Oh for godssake Martha. Joan is not rejecting you. Joan is exhibiting a serious mental condition and (*a hard look at Martha*) I damn well know where she got it from.

An arrow whizzes right past GEORGE's *head and finds a quivering home in the wall. The* DARKS *ignore it.*

JOHN: Look Mom it's raining again.

Blackout.

Lights up: JOAN'S ROOM. JOAN *alone. Rain runs under this monologue.*

JOAN: I hate the rain in this city. It falls like liquid sorrow, quenching the hotter emotions.

(*A troop of* BONFIRE GIRLS *stand around a campfire, trying to fan the coals into flames.*)

Nevertheless, the fire-starters are everywhere—the rain seems to inspire them. One of them was arrested last week near this house with a sodden box of matches. She admitted to nothing except a passion for the color red.

(*A* BONFIRE GIRL *is led away by* OFFICER RYAN. *She succeeds in setting his cap on fire.*)

I'm beginning to . . . <u>feel</u> the fires.

GEORGE AND MARTHA'S BEDROOM: *complete darkness.* GEORGE *lights a ciga-rette with two shaking hands; what is visible is a wavering flame and a trembling lit cigarette end.*

GEORGE: Martha Martha. <u>Martha</u>. Wake up. I had the same dream again.

Lights up.

MARTHA: The dream yawn about Joan yawn.

GEORGE: Of course it's the dream about Joan. That's the only dream I <u>ever</u> have Martha. She was in men's <u>clothes</u> Martha. In one of those bars full of <u>other</u> women in men's clothes. She was arm wrestling the only <u>real</u> man there and she was <u>beating</u> him for godssake. And every time she wrestled the man's arm to the table, the women in the bar made a kind of . . . <u>sound</u> Martha. I never heard anything like it in my life. (*with gestures*) It kindled in the diaphragm, seared up thru the esophagus, and flamed out over the soft palate. It was the sound of women <u>winning</u>, Martha. (*Pause, shudder*) And it was <u>awful</u>.

Pause

I'll drown her. I swear to god. If I ever see her in pants, if I ever see her flex-ing her muscles, if I ever see that she <u>has</u> muscles, I will throw her body into Puget Sound, see if I don't.

Blackout.

Lights up: JOAN'S BEDROOM. *She's having a dream.*

Lights up: JOHN AND JOHN'S BEDROOM. JOHN *and* JOHN *are suspiciously inter-twined. They're having* JOAN's *dream too.*

Blackout.

Lights up: DREAMLAND. GEORGE *and the* BOYS *are in a hazy space on the mar-gins of a dreamy seaside resort on the Oregon Coast. They are attired in beachwear and very enthusiastic. One* JOHN *carries a rubber ducky and the other* JOHN *carries a bucket and shovel.*

GEORGE: Did you try to sink her in the swimming pool?

JOHN: Sure Dad.

GEORGE: Did you weight her with stones and throw her in the sea?

JOHN: You bet Dad.

GEORGE: The bathtub. What about the bathtub?

JOHN: We tried that too Dad.

JOHN: We filled it real full Dad.

GEORGE: (*carefully, controlling himself*) Well boys. What happened in the pool, what happened in the sea, what happened in the bathtub.

JOHN: The pool is lousy with lifeguards, Dad.

JOHN They wouldn't let a stone sink.

JOHN: (*bitterly*) We couldn't've drowned a puppy.

JOHN: And the ocean is full of boats, Dad.

JOHN: Three huge sailors came churning thru the waves the minute we threw her in.

JOHN: Too much surveillance Dad.

JOHN: And the bathtub. That was the worst.

JOHN: No plug, Dad. Everybody at this resort takes showers.

JOHN: Finally we just filled up our toothbrush glasses and threw water on her.

JOHN: That was just for fun Dad. Dad?

JOHN: Dad? Dad?

JOHN: Honest Dad. We'll get her next time.

GEORGE: (*head in hands, moans softly*).

Blackout on **DREAMLAND**.

Lights up: **JOAN'S BEDROOM**. *She sits bolt upright in bed and clutches her bow and arrow.*

JOAN: (*gasps*) I've had this dream <u>before</u>. I've been like this <u>before</u>. (*looks down*) I feel . . . flames around the bed. There is . . . <u>fire</u> in my future.

GERTRUDE *and* MARLENE *appear at their posts.*

MARLENE: Joan darling. Put down that bow. C'est nous. And we are bringing some <u>very</u> . . . <u>hot</u> . . . news.

The CLOSET *barks twice. Then it howls.*

GERTRUDE: Oh will you listen to that Emily Brontë's left her dog in the closet again.

MARTHA: (*takes a whiff of the closet*) Mon dieu! And they say the <u>French</u> don't bathe.

PRINCESS ANGELINE, *daughter of Sealth, Chief of the Five Salish tribes of the Pacific Northwest, bursts from the closet, on a heavy tom tom roll. She's in native dress, much of which seems to be involved with fish scales and fins.*

ANGELINE: Hoo hoo. SURPRISE EVERYBODY. SURPRISE. Dog was not alone in that closet. (*to* MARLENE) Hoo hoo <u>look</u> at those legs. Like totem poles. Like fetishes. Very nice, luscious blond Venus. Hoo hoo <u>hoo</u>. (*turns to face* JOAN)

<u>I</u> am Princess Angeline, oldest child of Chief Sealth, rightful ruler of the Five Salish Tribes of this city. So who inherits the job of Chief when Papa Sealth swims to heaven? My dumb brother Dwayne, is who. Big drop in prestige if dumb brother Dwayne takes over tribal duties. Plus, trouble in Salish Nation has upset balance of nature. Salmon are swimming backwards, trees grow upside down, young girls start fires all over town, you get the picture. Therefore I, Princess Angeline, have put my foot on Path of War against all males of the Salish tribe. Hoo hoo. Such fun. I'm having a ball. And tonight I bring news that health of this city depends on heroic action by Joan Dark. But first, a little entertainment. (*another tom tom roll*)

(*chants*) Only good family man
Is dead good family man
Only good family man
Is dead good family man
Hoo hoo hoo hoo hoo
Hoo <u>hoo</u>.

GERTRUDE: (*over the chant*) Exactly how I would have said it myself Joan. The city is sick it is drowning and it is burning . . .

MARLENE: (*interrupts*) . . . and nobody knows <u>what</u> to do with the garbage.

GERTRUDE: You must restore Princess Angeline to her rightful place Joan—and heal (*a large gesture*) this embattled landscape.

The chant—and its accompanying dance—takes PRINCESS ANGELINE *up to the dresser where she stops vis-à-vis* GERTRUDE.

ANGELINE: Hoo hoo hooooooo. I know about <u>you</u>, Miss Gertrude Stein. Princess Angeline has <u>many</u> times shared her lodge with lovely Indian maidens. After night of wild pleasure we rub each other's bodies with salmon oil and seal urine. <u>Very</u> moving gesture and what a <u>heavenly</u> smell. You would perhaps like a bottle of salmon oil for your very own, large pale sister? (*she whips out a vial from her voluminous shawl*)

GERTRUDE: I'm totally and fully flattered Princess Angeline please accept this box of hand-rolled Cuban cigars in appreciation.

ANGELINE: Ah. (*smells them*) Mmmm. Very nice. (*takes one out*) Cigars are big in Five Tribes right now. All male Salish will fall into deep depression and jealous rage. Good gift large pale sister!

And Joan, I see you follow custom of my Lakota sisters with your bow and arrows. Excellent weapons, but geographically inappropriate. Here in Northwest Territory we use simple wooden spears to skewer the enemy. (*and she whips out a spear from her voluminous shawl*)

JOAN: Thank you Princess Angeline. I will carry it in your defense.

CLOSET *barks.*

ANGELINE: Hoo hoo. Good retort young heroine. I'll be back with instructions. (*lascivious look at* MARLENE) So sorry to leave your legs untouched Blond Venus. (CLOSET *barks again*) I must leave ladies, blood lust calls, I have many men to murder. (*she chants her way to the closet*)

Only good family man
Is dead good family man
Hoo hoo hoo hoo
Hoooo — move over doggie, it's Princess Angeline.

(CLOSET *barks again*)

EMILY: (*stepping thru the closet door, shuddering*) Ohhh. Who . . . who was it I just avoided in the closet. She had . . . she had a kind of <u>fish</u> feeling.

MARLENE: That was Princess Angeline darling. Isn't she divine? And did you see those trousers Joan? The world will <u>never</u> take you seriously if you wear a skirt. (*she pirouettes her trousers with great charm*)

GERTRUDE: Oh bloody hell what is the matter with Emily Brontë <u>now</u>.

EMILY: (*in a trance*) I smell smoke. I smell . . . <u>fire</u>.

Blackout.

Lights up: **SALISH LONGHOUSE.** *Meeting of Salish males around a smoking fire. They're dressed like sockeye salmon and they behave as though they're at a Men's Movement Weekend.* DWAYNE, *brother of* PRINCESS ANGELINE, *presides in the Salish language.*

DWAYNE: Warriors. Today we Salish swim in streams of cultural confusion.

WARRIORS: True, Dwayne.

DWAYNE: To survive, we must borrow from the old and steal from the new.

WARRIORS: True, Dwayne.

DWAYNE: So, warriors, I propose we deal with our threat directly.

WARRIORS: Good, Dwayne.

DWAYNE: Let us burn Princess Angeline at the stake, <u>then</u> donate her remains to science. Warriors. What do you think.

WARRIORS: (*they flap their fins in approval: swish swish swish swish*)

Good idea Dwayne.

Good idea Dwayne.

Good <u>thinking</u> Dwayne.

I didn't know Dwayne <u>could</u> think.

DWAYNE: (*an expansive gesture*) For <u>you</u>, warriors, even <u>that</u>.

WARRIORS: Good, Dwayne.

WARRIORS: FEED THE FIRE. FEED THE FIRE. FEED THE FIRE.

> *Blackout.*

> *Lights up: the* BONFIRE GIRLS, *slightly charred, are cruising a* BEACH, *looking for trouble. The view is beautiful, but they are oblivious.*

CINDY: How long since we had a fire Nancy.

NANCY: Oh, it's been two, three, hours at least.

ANNIE: I need another one, girls.

BECKY: I'm crazy about the color.

CINDY: I really dig the flames.

CANDY: I <u>adore</u> the ashes.

CATHERINE: (*simpering*) Fires are so romantic.

CINDY: <u>Can</u> it, Catherine.

NANCY: Okay okay. Let's start a fire <u>now</u>.

BECKY: Where's Joan.

ANNIE: She's never around when we do fires.

CANDY: I don't think she (*hesitates, a heresy*) . . . <u>likes</u> fire.

CINDY: This wood's awful wet.

NANCY: Hey we're Bonfire Girls. Wet wood's a <u>challenge</u>.

ANNE: Here's the kerosene.

CINDY: Can't we be more creative? Can't we burn something besides wood?

TRACY: How about a Brownie.

BECKY: Or a Cub Scout.

NANCY: I like tradition. Let's stick with wood.

ANNE: (*striking a match*) For now.

> *Blackout.*

> *Lights up:* JOAN'S BEDROOM, *now transformed to* FREDERICK AND NELSON'S,

Seattle's flagship department store in the 1950's. The fairy tale version. JOAN, MAR-LENE, GERTRUDE, *and* EMILY BRONTË *are on the longest wooden escalator in the world, passing ever upward thru astonishing displays of haute bourgeoise clothes for women.* EMILY DICKINSON *is in this scene too, but invisible.*

MARLENE: (*arm around* JOAN) Ach darling! Isn't this gemutlich. There is <u>nothing</u> like a really good department store.

GERTRUDE: (*glumly*) I am here steadily and without excitement but I am not happy.

MARLENE: Not happy in this monument to womanhood? Oh <u>Gertrude</u>.

GERTRUDE: (*glumly*) I could be happy in a houndstooth jacket but here I am sur-rounded by chiffon.

EMILY B: (*as they pass an outré negligé*) Is this what they wear for undergarments now? It wouldn't last a moment on the moors.

MARLENE: The only terrain that rag has to weather is a mattress, darling.

JOAN: Where is Emily Dickinson?

MARLENE: (*scanning*) There she is in notions, checking the needles. Escalators are not her . . . Ahh. Yes. Here we are. The top.

They arrive at the very top of the store and the escalator spills them out to face a huge decorative mirror.

GERTRUDE: Now I am getting excited and I could feel happy if I thought about it.

MARLENE: This is a special mirror Joan. Look carefully at yourself now. See who you really are. Then look again and you will see what you have been in the past.

They all look in the mirror. MARLENE *adjusts her coiffure.*

JOAN: (*recoiling*) I see fire. I see flames.

MARLENE: Is that all you see liebchen.

JOAN: I see . . . I see a woman I like. Her hair is very short and . . . she's wearing pants.

MARLENE: <u>Pants</u>? Ach, liebchen, what an opportunity! (*to* GERTRUDE *and* EMILY) Cue me girls.

GERTRUDE *and* EMILY *provide a concert pitch* (*and backup on the* "Joan darlings") *for* MARLENE, *who drapes herself over the mirror and sings:*

MARLENE: You must wear Pants
      Joan Darling
      Only Pants
      Joan Darling
      Long lovely Pants

That hold your legs
In their arms

. You must wear Pants
Joan Darling. . . .

(*spoken*) For the simple reason—and I have said this one <u>hundred</u> times be-fore—that no one will <u>ever</u> take you seriously if you wear a skirt.

JOAN: (*looks in the mirror in excitement*) St. Marlene! St. Marlene! The woman in the mirror looks like a hero!

MARLENE: Exactly Joan. Now look again.

JOAN: (*rising consciousness*) I see flames again. I see the woman in pants again. I see the woman <u>signaling</u> . . . <u>thru</u> <u>the</u> <u>flames</u>.

Blackout.

Lights up: PRESENT-DAY JOAN *in the* TRIUMPH.

JOAN: After that meeting in the mirror, everything changed for me. Despite my father's <u>violent</u> objections, I had a haircut, put on pants, and began to do things no one else could do. There was the incident with the car . . .

Projection: Seattle Times *headline:* DOCTOR'S DAUGHTER DRIVES CAR OFF QUEEN ANNE HILL. LANDS UNHARMED ON LAKE WASHING-TON FLOATING BRIDGE. *Superimposed on the headline is* YOUNG JOAN *in her* TRIUMPH *flying thru the air. Her hair is shorn.*

JOAN: And the archery contest . . .

A 50s portable radio begins to broadcast.

RADIO: This is your KOMO sports commentator with the week-end report on the international archery contest taking place in Volunteer Park. And let me tell you ladies and gentlemen if I hadn't seen this with my own eyes I wouldn't believe it. A local teenager—a <u>girl</u>—has beaten every archery contestant in the country . . .

JOAN: There was the resurrection of my infant cousin . . .

Lights up: YOUNG JOAN *at a christening lays hands on a very blue neonate who immediately turns pink, gurgles, and coos.* MARLENE DIETRICH *is the fairy god-mother complete with wand.*

JOAN: The National Science Award . . .

Lights up: YOUNG JOAN *appears with an astonishing invention that demon-strates the function of the ovaries.* GERTRUDE STEIN *stands benignly behind her in a doctor's coat.*

JOAN: The all-city high school song-writing contest . . .

Lights up: YOUNG JOAN *appears on a stage playing a song of her own composition—*THE BLUE OYSTER—*and all the band instruments as well.* MARLENE DIETRICH, *in her best seductive manner, sings the song while* GERTRUDE *and* EMILY *croon backup on the "please do's."*

MARLENE: I'm the OYSTER
   My dear
   And I'm silent
   And strange
   I'm the OYSTER
   My love
   And I won't
   Give my name
   And you don't
   Have my number
   And you can't
   Guess my game
   Come nearer
   My dear
   Please do
   Please do
   Come nearer
   My dear
   Please do

JOAN: And the state-wide haiku competition.

Lights up: YOUNG JOAN *in kimono and Nipponese accent recites a haiku of much beauty—*

I run fluttering
  like a frightened little girl
   after her mother.

—*and is crowned with cherry blossoms.* GERTRUDE *and* EMILY *flank her, beaming. Blackout on* YOUNG JOAN.

Lights to full: ADULT JOAN *standing by her* **TRIUMPH.**

JOAN: Along with these . . . special circumstances came a flood of memories of what seemed to me to be a life I had once lived or was still living or would continue to live in constant counterpoint to my present life. This other life was completely real to me. And I believed in it.

Lights up: **JOAN'S BEDROOM.** MARLENE, GERTRUDE, *and* EMILY BRONTË *are gathered round* YOUNG JOAN.

JOAN: (*agitated*) It happened <u>again</u> today. I felt myself <u>again</u> today dressed in armor, holding a banner, riding a horse at the head of ten thousand men.

MARLENE: Ten thousand <u>men</u>! How <u>marvelous</u>, darling.

EMILY: It is true, Joan. This did happen to you.

JOAN: It happened to me in <u>geometry</u> class this afternoon St. Emily and it was not pleasant.

GERTRUDE: Geometry is never a pleasant subject to sit thru it makes us measure angles when we want to calculate curves.

JOAN: And then yesterday, right in the middle of Social Studies, I thought I was in a courtroom. Inside myself I mean. I was in a courtroom testifying to a long line of old men about a crime of which I had no consciousness.

EMILY: This, too, happened to you Joan.

GERTRUDE: The study of law or at least the study of lawyers is not a dull one it is a necessary one it is always lawyers who stand between a woman and justice.

MARLENE: (*dreamily*) I have never made love to a lawyer. (*snaps back*) Or to a judge for that matter.

JOAN: And just now, I have such a clear bright vision of what I can do. Everything is so . . . simple for me. I have almost . . . another voice. And the world is so large . . . so lovely . . . and I see . . . I can see . . . (*trails off*).

EMILY: (*in a light trance*) I can see it too Joan. But these things are not for <u>now</u>. This age is too debased and threaded thru with tiny terrors. Why even the moors are smaller <u>now</u> . . . (*deep trance*).

GERTRUDE: Oh for godssake Marlene there she <u>goes</u> again how are we going to haul Joan out of this room and into history with <u>this</u> one (*points to* EMILY B) in a trance and <u>that</u> one (*points to* EMILY D *in closet*) in a closet and Princess <u>Angeline</u> banging the bongos all night long . . .

MARLENE: (*an arm around* GERTRUDE) Now Gertrude darling. Can't you see Joan is having a *petite crise de foi*. Let us be calm, let us be quiet, let us be a little more <u>saintly</u> . . . (*her voice dies away under the voice of* ADULT JOAN).

JOAN: And so they set me on my path, those three wonderful women. Emily Brontë, whom no one believed, Gertrude Stein, whom no one read, and Marlene Dietrich, whom no one took seriously. The one thing they didn't prepare me for was the <u>only</u> thing I had in common with other teenagers. (*lights a Gauloise*)

Blackout on ADULT JOAN.

Lights up: a **SOFA.** YOUNG JOAN *and* GILLES DE RAIS.

JOAN: You're my first friend who's a boy, Gilles. It's funny you should have a girl's name.

GILLES: Gilles is not the name of a <u>girl</u>, *chérie*, it is the name of a <u>French</u> <u>person</u>. And you Joan are my first friend of <u>any</u> gender—so it is amusing that you should wear boy's clothes. Amusing and . . . quite attractive. I suppose you cannot help it. (GILLES' *eyes glitter and, oops, we see all is not well with him as he stretches out a blackened hand*) Look at this Joan. Here is something <u>I</u> cannot help. And I cannot help . . . my unusual tastes.

JOAN: (*suddenly, a weird new world*) What . . . tastes . . . Gilles? What do you mean . . . <u>tastes</u>?

GILLES: (*mildly shocked*) <u>Chérie</u>. This is the sort of predeliction any French adolescent would understand without explanation. Must I spell the words for you?

JOAN: I think just <u>saying</u> them would be enough, Gilles.

GILLES: As you wish, *chérie*.

GILLES *leans over and begins whispering in* JOAN's *ear. Her eyes widen.*

JOAN: <u>No</u>. Really?!

Blackout.

Lights up: the **DARK HOUSE**. *A sofa.* DR. GEORGE *and* MRS. MARTHA *are smoking.*

GEORGE: Thank <u>god</u> for that boy what's his name, Martha. Thank <u>god</u> for him is all I can say.

MARTHA: Well I'm sure I don't know what you're so excited about George. He's not even an American boy for heaven's sake. And he's quite likely (*lowers her voice*) a Catholic.

GEORGE: Martha, I wouldn't care if he worshipped in a snake cult in South Carolina. Dating that boy is the first sign of normalcy Joan has shown in. . . . in . . . (*can't think of when she was last normal*) <u>whenever</u>. Besides, the boy's father is an ambassador. If he's good enough for the U.S. government, he's good enough for me Martha.

MARTHA: I suppose you're right George. There's just something about that young man that makes me. . . . shiver.

GEORGE: It's the damp Martha. That's why you're shivering. Can't you see it's raining again. (*looks around*) Now where are those boys?

Blackout.

Lights up. JOHN *and* JOHN, *sneaking and peeking outside* **JOAN'S ROOM**.

JOHN: (*very nervous and obsessed*) You think that Gilles-guy got her yet John. You think he picked her cherry. I mean if anybody's gonna do it it should be <u>us</u>. We're her <u>brothers</u>, fer chrissake.

JOHN: Too late John. Gilles got there first. That's what we're telling everyone so it must be true. He got there first and there's nothing we can do about it.

JOHN: There's nothing I <u>wanna</u> do about it, jerkface. The guy's a frothing <u>nut</u>. Did you see his hand.

JOHN: Uh . . . which hand John.

JOHN: His <u>other</u> hand flatnose. It's black. It's black as night and all crusted over. Like he stuck it straight into hell. And his <u>hair</u>. Didja catch his hair.

JOHN: (*anxious to seem alert*) No crewcut, no DA, light brown, down to his shoulders in a pageboy.

JOHN: Like I said, a fruitcake.

JOHN: I wonder why I didn't see his hand.

JOHN: Aw hell, the air's so damn wet your glasses prob'ly fogged up. Lookit. They're fogged up right now.

John takes off his glasses and looks at them.

Blackout.

Lights up: the **DARK HOUSE**. GEORGE *and* MARTHA, *both smoking furiously. A fireplace burns sullenly.*

GEORGE: Martha I can tell by your expression. You've been looking at the boys' dirty magazines again.

MARTHA: No George. I have not been <u>looking</u> at the boys' dirty magazines, I've been <u>burning</u> the boys' dirty magazines. (*a glance at the fire*) <u>Smoldering</u> might be a better word.

GEORGE: <u>You</u> look like the one who's smoldering. Martha. Uh. Dear.

MARTHA: You're damnright I'm smoldering George. Those boys are slandering their sister all over Seattle again. John and John are saying that Joan is not a virgin George and I want to know <u>why</u> and I want to know <u>now</u>.

GEORGE: Oh boys. Oh <u>boys</u>.

Blackout.

Lights up: GEORGE *and the* BOYS. *The* BOYS *take turns burning each other with matches as they speak.*

JOHN: Aw Dad do we gotta? Ow you're <u>burning</u> me jerkhead.

JOHN: Jeez Dad I don't think that's such a hot idea. <u>Watch</u> it, zitface.

GEORGE: Boys. <u>Boys</u>. You <u>know</u> how sensitive your sister is about her . . . habits. And yet, I must penetrate the secrets of her brain.

JOHN: But Dad. Her <u>diary</u>?

JOHN: We don't even know what it looks like.

JOHN: We don't even know if she's <u>got</u> one.

GEORGE: All adolescent girls have diaries boys. And all those diaries have pastel covers and little heart-shaped locks.

JOHN: Uh what is heart-shaped Dad.

GEORGE: Actually John, the shape of a heart (*draws it in the air*) is the shape of a vulva. (*uncomprehending glance from* JOHN) A young woman's pudendum, John.

JOHN: (*another blank look*)

JOHN: <u>Pussy</u> John. Dad means it's the shape of a pussy. We'll be looking for a book with a <u>pussy</u> on its cover. (THE BOYS *laugh hysterically,* GEORGE *looks glum*)

Blackout.

Lights up: YOUNG JOAN, *in the* TRIUMPH. *Doves flutter around her.*

JOAN: (*to the Audience*) I'm getting flashbacks again. Symptoms from my other life. They're . . . confusing me.

Lights up: YOUNG JOAN *remembers her other life. A kind of suspended cage drops over the* TRIUMPH. *We hear and see* JOHN *and* JOHN *running round and round her, leaping up to look.*

JOAN: (*alone in deep space*) They won't let me sleep. They want me to die. And before I die, they'd like to violate me. Two of my jailors and one of my judges have already put their hands on me. I am . . . so tired. (*pause*) I read somewhere that sleep is a rehearsal for death. You'd think they'd let me have the practice. (*pause. Shakes her head*) No! I'm dreaming backward now to that . . . other time, the time in the mirror, the time of the stake and the fire.

I must stop it. (*shakes head again*) I must stop it. (*screams suddenly, to the still-leaping* JOHNS, *to herself*) STOP IT! STOP IT! STOP IT!

We see JOHN AND JOHN, *electrified by her scream, frozen in the air in mid-leap in a sudden . . .*

Blackout.

Lights up: DR. DARK'S LAB. GEORGE *and his Salish Indian assistant,* PRINCE DWAYNE. GEORGE *drinks port expansively,* DWAYNE *breaks things deliberately.* GEORGE *looks at glass slides.* DWAYNE *cleans up.*

GEORGE: I'm so close, Dwayne. So close. Fifteen years of research on the ways of women and I <u>know</u> the secrets of their sex are buried in the virgin brain. (*holds up slides*) See this. Now look at <u>this</u> abnormality. Right under my nose. In my own family. Oh for the opportunity to operate!

DWAYNE: (*breaks a retort, a petri dish, and a glass slide in rapid succession*) Ooops. Wooops. Aooww!

GEORGE: Dwayne . . . (*about to admonish, but notices him suddenly*) Uh . . . Dwayne. Do <u>you</u> have a family?

DWAYNE: Dead, Dr. Dark. All dead. Except for honored father and troublesome renegade sister.

GEORGE: A <u>virgin</u> Indian sister? (*hungrily*) Perhaps your sister should be looked at Dwayne. <u>Examined</u>. Brought under the bright lights of science.

DWAYNE: Angeline is virgin Indian <u>Princess</u>, Dr. Dark. She cannot be touched.

GEORGE: You're the son of a <u>chief</u> Dwayne? You're . . . (*incredulously*) Indian <u>royalty</u>?

DWAYNE: (*picks up his broom and begins to sweep*) Yessir Dr. Dark. Dwayne is royalty-in-waiting. Just like Prince of Wales. (*sweeps harder*) But Princess Angeline does not treat Dwayne like royalty. Princess Angeline treats Dwayne like <u>fish</u> food, like <u>moccasin</u> dust.

GEORGE: (*uninterested, yawns a bit*) <u>Does</u> she, Dwayne.

DWAYNE: Princess Angeline thinks I am stupid because I work for <u>white</u> man.

GEORGE: (*<u>very</u> interested*) Because you work for (*mouths the word "<u>me</u>" and points to himself in astonishment*) Tch. <u>Women</u>, eh Dwayne. <u>Women</u>.

DWAYNE: So right, doctor. Another specie entirely.

GEORGE: Hah. Another specie. Ha ha. That's funny Dwayne. I didn't know you people could be <u>funny</u>.

Blackout.

Lights up: JOHN *and* JOHN *burst into the* **LAB,** *waving a book.*

JOHN: Got it Dad!

JOHN: Here it is Dad!

JOHN: It took us <u>hours</u> Dad

JOHN: <u>Many</u> hours Dad.

JOHN: But we finally figured it out.

JOHN: Under the bed Dad.

JOHN: That's where she hid it.

JOHN: It's just like you said, chartreuse cover and pussy on the front.

GEORGE: (*holding his temper, barely*) This <u>is</u> a chartreuse cover, boys, but that is a heart-shaped <u>face</u> not a <u>lock</u>. The face of the author of this book.

JOHN: It's not a diary Dad?

JOHN: It's not a lock Dad?

JOHN: That's not a pussy Dad?

GEORGE: (*steely*) This, boys, is a book by the American poe<u>tess</u> Emily Dickinson. The bookmark holds the place of a poem that begins (*he reads with real disgust*):

Wild nights wild nights
Were I with thee
Wild nights would be
Our Ecstasy

Grim silence

JOHN: (*shrugging disingenuously*) Sounds like pussy to me.

JOHN: Dad? Dad?

GEORGE: (*head in hands, groaning*)

Blackout.

Lights up: **NANCY DETWILER'S BASEMENT.** *Before a* **BONFIRE GIRLS** *meeting.* NANCY *and* JOAN *confer. The* BONFIRES *are comparing bras, smoking, drinking, doing their nails.*

NANCY: You know what an honor this is.

JOAN: (*firmly*) I do.

NANCY: You know I've never let anyone hold the ceremonial match <u>or</u> light the sacred fire before.

JOAN: I know.

NANCY: Leading a Bonfire meeting is a <u>huge</u> responsibility . . .

JOAN: I take it very seriously.

NANCY: . . . and I generally have a slug of Thunderbird before we get started.

JOAN: (*looks as though she might assent, but her* VOICES *have other ideas. She speaks regretfully*) I think I'm fine without it, thank you.

NANCY: Alright then. This better be good.

JOAN: (*raps for attention with the bottom of her bow*) Bonfires. Bonfires. I have something to tell you.

CANDY: The fire, Joan. You have to light the fire.

CINDY: Don't be an asshole, Cindy. This is her first time. She doesn't know. Before you speak Joan, we have to have fire . . .

CANDY: We have to see burning. . . .

NANCY: We have to feel flames.

BETTY: Strike the match, Joan. Light the fire.

ALL: FEED THE FIRE. FEED THE FIRE. FEED THE FIRE.

JOAN: (*horrified, drops the match*) I can't do it. I won't do it.

Blackout.

Lights up: **GEORGE'S LABORATORY.** GEORGE *with a letter,* DWAYNE *watches carefully.*

GEORGE: It's a big grant, Dwayne. It's a generous grant. It's the largest grant the state government has ever made to a private hospital and they're giving it to me, Dwayne. To me. For scientific research whose proofs I have . . . uh . . . abridged. More or less . . . enhanced. Oh what the hell. Totally fabricated. I needed a young virgin's brain, Dwayne, and where, in all America, could I get my hands on that? The theory is perfect Dwayne. But there are no glass slides to support it. (*grabs* DWAYNE *and shakes his lapels on each word*) Where (*shake*) are (*shake*) those (*shake*) slides, (*shake*) Dwayne? WHERE ARE THEY?

DWAYNE: (*slyly*) Gee doctor, sir, I thought you only collect rat slides.

GEORGE: Rodents do not make a career, Dwayne. Discoveries in human medicine make a career. I must see a virgin's brain, Dwayne. And I must see it soon.

Blackout.

Lights up: **GEORGE'S LAB.** DWAYNE *alone. He speaks in Salish.*

DWAYNE: (*fingering tissue slides*) What are the rules here? (*pause*) Who makes them? (*pause*) The Chief makes the rules. (*pause*) When I am Chief, I will decide whose skin is spread out on a glass slide. (*pause, evil smile*) When I am Chief, my glass slides will hold pieces of Princess Angeline. (*he smiles broadly*)

Blackout.

Lights up: **OUTSIDE JOAN'S ROOM.** JOHN *and* JOHN, *their eyes to the keyhole in nervous alteration.*

JOHN: You think those old babes got titties John.

JOHN: You bet they got titties. Maybe more than the usual number. Lookit that big fat one she's probably got three or four sets of 'em.

JOHN: And pussies. You think they got pussies too.

JOHN: You bet they got pussies. Just like in the magazines. (*sagely*) Age makes no damn difference.

JOHN: (*reasoning with extreme difficulty*) Well if they got tits and they got pussies we might be able to do things to 'em.

JOHN: You bet we can do things to 'em.

JOHN: Like what John. Like what could we do.

JOHN: Like anything we wanted.

JOHN: Yeah but like what.

JOHN: Like we could . . . we could like undress 'em and rape 'em and stuff. Like in the magazines.

JOHN: I don't exactly understand how you do that John.

JOHN: (*disgusted*) Y' mean y' never raped anyone before.

JOHN: (*thinking quickly*) I never said that. I said I didn't understand how <u>you</u> do it.

JOHN: Y' want a magazine.

JOHN: That would be helpful.

JOHN: Asshole. Rape is like what I used to do to you at night when you were a kid.

JOHN: (*darkens*) I didn't like that John. Not at all. (*brightens*) But I'd like to <u>do</u> it.

GEORGE: (*offstage*) Oh <u>boys</u>.

Blackout.

Lights up: YOUNG JOAN *in her* TRIUMPH, *stopped at the top of* Queen Anne Hill, *ringed by mountains, beautiful blue waters at her feet. A flock of doves flutter around her head.*

JOAN: (*ecstatic, she stands in the car, arms open wide, ringed by exhaust smoke*) I see you, Seattle, I see you completely. I know I can heal you. I bring you my old self and also the new. I offer you . . . I offer you . . . (*the arms and the attitude come down; she's a little confused*). St. Marlene. What is it that I have to offer again?

MARLENE: (*voice only—but strictly from heaven*) Purity, liebchen. You have purity. And you're going to need it, <u>believe me</u>.

Blackout.

Lights up: PRESENT-DAY JOAN *in the* TRIUMPH, *stopped at the top of Queen Anne Hill, ringed by mountains, beautiful blue waters at her feet. A flock of doves flutters around her head.*

JOAN: In the old days, being a virgin meant simply being a woman who chose not to marry. It had nothing to do with the state of your experience. (*pause*) As a teenager, I always had burning desires . . . but they weren't the usual ones . . . (*trails off*)

Blackout.

Lights up: JOAN'S ROOM. YOUNG JOAN *on her knees in front of the altar, supplicating. All her figures and icons are smoking with the intensity of her devotion.*

Blackout.

Lights up: the DARK HOUSE. GEORGE *and* MARTHA, *smoking. As* GEORGE *lectures, he sounds crazier and crazier.*

GEORGE: No no Martha. The intactness of the hymen is <u>not</u> indicative of virginity. <u>Anything</u> can puncture a hymen, Martha. A good volleyball game, a bicycle ride, a fall from a horse . . . The real test for virginity is in the <u>brain</u>, Martha. A virgin's brain has a special hue, a particular cortical construction. Her thinking moves in a certain electromagnetic pattern, and that pattern is entirely controlled by chemicals deep within the frontal lobes of the brain. The only way to examine Joan for virginity, Martha—and I recommend this on an annual basis—is to <u>inspect her brain</u>.

MARTHA: (*calmly, lighting another cigarette*) George. Dear. If you dare to approach my daughter with a surgical tool or a psychological theory, I will cut off your . . . (*pauses significantly to stare at his fly*) . . . operating hand with my cake knife.

Blackout.

Lights up: JOAN'S BEDROOM. YOUNG JOAN *still on her knees in front of the altar.* MARTHA *sticks her head in.*

MARTHA: Yoo hoo Uh. Joan darling.

JOAN *rises quickly, flustered.*

JOAN: Mom.

MARTHA: (*making an attempt*) That's alright dear. You go right ahead and pray if you have to.

JOAN: I don't have to Mom. Is there something I can do . . .

MARTHA: (*overlapping*) I just wanted to . . .

JOAN: What?

MARTHA: What?

JOAN: I'm sorry Mom.

MARTHA: No no, it's me. I always speak too quietly.

Silence

MARTHA: (*very low, very intense*) Joan, listen to me. Stay away from your father. He wants to . . . he wants to . . .

JOAN: He wants to hurt me.

MARTHA: Something's wrong with him Joan.

JOAN: I know Mom. Thanks. I'll take care of it.

MARTHA: (*relieved*) You will, darling?

JOAN: Don't worry Mom. I've got . . . <u>friends</u>.

Blackout.

Lights up: **JOAN'S BEDROOM.** MARLENE, GERTRUDE, *and* EMILY BRONTË, *all smoking and distracted.*

MARLENE: Ay yi yi.

GERTRUDE: Fathers are depressing.

EMILY: I wonder if the man can be bought off. He has a lean and hungry look . . .

MARLENE: (*shaking her head*) Ay yi yi not that one, darling. You don't buy <u>that</u> one off. That one is <u>beyond</u> money.

GERTRUDE: Marlene is right unfortunately the doctor is not working for Mammon he is working for god.

MARLENE: For <u>god</u>? Ay yi <u>yi</u>.

Sound of drums from closet. PRINCESS ANGELINE *emerges from the closet, dancing and chanting.*

ANGELINE: Only good doctor man
Is dead good doctor man
Only good doctor man . . .

(*to* MARLENE) Hello blond Venus. And all you other white ladies. (*to Marlene*) I wonder, Divine One, if you know what your pitiful cry—ay yi yi—<u>means</u> (*a sug-*

gestive leer) in Chinook? No? Another time, Blond Venus, and I will <u>show</u> you. So. Darling Joan's evil Papa is misbehaving again? My dumb brother Dwayne has also stepped out of line. Perhaps we can pierce two crows with one spear. Let us sit down, have a smoke, and think together of ways to stop the he-devils.

They smoke and think.

GERTRUDE: We could . . . no. That's not right.

EMILY: Perhaps there's a . . . no. That's not possible.

ANGELINE: I could maybe . . . no. Not enough time.

MARLENE: (*a spreading smile*) Ahhh . . . Of course. I have it. (*everyone looks at her as her smile broadens*) An <u>American</u> solution. The Bonfire Girls.

Blackout.

Lights up: the BONFIRE GIRLS *sneaking thru* DR. DARK'S LABORATORY *window.*

CINDY: Ooo this is so much fun Nancy.

NANCY: Shuddup Cindy.

ANNIE: Our first commission.

NANCY: Shuddup Annie.

ALICE: God I love starting fires.

NANCY: Shuddup Alice.

ANNIE: What an opportunity.

CATHERINE: (*tossing her hair*) It's just like a fairy tale. Something . . . <u>French</u>.

NANCY: Something <u>German</u> dearie. We're gonna blow these bastards straight to hell and burn their stinking lab to <u>ashes</u>!!

ALICE: Ready on the fuse, Nancy.

ALL: FEED THE FIRE. FEED THE FIRE. FEED THE FIRE.

Blackout: Boom. Huge explosion. Boom. Another one. Sound fizzles.

NANCY: (*in the blackout*) Damn. The charge was too small!

Lights up: LAB. DWAYNE *and* GEORGE. DWAYNE *with ill-concealed pleasure at the explosion.*

DWAYNE: Dr. Dark! Dr. Dark! Strange blow-up in rat room!

GEORGE: Dwayne. How many times have I told you not to dist . . .

DWAYNE: Bunsen burner blew hole thru ceiling, Dr. Dark. Lab is dripping with infected fluids.

GEORGE: That's impossible Dwayne. Those cultures were over on the . . .

DWAYNE: Then explosion in retort blasted rats from cages. Big rodent convention now taking place among flames and rubble.

GEORGE: Flames? For godssake Dwayne! <u>Flames</u>? In the <u>lab</u>?!

DWAYNE: (*helpfully*) You think I should maybe call Fire Department? Or just wait for thunderstorm to put huge conflagration out.

GEORGE: (*his head sinks slowly into his hands, groans*) Ohhhh . . .

Blackout.

Lights up: **JOAN'S BEDROOM** *and the circle of smoking ladies. They have* JOAN's *diary and are passing it around, giggling affectionately.* "Look at this." "No look at this." "Isn't she sweet." MARLENE *reads this quote collapsed in laughter:* "I think I'm supposed to be a virgin."

Blackout.

Lights up: the **DARK HOUSE.** JOAN *and* GILLES, *back from a date.* GILLES *very James Dean, but more dangerous.* JOAN *in her Jean Seberg hair. They both wear leather jackets.*

JOAN: Well here we are, Gilles.

GILLES: Ouais. We are here. (*looks around*) And it's very bourgeois. So what is next *chérie*.

JOAN: (*earnestly*) Would you like to see my bow and arrows. Or my spear.

GILLES: I am not particularly interested in pointed instruments, *chérie*.

JOAN: Well . . . uh . . . how about some sacramental wine.

GILLES: *Écoute* Joan. Let me be honest. I think we are supposed to <u>do</u> something.

JOAN: (*quickly*) We don't have to Gilles. Nobody says we have to.

GILLES: Nevertheless I feel something in me rising, stiffening, and pointing towards you.

JOAN: (*matter of fact*) It's probably just your penis, Gilles.

GILLES: (*coldly*) You are right *chérie*. That's what it is. But what do you know about penises.

JOAN: My saints told me you'd be trying something sexual. They used the word penis.

GILLES: *Mon dieu.* And what else did the old beasts say.

JOAN: (*conscientiously*) St. Marlene told me not to let you slip your hand under my angora sweater. St. Gertrude Stein showed me where to kick you if you tried to force yourself on me. And the two Emilies gave me their best fountain pens and advised me to go for your eyes with the points if I had to.

GILLES: *Jésu.* The old goats play rough.

JOAN: (*straightforward as she is in everything*) I think, I mean I'm not really sure about this Gilles, because everything is still developing <u>thru</u> me, but I think I'm supposed to stay a virgin.

GILLES: Oh, *ça va*, Joan, it's alright. I'm not really interested in girls. But don't you think we should do <u>something</u>. I mean we're teenagers out on a date, *par dieu*. What about a little oral sex.

JOAN: I don't know what that is, Gilles.

GILLES: It will be my pleasure to show you *chérie*. Just take your pants off, here let me help you, the underwear also, and lie back on the sofa. No hands, no generative organs, just the tongue. My own uncle taught me this technique — and on my own body I might add. The old girls will be very pleased, I can promise you that.

JOAN: And no penetration, Gilles. Remember that.

GILLES: *Ne t'inquiete pas chérie.* This is the 1950's and nobody penetrates <u>any</u>-<u>thing</u>. I'm just going to define your clitoral range for you. It will give you something to explore in those rare moments when you're alone in your room. Lie back, *chérie*, close your eyes, and if I'm right about what your sexual tastes would be if you had them, you're going to enjoy this very much.

Blackout.

Lights up: OUTSIDE THE DARK HOUSE. JOHN *and* JOHN, *ears and eyes to doors, windows and keyholes as they run, vault, and leap around the outside of the house, looking for the best view of what they hope (and fear) is the defloration of their sister.*

JOHN: Is he <u>in</u> her yet John. Is he <u>doing</u> it. Jeez get outta the way, I can't see a <u>thing</u>.

JOHN: He's doing <u>something</u>, alright. He's got her damn pants off.

JOHN: God I didn't think <u>anybody</u> could get the pants off Joan. (*jumping up and down*) For Chrissake will you <u>move</u>! I can't <u>see</u>.

JOHN: (*the moralist*) This just isn't right. If anybody should do it to her it's you and me, right? I mean we're her <u>brothers</u>.

JOHN: Well I <u>tried</u> John, I tried to do it on various occasions but the girl is made of marble.

JOHN: She's stronger than you isn't she.

JOHN: She's a <u>lot</u> stronger than me and those legs of hers don't spread.

JOHN: (*back to the window*) Well they're spreading now John. WOW. They are certainly spreading now.

JOHN: Get outta my sight line, ya moron. Get outta my sight line or I'll beat you up for the rest of your life!

Fadeout: one JOHN *pulls the other to the ground and starts punching him and stomping on his face. Neither of them, as a consequence, sees anything.*

Lights up: GILLES *goes down on* JOAN; *she has a short, sharp, almost immediate orgasm and, as she cries out, a dove flies from her mouth.*

GILLES: Holy cow!

Blackout.

End of Part I

Entre-acte

Lights up: **JOAN'S ROOM.** MARLENE, GERTRUDE, *and* EMILY BRONTË *are still on the floor smoking and drinking. They're quite tipsy.*

MARLENE: (*raising her glass*) Well darlings. Here's to Joan's first sexual experience.

GERTRUDE: Hmph. It should have been with a woman.

EMILY: (*slyly*) Or a dog.

The CLOSET *barks.*

GERTRUDE: (*a confirming look at* EMILY *and the closeted dog*) Hah. I <u>knew</u> it.

MARLENE: (*preventing an argument*) Joan has had her experience, my dears, but, <u>heureusement</u>, she has not suffered the effects. Heaven knows why, but she really is supposed to remain a virgin.

EMILY D: (*erupting from the closet*) Wild nights! Wild nights!

MARLENE: (*calls to the closet*) I don't think so darling. More like an unbridled quarter of an hour.

GERTRUDE: I wonder if she'll develop a taste for it.

EMILY B:
EMILY D: (*they look at each other, then shake their heads vigorously*) NAAAHHHHH.
MARLENE:

Blackout.

End of Entre-acte

Part II

Lights up: **HOSPITAL. GEORGE'S LAB.** GEORGE *and many white-coated colleagues gathered for a conference, accompanied by an* EAGLE SCOUT. PRINCE DWAYNE *sweeps steadily around them.*

GEORGE: Gentlemen. And . . . uh . . . Eagle Scout. The subject for discussion here tonight is an adolescent virgin female in her seventeenth year. She behaves in ways I cannot explain. (*accelerates*) She dresses unacceptably. (*a failed attempt at quiet control*) I <u>hate</u> <u>her</u> <u>haircut</u>!! (*calms a bit*) I am clearly too close to the subject gentlemen . . . You've read the case history, you've seen the blood work-ups, and you've scanned the charts. Now give me the benefit of your wisdom.

ALL: (*answering the wrong question*) It's your daughter isn't it.

GEORGE: (*raises his hands*) GENTLEMEN. Yes it's my daughter. Now what am I to do with her.

DR.: Take a cell culture.

DR.: Examine the menstrual flow.

DR.: Do an estrogen count.

DR.: X-ray the heart, the brain, and the liver.

DR.: Inspect the vagina.

DR.: Read her diary.

DR.: Inspect the vagina <u>again</u>.

DR.: Take a family history.

DR.: Operate.

DR.: Psychoanalyze.

DR.: Operate.

All the DOCTORS *begin to argue heatedly amongst themselves. The words: "lobotomy," "electroshock," and "sanity hearing" bubble up above the babble.*

GEORGE: (*holds up his hands*) Thank you gentlemen. I have done or contemplated all those things. Can we hear from the Eagle Scout?

SCOUT: (*laconic*) She's a Bonfire Girl. <u>Burn</u> her.

Blackout.

Lights up: GEORGE, *overcome, his head down on his* **LAB** *table. He looks up, appears to notice the Audience, pauses, then makes a visible decision to unburden himself.*

GEORGE: (*agonized*) Virginity, ladies and gentlemen. The subject is always female virginity. Now <u>why</u> we do we desire it and <u>what</u> do we know about it? Ladies and gentlemen? Ladies? <u>Gentlemen</u>?

GEORGE'*s head returns to the table—klonk—as he realizes there will be no response to <u>this</u> burning desire.*

Blackout.

Lights up: GEORGE *and the* BOYS. GEORGE *is obsessed and lecturing.*

GEORGE: (*shaking his head*) Boys. Boys. You would not believe what we removed from vaginas in the old days. In the old days women were so much more creative. The restrictions on their lives inflamed their minds and there was no limit to what they could imagine. In my laboratory alone, in one six month period, I personally removed from the vaginas of otherwise perfectly healthy women, a tin pepper box, a drinking glass, an inkwell, a spring hat, fistfuls of hair pins, a can of vegetable soup, and a fountain pen.

A small silence.

JOHN: What kind of fountain pen Dad.

GEORGE: A Mont Blanc John. The very best.

JOHN: That's cool Dad.

A small silence.

JOHN: Any . . . ink in the pen Dad?

Blackout.

Lights up: a **GARAGE.** ADULT JOAN *stands in front of the raised hood of the* TRIUMPH *while a mechanic frenziedly pulls out endless quantities of coils, gaskets, plugs, etc.*

JOAN: There was no stopping my father once he formed a theory. The more I did what I was meant to do, the more he tried to do <u>to</u> me.

Blackout.

Lights up: **DR. DARK'S OFFICE.** YOUNG JOAN *stands in front of her father, wearing her quiver and bow, arms folded. She's refusing something.*

JOAN: Forget it Papa.

GEORGE: I cannot forget medical science Joan dear. I cannot forget the exploratory principles of <u>brain</u> surgery.

JOAN: I have things I'm supposed to do, Papa. You'd <u>better</u> forget it.

GEORGE: (*picks up a syringe*)

JOAN: (*reaches for an arrow*) I'll <u>make</u> you forget it Papa.

GEORGE: (*smiles and holds up a hand to stop her*) Let us pause a moment to review your options, my dear. (*ticks them off on his fingers*) A minor child, the daughter of a respected medical professional, that professional has just recommended a course of treatment for your condition . . .

JOAN: What <u>condition</u>, Papa. <u>What</u> <u>treatment</u>.

GEORGE: (*corrects himself suavely*) . . . a course of <u>experimental</u> treatment for your <u>suspected</u> condition and you're going to have to allow me to <u>do</u> it, Joan. You're going to have to allow me to do what I <u>want</u> to do or what I <u>decide</u> to do or what I <u>feel</u> like doing because that is the way medical science works, Joan. Dear. (*an attempt at levity*) What have I told you ever since you were an infant? Hmmm? What? (*playfully wags a finger*) The Doctor . . . knows . . . best.

JOAN: (*fitting an arrow to her bowstring, as she backs out of the office*) The . . . doctor . . . knows . . . <u>nothing</u>, Papa. And the doctor will <u>not</u> touch me again.

Blackout.

Lights up: the BEACH. *The* BONFIRE GIRLS *are feeding a huge fire, cutting driftwood with their regulation tomahawks.*

NANCY: Listen Annie. This is something I wanna do. This is something I <u>gotta</u> do. The desire to kill is <u>hormonal</u>. I feel it <u>right</u> <u>here</u>. (*presses her ovaries*)

ANNIE: I'm not surprised Nancy. <u>Every</u>body's at war in <u>this</u> town.

CINDY: Who said war?

BECKY: Nancy did.

CINDY: Annie did.

DOT: What war? Which war?

ANNIE: War with our historical enemies of course.

CINDY: Truant officers?

BECKY: School principals?

DOT: <u>Doctors?</u>

NANCY: No no <u>no</u>.

ALL: (*looking gleefully at each other*) THE BOY SCOUTS!

NANCY: Right girls. Go home. Sharpen your tomahawks. Start hoarding those fireplace matches. It's Scout hunting season and I got a <u>helluva</u> battle plan!

ANNIE: It's <u>Joan's</u> battle plan, isn't it Nancy.

NANCY: (*reluctant*) Yeah. Well. More or less.

ANNIE: Which is it Nancy. <u>More</u> Joan's plan or <u>less</u>.

NANCY: Alright. It's <u>more</u>. It's <u>more</u> Joan's and <u>less</u> mine.

CINDY: (*looking around*) Where . . . <u>is</u> Joan?

The fire flares up violently.
Blackout.

Lights up: **BOY SCOUT CAMP.** A SCOUT *troop, huddling for warmth, tries unsuccessfully to light their campfire thruout the entire scene.*

SCOUT: What've you heard.

SCOUT: Not that much.

SCOUT: Billy met with the Surgeons.

SCOUT: Oh yeah?

SCOUT: What about.

SCOUT: I dunno. He's not back yet.

Pause

SCOUT: The Salish are gathering for war.

SCOUT: Oh yeah?

SCOUT: Well they're too lazy to gather for anything else.

SCOUT: That's for damn sure.

Pause

SCOUT: What about the Bonfire Girls.

SCOUT: They picked off a scout in Evergreen Troop this week.

SCOUT: Got one in Alki Troop too.

SCOUT: We get any a <u>them</u>?

SCOUT: Are you kidding?

SCOUT: We <u>never</u> get any of them.

SCOUT: At this rate, we never will.

Small pause

SCOUT: <u>That's</u> depressing.

SCOUT: God yes.

SCOUT: That's <u>really</u> depressing.

The SCOUTS, *incredibly depressed, let their tiny fire flicker out.*
Fadeout.

Lights up: **VOLUNTEER PARK.** PRINCESS ANGELINE. *It's dusk and she's surrounded by rowdy* BONFIRE GIRLS.

ANGELINE: (*holds up her hands with a Mahatma Gandhi smile*) Quiet please, pale teenagers. SILENCE now troubled adolescents. SHUT YOUR MOUTHS NOISY JUVENILES! Or my sisters of the Lakota tribe will have your scalps on their lodgepoles tonight.

Complete and instant silence.

ANGELINE: So happy to have your full attention young Americans. I, Princess Angeline, am reduced to leading little rich white girls in ersatz Indian-wear against males of my own tribe. Paradoxical, no? But Marlene Dietrich says life is cruel joke and you are toughest kids around. So. Who wants to show me how tough?

In one smooth motion, NANCY DETWILER *punches the lights out of* CATHERINE *of New Rochelle.*

NANCY: How's that your highness.

ANGELINE: Ooooo hoo hoo. Solid right cross young troop leader. Who else has something for Princess Angeline?

CINDY *gets up, bites off a plug of tobacco, spits it across the stage.* ANNE *smokes five cigarettes at once.* LINDA *hog-ties a struggling* GRETCHEN, *and* SALLY *attempts to strangle* DOT *with her bare hands.*

ANGELINE: (*admiring*) Alright. Alright. You girls are plenty mean. I think we gonna turn you into real killers.

Heavy cheering from the BONFIRE GIRLS.

ANGELINE: But first we gotta give you some warrior discipline. Follow me girls! (*whirls out her drum*)

Only good enemy male
Is dead good enemy male

She begins an Indian step dance.

Only good enemy male
Is dead good enemy male

The GIRLS *form a line and snake dance behind* ANGELINE.

Only good enemy male
Is dead good enemy male
Hoo hoo hoo hoo hoo hoo hoo.

NANCY: Your highness. Your highness. Request permission to speak.

ANGELINE: Ho ho. Make it brief warrior girl, we got four hours of heavy drill ahead.

NANCY: Your highness. How come you recruited <u>us</u> for this battle. Your highness.

CINDY: Yeah your highness. Aren't there any Indian maidens available.

CATHY: Shut up and let Princess Angeline answer Nancy's question.

ALL: (*to each other*) Yeah c'mon. Shuddup. Shuddup. No <u>you</u> shuddup. <u>Every</u>-body shuddup. (*they start to chant*) An-ge-line. An-ge-line. What's the answer An-ge-line. (*a lone voice emerges*) What <u>is</u> the answer?

ANGELINE: (*stops the snakeline with an upheld hand*) What is the question pale children.

GERTRUDE STEIN *appears curled around a tree branch like the Cheshire Cat, expresses maximum disapproval with facial expressions, then fades away).*

ANGELINE: (*to the Audience*) Hoo hoo <u>writers</u>. <u>Sooo</u> touchy.

NANCY: The question your highness was why <u>us</u>.

ANGELINE: Ahh yes. The canoe of memory glides thru the waters of conscious-ness once again. Sad to say, all maidens of my tribe eat, sleep, or otherwise en-gage themselves with enemy Indian males. So I am forced to cross cultural lines and call upon Girls of the Bonfire for the dirt work.

ALL: Good answer princess. Hooray for us! Yippeee! Woo hoo! We're <u>real</u> dirty! We'll get em for you! (*etc. etc.*)

ANGELINE: OK enough joy pale maidens. Back to basic training. Who here knows how to take a scalp?

Delighted, the whole troop steps forward in anticipation.
Blackout.

Lights up: still the GARAGE. ADULT JOAN, *facing upstage, talks to the* MECHANIC *in exasperation.*

JOAN: The valve-lifters sound like castanets, the brake-lining is gone, and I can put my fist thru the frame! This car has <u>got</u> to go back on the road.

MECHANIC: Classic car parts are <u>murder</u> to find, lady. It's gonna cost ya, it's gonna cost ya <u>big</u>.

JOAN: It won't be the first time. (*to the Audience*) What was I saying. Oh yes. My father. I began to smell smoke and feel fire everytime I saw my father . . .

YOUNG JOAN *appears, climbs in the car, and seems to drive out of the garage.* ADULT JOAN *continues to speak.*

JOAN: But I was so excited at the prospect of restoring Princess Angeline to power and the city to health, I forgot to watch him. I paid for <u>that</u> in a large way.

Blackout.

Lights up: JOAN *and* GIRLS *in the* **TRIUMPH** *at a drive-in movie. It's Dreyer's* The Passion of Jeanne d'Arc *and the trial scene is playing. They respond to the film for awhile, then . . .*

GILLES: (*coolly*) I think the *truc* with your father is serious, *chérie*. To make you the subject of a hospital seminar . . . ooo la la.

JOAN: (*unconcerned*) He's been X-raying me for years, Gilles. (*pause*) But I can feel it. He's up to something new, <u>this</u> time.

GILLES: Something ghoulish, *chérie, sans doubte*. Doctors are not the most balanced class of people. *Mais ne t'inquiète pas.* I have decided to be your . . . companion-at-arms. Your guardian devil. Your . . . <u>spy</u>. I shall penetrate the <u>luscious</u> flanks of the enemy and—how do you Americans call it—bring home the bacon. (*he tentatively reaches out his black hand for the popcorn*)

JOAN: What a kind thought Gilles.

GILLES: (*immediately depressed*) I know *chérie*. I hate myself for it.

Blackout.

Lights up: **VOLUNTEER PARK.** PRINCESS ANGELINE *looks down at the bound and gagged body of* OFFICER RYAN.

ANGELINE: Not a great idea, girls. Kidnapping lawman for scalping practice is <u>not</u> a great idea.

NANCY: (*nonchalantly*) We were in a hurry princess.

CINDY: (*scornfully*) Yeah princess. We didn't have time to grab a Cub Scout.

ALICE: (*helpfully, pulling the cop's hair*) Look at this hair princess. And the nice loose scalp. He's a good candidate.

ANGELINE: Crossing the law is an <u>obvious</u> act pale teens. You got that? Now go and catch me something <u>subtle</u>.

Blackout.

Lights up: **BOY SCOUT MEETING.** GILLES *in Scout drag, spying for the* BONFIRE GIRLS. *He's a very unconvincing Scout.*

SCOUT: Who's <u>he</u>?

SCOUT: He's the new guy.

SCOUT: Whadda creep.

SCOUT: I'm not sleeping in <u>his</u> tent.

SCOUT: What is he a <u>foreigner</u> or something.

SCOUT: A foreigner and some kinda cripple. Lookit his <u>hand</u>.

SCOUT: Uk.

SCOUT: Yuck.

SCOUT: Puke.

HEAD SCOUT: Listen we can't crap around ranking on what's his name there, we gotta get our plans laid. The Bonfire Girls are after <u>us</u> now.

SCOUT: Well <u>I'm</u> not afraid.

HEAD SCOUT: Then you're an asshole. The Bonfires are the most dangerous bunch of Scout-hating butches since . . . since . . .

SCOUT: Since the Amazons.

SCOUT: Yeah. The <u>Amazons</u>.

HEAD SCOUT: They're smart and they're vicious and they can set fire to <u>anything</u>.

SCOUT: I heard they tried to incinerate a <u>doctor</u>.

SCOUT: I heard they tried to blow up a <u>hospital</u>.

HEAD SCOUT: Damn right. And all the doctors <u>in</u> that hospital wanna join up with us against the Bonfires. (*the* SCOUTS *look sceptical*) Listen, those doctors are professionals with pointed instruments. They could arm us to the <u>teeth</u>.

SCOUT: And just what are we doing for them, Billy.

GILLES: Adding a little youth and beauty to their dreary fantasies, I would imagine. (*conversation stops dead*) Ah. I see I have had my usual effect upon a group. I am Gilles de Rais, your very newest member and I am prepared to offer you some in-ter-esting information about your enemies the Bonfire Girls. Like, for instance, where to find them. (*smiles evilly*) Well? Go ahead boys. <u>Ask</u> me.

Blackout.

Lights up: the **BEACH.** MARLENE, GERTRUDE, EMILY BRONTË. *They're eating fried claims.*

MARLENE: (*licking her fingers*) My darlings, I feel things are coming to a head. Have a clam Gertrude.

GERTRUDE: Umm very tasty. They're coming to much more than a head Marlene Dr. Dark is after Joan's <u>brain</u> and <u>where</u> are those Bonfire Girls.

EMILY: They are young, Gertrude. Tho' well-versed in the ways of evil. You cannot rely upon children.

MARLENE: I <u>believe</u> the Bonfires are learning the manly art of war from Princess Angeline.

EMILY: Ah Marlene. That <u>is</u> good news. Their simple savagery will dissolve in her native ruthlessness like red wine in water and produce a <u>brutal</u> effect. (*a visionary state*) I can see it now.

GERTRUDE: (*brightens*) Pass those french fries Emily Brontë I think I'm getting an idea. (*takes a bite and chews audibly*) It's hard being a genius.

Blackout.

Lights up: JOAN'S BEDROOM. JOAN *and* GILLES.

GILLES: Jesus *chérie.* Are you sure you want to meet in here? I feel as though I'm defiling a convent. (*brightens with pleasure at the realization*)

JOAN: This is the only safe place in the house, Gilles. Papa never comes in here alone.

GILLES: I must say, *chérie,* your father is quite a bastard.

JOAN: The goddess Diana always thought so.

GILLES: I cannot comprehend why a man would want to *fillet* <u>and</u> *sauté* his only daughter.

JOAN: I think he wants other people to do it, Gilles. I think he only wants to <u>watch</u>.

GILLES: Still, *chérie.* Lobotomy, as any German knows, removes a significant part of your brain, and electroshock, as any Frenchman can tell you, burns up the rest of it. This is not friendly, *chérie.*

JOAN: Papa is peculiar Gilles. If he can't understand something, he destroys it.

GILLES: (*shaking his head*) So American.

JOAN: (*a visionary voice, as tho' at the Trial of 1431*) I know what he wants, Gilles. He wants me to recant. To take back what I said I saw. He says he'll spare my life if I do this. But what is my life worth without my saints? And what am <u>I</u> worth without my inspiration. (*pause, then with unusual force*) I'll take back nothing. I might be the one to burn—but <u>he'll</u> be the one to go to <u>hell</u>!

Blackout.

Lights up: the DARK HOUSE. GEORGE *alone. He holds a labeled X-ray of* JOAN'S *cranium. A skull sits on his desk.*

GEORGE: (*a crescendo*) Here in my own household. My perfect patient. My sublime subject. My <u>inspiration</u>. I owe it to <u>science</u> to cross examine her. I owe it

to <u>medicine</u> to operate on her. I owe it to <u>god</u> to <u>understand</u> her! (*deflates*)
The sanity hearing is just a formality.

Blackout.

Lights up: **VOLUNTEER PARK.** BONFIRE GIRLS *dump the bound bodies of* JOHN
and JOHN *in front of* ANGELINE. *She grins and flourishes her tomahawk.*

Blackout.

Lights up: **GEORGE'S LAB.** DWAYNE *is sterilizing scalpels. He fingers them reflectively and grins.*

DWAYNE: Big doctor. Big Doctor with his sharp knives. Gonna cut his own
daughter. <u>Not</u> for sacred lands. <u>Not</u> for tribal power. (*Pause. Real wonderment.*) Who can figure these pale people out?

Blackout.

Lights up: the **DARK LIVING ROOM.** *A family conference.* GEORGE, MARTHA,
JOHN *and* JOHN. *There are still quivering arrows stuck everywhere.* JOAN *is obvious
by her absence, while* JOHN *and* JOHN *are conspicuous by their lack of hair (scalping practice by the* BONFIRES).

MARTHA: (*smokes feverishly*) This . . . obsession with Joan can't go on George.
You are frightening me and you are frightening the boys.

JOHN: Naah, Dad's not frightening me, Mom.

JOHN: You're frightening <u>me</u>, Dad. A <u>lot</u>.

GEORGE: (*smokes silkily*) I'm glad to hear it John. A <u>little</u> fear is useless. Now
boys, tell me where your sister is.

JOHN: (*casual*) Haven't seen her Dad.

JOHN: (*intensely nervous*) I haven't seen her either Dad. But I'd tell if I had, Dad.
You <u>know</u> I would. <u>Honest</u>.

GEORGE: You see Martha? (*points*) This John has a little fear and <u>this</u> one
(*points*) has a lot. And it is <u>this</u> John (*points to the scared one*) who will be the
useful one.

Blackout.

Lights up: JOAN *in* **NANCY DETWILER'S BASEMENT.** *She's in the center of a
group of* BONFIRE GIRLS *surrounding* NANCY, *who is putting pins in a big war map.*

JOAN: It <u>has</u> to be in Volunteer Park, Bonfires. We <u>have</u> to fight them in Volunteer Park. Gilles says that's where the Surgeons and the Salish and the Scouts
are gathering—and Gilles is <u>always</u> accurate about men. I have studied every
bas relief map in this city and Volunteer Park has enough hills and forests and

basins to conceal us forever. (*dreamily*) Besides, there are voices in those woods. I've heard them.

NANCY: Can we keep this short, Joan. I'm trying to schedule a war, here.

CINDY: It doesn't have to be <u>that</u> short, Nancy, we <u>like</u> Joan now.

CANDY: (*judicious*) She drives well.

PATTY: (*judicious*) And she's got real leadership potential.

JOAN: Thank you. I'm flattered. Honestly.

NANCY: (*smoking heavily*) Okay, we like her. But right now I'm juggling battle plans from Princess Angeline, Marlene Dietrich, and the Bonfire Girl National Council. I'm up to two packs a day with the pressure.

BETTY: (*with asperity*) We're <u>all</u> very nervous and incapacitated, Nancy.

CINDY: I haven't stolen a lipstick in a week.

PATTY: I haven't started a fire in ten days.

CAROLINE: My White Lady's bridal veil is torn and she cries all the time. (*weeps herself*) I think she's been jilted.

GIRLS: HA HA HA HA Serves her right HAW HAW HAW Serves <u>you</u> right, (*etc. etc. etc.*)

JOAN: (*holds up her hand, instant silence*)

PATTY: (*whispers*) I <u>told</u> you she was a leader.

JOAN: (*very direct*) The health of this city—and my own safety—depends on our next maneuver. I have listened to my voices, I have thought carefully about the consequences, I have . . . <u>prayed</u> for guidance, and now I will tell you <u>exactly</u> what we are going to do.

Blackout.

Lights up: **DUCK BLIND IN VOLUNTEER PARK.** ANGELINE, GERTRUDE, EMILY, *and* MARLENE. *Arrows and scalpels fly overhead.*

GERTRUDE: WOW THAT WAS CLOSE!

MARLENE: Ach, darlings. It's just like old times at the French Front. Did I ever tell you . . .

ALL: Yes!!!

MARLENE: Well I'm saving my <u>best</u> stories for the victory celebration. Princess Angeline, darling, just when will that be.

ANGELINE: No idea, Blond Venus. I lost radio contact with Joan and Bonfire Girls twenty minutes ago.

MARLENE: *Mon dieu*, Angeline, don't tell me the girls are out on their own!

GERTRUDE: Those girls are better trained than the Wehrmacht Marlene I would pray for the doctors and the scouts if I were you.

ANGELINE: (*peeping over the* DUCK BLIND's *rim*) And the Indians, Marlene. Pray for the Indians. Bonfire Girls are practicing scalping skills on cousin Larry Twelvetrees. Hoo hoo. Not bad for beginners. Not bad at <u>all</u>.

EMILY: (*in a sudden trance*) I see Joan successful. I see Joan immortal. I see . . . (*horrified*) I see Joan <u>captured</u>!

Blackout.

Lights up: JOAN *in* **DEEP SPACE**. *Surrounded by fluttering doves. Flames are below her.*

JOAN: There is fire in my future. I smell the smoke. I try to pull back from the edge of the conflagration but I feel myself falling into the flames. Oh! For the wings of a dove.

Blackout.

Lights up: **VOLUNTEER PARK**. GEORGE *beating the bushes for* JOAN, *his nose twitching.*

GEORGE: (*muttering distractedly*) I'll find her myself. I'll . . . Snif Snif. I smell smoke. There is smoke here somewhere. And wherever there is smoke, Snif Snif, there is usually someone . . . (*big smile*) <u>burning</u>. I'll follow the smoke and when I find her . . . that will be the day. Oh that will be the day for me.

Blackout.

Lights up: GILLES *with one of* JOAN's *brothers in each hand.*

GILLES: Alright criminals. I offer you a choice. A <u>Christian</u> choice. Where has the old villain scheduled Joan's sanity hearing? Speak to me and live. Keep silent and I barbecue you. (*he shakes them hard*)

JOHN: Okay Okay I'll talk, I'll <u>talk</u>.

JOHN: (*totally attracted*) Jeez John. He's even scarier than <u>Dad</u>.

Blackout.

Lights up: **VOLUNTEER PARK**. *Battlefield scene. A battalion of angry* SURGEONS, *a tribe of* SALISH *males, and a troop of* BOY SCOUTS *are herded together and circled* *by a perfect ring of fire, set and tended by the* BONFIRE GIRLS *who are doing the dance* PRINCESS ANGELINE *taught them. They chant as they dance and desultorily wave spears, tomahawks, and outsize fireplace matches.*

GIRLS: Only Good Salish brave
        Is dead good Salish brave
        Only good doctor man
        Is dead good doctor man
        Only good young boy scout
        Is dead good young boy scout
        Hoo hoo hoo hoo hoo hoo <u>hoo</u>.

    GILLES DE RAIS *stands off to the side, disdainfully, his only sign of interest is in a good-looking* BOY SCOUT *venturing too near the circle of flames.* GILLES *puts his black hand thru the flames to touch the boy's cheek.*

GILLES: Careful *chéri*, it's hot in there.

    The BOY SCOUT *faints, not from the heat, but from* GILLES' *touch.*

GILLES: Ah. *Merci bon dieu.* I haven't lost my touch.

NANCY: (*stopping mid-chant*) Hey! Where's Joan?

    Blackout.

    Lights up: GEORGE *with his hand over* JOAN's *mouth, spirits her away.*

    Blackout.

    Lights up: **BATTLEFIELD** *and* BONFIRE GIRLS.

ANNE: And where's Joan's father?

    Blackout.

    Lights up: the **DUCK BLIND.** MARLENE, ANGELINE, GERTRUDE, *and* EMILY.

ANGELINE: Oh oh Ladies. Very bad news.

EMILY: Fatal news.

GERTRUDE: We cannot intervene.

EMILY: We're not allowed.

GERTRUDE: This is quite a pickle girls quite a pickle quite a pi . . .

MARLENE: Wait a minute, darlings. Princess Angeline is not like <u>us</u>. (*her eyes light*) Princess <u>Angeline</u> is <u>mortal</u>. (*smile*) Princess <u>Angeline</u> is <u>local</u>. (*bigger smile*) Princess <u>Angeline</u> can intervene in <u>anything</u>. (*triumphant smile*)

    Blackout.

Lights up: JOAN's **TRIUMPH.** *All four ladies are somehow stuffed in it.* GERTRUDE *is on the tiny backseat ledge,* EMILY *is crumpled into the boot,* MARLENE *drives, apparently very badly, and* ANGELINE *is in the passenger seat.*

ANGELINE: Ooooh Blond Venus! Where did you learn to drive like <u>that</u>.

MARLENE: (*dimpling as for a compliment*) I'm an actress, Angeline. I can imitate <u>any</u> action.

GERTRUDE: (*holding tight*) Take comfort Emily, we can't die twice.

EMILY: (*exhilarated, yells back*) I'm <u>enjoying</u> myself, Gertrude!

Boom. Ack ack ack. The awful sound of an engine backfiring. Smoke envelopes the TRIUMPH *and it coughs and sputters to a stop.*

ALL: (*thru the smoke*) OH NO!

Blackout.

Lights up: ADULT JOAN. **IN FRONT OF THE HOSPITAL.**

JOAN: By this time, my father simply couldn't help himself. He was going to prosecute the sanity hearing that would deliver me into his scrubbed and gloved surgeon's hands. (*pause*) I had always known, my voices had always told me, that a man would stand between me and the law.

Blackout

Lights up: **GEORGE'S LABORATORY.** YOUNG JOAN *strapped to a gurney,* GEORGE *busying himself with pre-operative matters. Faggots surround the gurney and* JOHN *and* JOHN *add to them enthusiastically thruout her monologue.*

JOAN: Now I remember. Everything. The <u>heat</u> of those flames. They kept that fire burning all day long. They kept it burning with wood and with olive oil and with their fear of me. Of <u>me</u>. And when all that had been me was consumed by the fire, when my bones were burned to ash, and my liquids boiled to steam and my tissues charred to carbon—there was still my heart. Beating there on the ground for all to see. It would not burn. And the executioner had to throw my beating, bleeding, <u>stubborn</u> heart into the river Seine. (*pause*) Because it just . . . <u>refused</u> . . . to burn. (*pause, to the Audience*) I absolutely . . . <u>love</u> that part of the story.

Blackout.

Lights up: the stranded **TRIUMPH.** MARLENE, GERTRUDE, *and* ANGELINE *are sitting glumly in and on the reeking, smoking car.* EMILY BRONTË, *unnoticed by her sister saints, is busily at work on the unhooded engine.*

MARLENE: (*holding her head and waving her cigarette holder indiscriminately*) Ay yi yi. AY YI <u>YI</u>.

GERTRUDE: (*ponderously*) I think I have a proposition for our predicament does anyone want to hear a proposition which I thought of while dismounting the rumble seat.

ANGELINE: (*brightening momentarily*) Ahh Gertrude Stein. I would <u>love</u> to hear a proposition.

MARLENE: Ay yi yi. We will <u>never</u> arrive in time to save darling Joan. Ay yi yi. I <u>knew</u> we should have taken a limousine. (*waves away smoke with her cigarette holder and stops dead as* EMILY *cranks the engine*) Why Emily Brontë. You've fixed the . . . whatever it was. And . . . (*inhales her cigarette dramatically*) . . . My dear. You did a <u>marvelous</u> job.

EMILY B: (*dimpling with pleasure and waving a dipstick*) It was a nineteenth century solution, Marlene. I cleaned the carburetor with a hairpin and straightened the valve-lifters with my barrette.

ANGELINE: (*snippy*) Hoo. Better you than <u>me</u>, little white writer. Princess Angeline does <u>not</u> haul water for the leisure classes.

EMILY B: (*snippier*) <u>I</u> used to work as a <u>governess</u>, Angeline. Hauling water would have been a <u>delightful</u> alternative.

GERTRUDE: (*stealing the focus*) Well come on girls let's hop back in the Hupmobile here time is just a dimension but it is filling up very fast.

MARLENE *and* EMILY *look at each other and mouth* "<u>What</u> did she say?"

ANGELINE: (*to* GERTRUDE) Allow me to translate large pale sister. (*to* MARLENE) Gertrude Stein says: "Step on the gas screen goddess or Joan Dark will die once again!!"

Blackout.

Lights up: the OPERATING THEATRE. *A few ancient physicians, arranged like a jury high above, are in the glass-enclosed spectator seats.* GEORGE *is below with* JOAN, *still strapped to the gurney.*

OUTSIDE THE HOSPITAL. *The* TRIUMPH *stops at the hospital door.* GERTRUDE, *hands over eyes,* EMILY, *exhilarated,* ANGELINE, *determined, and* MARLENE, *very proud of her ability to find the brakes in time, dismount and step up to the hospital door. Which is barred.* MARLENE *snaps her fingers. Lights bump out then up and* MARLENE, GERTRUDE, *and* EMILY BRONTË *are materialized on the other side of the door.* PRINCESS ANGELINE *taps her toes with impatience outside.* MARLENE *coolly lights a cigarette, then snaps her fingers again. Lights bump out then up again and* ANGELINE *is inside.*

GEORGE: In conclusion, gentlemen, I ask you to weigh the evidence — erratic interaction with family and friends, auditory and visual hallucinations on private and public occasions, overtly aggressive behavior towards males in the "help-ing" professions . . .

GEORGE'S *mouth keeps moving but his speech dies out as* PRESENT-DAY JOAN'S *voice takes over the scene. She's back by the* TRIUMPH.

JOAN: Papa presented an excellent case to the few hospital doctors who were not on the field of battle. Unfortunately the doctors were so old, that the ones who could still hear <u>him</u> (*ear trumpets and opera glasses are brought out by the an-cient doctors*) couldn't see <u>me</u>. But it really didn't matter. As Papa said, the sanity hearing was merely a formality.

DR.: (*very ancient, he rises and intones*) Before we pronounce judgment, does the patient have anything to say for herself?

Projection: JOAN *in 1431, bound to the stake, about to be burned. Doves fly around her. Her face is turned upwards in dignity and distress.*

JOAN: (*on the gurney*) If I were to say that God had not sent me, I should be damning myself, for it is true that God did send me. Alas, that I should be treated so horribly and cruelly, that my whole body, never yet corrupted, should today be consumed and burnt to ashes!

DR.: (*turns to colleague*) She's nuts alright.

DR.: (*raises his ear trumpet*) What? What did you say?

DR.: I can't see a <u>thing</u>.

DR.: This commission certifies the patient Joan Dark to be insane. (*to* GEORGE, *with avidity*) Do anything you want with her. We'll watch.

GEORGE: (*smiles a big smile*)

Blackout.

Lights up: VOLUNTEER PARK. *The* BONFIRE GIRLS *are still circling the ring of fire, taunting prisoners, etc. The activity has clearly exceeded the length of their at-tention spans.*

ANNE: Nancy this is the most boring thing we've ever done!

PATTY: Why do we have to keep 'em prisoner?

CINDY: Why don't we just roast 'em?

BETTY: Or hang 'em?

CATHERINE: (*truly vicious*) Or cut out their intestines and use them for jump ropes!

PATTY: (*delighted*) Catherine, what an <u>inspiring</u> thing to say.

CINDY: And so uncharacteristic.

CATHERINE: (*hand to mouth, horrified*) It just slipped out!

NANCY: (*hideously reluctant to speak*) There's something I have to tell you Bon-fires. (*shamefaced and reluctant*) Joan asked me not to hurt anyone. (*very reluctant*) And I promised her we wouldn't.

ALL: Eeeuuuwww. How disgusting! No! You <u>didn't</u>!

NANCY: (*disingenuously*) I gave my <u>word</u>. A Bonfire Girl has to keep her word. Or other Bonfire Girls can't trust her.

ALL: True. That's right. She's got a point. A <u>tiny</u> one.

CINDY: (*a spreading smile*) Well, now, you didn't promise not to <u>frighten</u> them to death, did you? Bring in the cannons, Bonfire Girls! Let's have some <u>fun</u>!

Four BONFIRE GIRLS *immediately roll four cannons from the park's military display to the four imagined corners of the ring of fire. The cannons are pointed slightly heavenwards and the* BONFIRE GIRLS *front-load them, whistling while they work.* GILLES DE RAIS *climbs astride one cannon, grinning broadly, waiting, clearly, for the thrill of his life.*

The SURGEONS, *the* INDIANS, *and the* SCOUTS *gibber for mercy in the circle's center.*

NANCY: Alright Bonfires. Altogether now.

The men drop to the ground, hands over their ears.

Huge light show in the sky. The cannonballs head for some high cumulus formations and the stage darkens precipitously. The cannonballs pierce the clouds. Dramatically. The rumble of thunder is heard.

Lights up: the **OPERATING THEATRE.** JOAN, *on the gurney, suction cups on her head.* MARLENE, GERTRUDE, EMILY, *and* ANGELINE *have joined the audience of ancient doctors. They are concentrating very hard and* ANGELINE *is frantically searching her voluminous cloak for the spear she presented to* JOAN *in Part 1. Quite naturally, she finds nothing.*

GEORGE: We will begin with the electroshock treatment.

The rumble of thunder is suddenly very loud. Lightening is heard—and somehow felt. The stage becomes very electric and ANGELINE, *suddenly inspired, begins a rain dance learned, apparently, from her Hopi sisters.*

GEORGE: (*shouting above the thunder*) The side effects are unpleasant, but after we've quieted her down and ascertained the damage, I have developed a <u>beautiful</u> exploratory procedure to perform on the frontal lobe. Here we go.

GEORGE *puts his hand on a huge side-arm lever. He pulls it.* ANGELINE *dances harder.*

An enormous biblical bolt of lightening strikes the hospital, illuminates it, then burns its electrical system to a crisp. Everyone in the operating theatre is momentarily irradiated.

Complete blackout.

Lights up: a smoldering **BLACK STAGE.** *Pieces of ash fall from it. Voices of the* BONFIRE GIRLS. *Wistful, post-apocalyptic.*

CINDY: Whatever happened to Joan of Arc?

CANDY: They burned her, didn't they?

PATTY: I thought she died in the war and <u>then</u> they burned her.

ANNIE: What war? Which war?

BETTY: Whichever war they were having at the time. She died in the war and then they burned her.

NANCY: That's not how it happened. She was a real hero. And she had the <u>life</u> of a real hero.

CANDY: That's right. (*enumerates*) Her friends betrayed her, her enemies imprisoned her, and her church burned her <u>alive</u>.

CATHERINE: Why would they want to do <u>that</u>?

NANCY: So there wouldn't be anything left, any relics. You know what I mean. Fingers, a piece of her chin, things like that.

CINDY: That's right. <u>Body</u> parts. Body parts attract crowds. People will pay anything to see body parts of the famous.

ANNIE: Well, if they were going to make her a <u>saint</u>, you'd think they'd want to <u>keep</u> her body parts. Why did they burn her if they were going to make her a saint.

CINDY: I don't know.

BETTY: I don't know.

Slight pause.

NANCY: (*definitive*) <u>Politics</u>.

Lights up: **OPERATING THEATRE.** GEORGE, *frozen and still smoking slightly, his hand on the melted lever.* PRINCESS ANGELINE *is unstrapping* JOAN *from the gurney,* MARLENE *and* GERTRUDE *are shaking hands.* EMILY BRONTË *opens a supply cabinet and* EMILY DICKINSON's *voice floats out:*

After great pain
A formal feeling comes
The nerves sit ceremonious
Like tombs . . .

EMILY BRONTË *shuts the supply closet.*
Blackout.

Lights up: **VOLUNTEER PARK.** DWAYNE, *the* HEAD SURGEON, *and the* BOY SCOUT TROOP LEADER *are formally signing a treaty of surrender to the* BONFIRE GIRLS. GILLES DE RAIS *is consoling the attractive young* SCOUT. *The rain is torrential.*

JOAN: (*still attached to the* TRIUMPH) Well of course he didn't burn me. How could he? Even Seattle had never seen a rainstorm like that. Princess Angeline, soon to be <u>Chief</u> Angeline, and my darling saints, escorted me in triumph, <u>in</u> the Triumph actually, to the signing of the peace treaty.

Lights up: JOAN OF ARC, *1431, tied to the stake, enveloped in flames, doves fluttering above her. Torrential rains instantly quench the fires.* ST. MICHAEL, ST. MARGARET, *and* ST. CATHERINE, *halos glowing, untie her, crown her with laurel, and lead her to safety thru the adoring throng. They all become* YOUNG JOAN, MARLENE DIETRICH, GERTRUDE STEIN, *and* EMILY BRONTË (MARLENE, EMILY, *and* GERTRUDE *fling their halos to the ground*) *in Volunteer Park—watching the* BOY SCOUTS *and the* BONFIRE GIRLS *shake reluctant hands and the* SURGEONS *and the* SALISH *dance to* PRINCESS ANGELINE'S *tom-tom.*

JOAN: (PRESENT-DAY JOAN) Daddy and the boys were packed off to a convenient halfway house where they live to this day in a kind of twilight sleep of testosterone.

Lights up: A momentary illumination. **MENTAL HOSPITAL.** JOHN *the younger bites an attendant,* GEORGE *does an air guitar operation and* JOHN *the elder slobbers over the breasts of a giant nurse.*

Blackout.

Lights up: PRESENT-DAY JOAN *with her* **TR-3** *silhouetted against the Seattle skyline.*

JOAN: It was amazing how much Mama cheered up when the household cleared out. She stuck to me like glue in the aftermath of the, I guess you could call it, <u>miracle</u>, and in her support of me she was admirable and <u>very</u> spirited.

Lights up: A momentary illumination. MARTHA *bashes an ancient doctor with her handbag.*

Lights up: YOUNG JOAN, *standing by the* TR-3, *outlined against the city and surrounded by the beaming, gleaming, celebrating* MARLENE DIETRICH, GERTRUDE STEIN, EMILY BRONTË, *and* ANGELINE, *Chief of all the Indians.*

YOUNG JOAN: What I finally realized was this. That my mission, my <u>real</u> mission, was to be put here, in this time and place, and to be made uncomfortable enough to tell my story.

JOAN: And so I was.

And so I have.

MARLENE: And I helped you my darling. I helped you vewy vewy much. And I want my name above the title on the marquee, darling. I put it in the contract. (*waves the document*) You see? It's <u>right</u> <u>here</u> in the small print.

The BONFIRE GIRLS, *the* SCOUTS, *the* SALISH, *and even the* SURGEONS *celebrate with* CHIEF ANGELINE *and the triumphant young* JOAN *as* ST. MARLENE, ST. GERTRUDE, *and* ST. EMILY BRONTË (*in a good mood and holding an oil dipstick*) *wave cheerily to the Audience.*

The celebration continues into the blackout. Sound of rain.

Finis

University Press of New England publishes books under its own imprint and is the publisher for Brandeis University Press, Dartmouth College, Middlebury College Press, University of New Hampshire, University of Rhode Island, Tufts University, University of Vermont, and Wesleyan University Press.

Joan Schenkar is a well-known experimental playwright whose works are produced, taught, and read across North America and Western Europe. She is the recipient of more than thirty-five grants and awards, has had more than three hundred productions of her plays throughout the world, and has been a guest artist in many venues in North America. Her works are published by Samuel French, Applause Books, Kenyon Review, TDR, and others; she is invited to speak about her plays at colleges and theatre festivals around the country.

Vivian Patraka is Professor of English at Bowling Green State University; she also serves as Director of the Institute for the Study of Culture and Society at Bowling Green. She is co-author of *Sam Shepard* (1985), co-editor of *Feminist Re-Visions: What Has Been and Might Be* (1983), and a contributor to numerous journals and anthologies. Her most recent book, *Spectacular Suffering: Theatre, Fascism, and the Holocaust*, is forthcoming in the Unnatural Acts: Theorizing the Performative series from Indiana University Press.

Library of Congress Cataloging-in-Publication Data

Schenkar, Joan.
Signs of life: Six comedies of menace / Joan M. Schenkar; edited and with an introduction by Vivian Patraka.
   p. cm.
   Contents: Cabin fever — Signs of life — Fulfilling Koch's Postulate — The Last of Hitler — The universal wolf — Burning desires.
ISBN 0–8195–6322–6 (alk. paper). — ISBN 0–8195–6323–4 (pbk. : alk. paper)
I. Patraka, Vivian. II. Title.
PS3569. C4829S5 1997
813'.54 — dc21   97–17910